'This book is a much needed addition to the available texts on courses related to careers in criminal justice. Not only does it provide a thorough and empirical overview of the trends regarding careers in criminal justice, a noteworthy omission in many curricula, this book also offers valuable, practical, and empirically-based advice on how best to consider a career within criminal justice. Another important feature of this book is that it provides important insight into the nature of the internship experience for students. In short, the book is comprehensive, timely, practical, and makes a valuable contribution to the field.'

Robert McNamara, Ph.D., The Citadel

'Ronald G. Burns has written the career guide our criminal justice students need, and I wish it was available when I was an undergraduate student. *Careers in Criminal Justice and Criminology* provides an organized, well-researched, and engaging look at possible careers, and includes insight from those who have held some of the most interesting and highly sought-after positions in the field.'

Charles Crawford, Ph.D., Western Michigan University

Careers in Criminal Justice and Criminology

This book provides a thorough and directed focus on successfully identifying, obtaining, and succeeding in a career in criminal justice or criminology. With empirically based, research-focused information on how students can prepare for and ultimately join the criminal justice or criminology workforce, it covers the positions available in criminal justice and criminology, how to get a job in the field, and what can be expected upon obtaining employment. The book contextualizes career opportunities within criminal justice and criminology, providing information about the nature of the work and how various positions fit within the criminal justice system as a whole.

Part 1 provides an overview of the book, an examination of the history of careers, and coverage of job opportunities and the nature of working in criminal justice and criminology. Part 2 addresses preparation for entering the field, including coverage of internships and overall professional development. Part 3 of the book addresses careers in the primary components of the criminal justice system, juvenile justice, and other areas. An epilogue addresses promotion issues, and a series of helpful appendices provide practical tools for working toward a career in criminal justice or criminology.

This book is suitable for any reader considering employment in criminal justice or criminology, and ideal for instructors who supervise and guide students as they gain practical experience and move toward careers.

Ronald G. Burns is Full Professor of Criminal Justice in the Department of Criminology and Criminal Justice at Texas Christian University. He earned his degrees from the University of South Carolina and Florida State University, and has published more than 70 scholarly articles. Burns has also authored, coauthored, or edited ten books, including *Criminal Justice: The System in Perspective* and *Multiculturalism, Crime, and Criminal Justice* (3rd edition). His teaching and research interests primarily pertain to law enforcement, white-collar crime, and criminal case processing.

Careers in Criminal Justice and Criminology

Ronald G. Burns

Routledge
Taylor & Francis Group
NEW YORK AND LONDON

Designed cover image: Ryan Burns

First published 2023
by Routledge
605 Third Avenue, New York, NY 10158

and by Routledge
4 Park Square, Milton Park, Abingdon, Oxon, OX14 4RN

Routledge is an imprint of the Taylor & Francis Group, an informa business

© 2023 Ronald G. Burns

The right of Ronald G. Burns to be identified as author of this work has been asserted in accordance with sections 77 and 78 of the Copyright, Designs and Patents Act 1988.

All rights reserved. No part of this book may be reprinted or reproduced or utilised in any form or by any electronic, mechanical, or other means, now known or hereafter invented, including photocopying and recording, or in any information storage or retrieval system, without permission in writing from the publishers.

Trademark notice: Product or corporate names may be trademarks or registered trademarks, and are used only for identification and explanation without intent to infringe.

ISBN: 978-1-032-41877-3 (hbk)
ISBN: 978-1-032-41293-1 (pbk)
ISBN: 978-1-003-36016-2 (ebk)

DOI: 10.4324/9781003360162

Typeset in Bembo
by Newgen Publishing UK

Access the Support Material: www.routledge.com/9781032412931

Contents

PART I
The Criminal Justice and Criminology Workforce   1

1   An Overview of Careers in Criminal Justice and Criminology   3

"Graduation Day Trauma" 3
Criminal Justice, Criminology, and the Criminal Justice System 4
What's Ahead? 5
Summary 8

2   A History of Criminal Justice Focused on Employment and Academic Study   12

Why History? 12
The Evolution of Criminal Justice Practices and the Creation of Jobs 13
   1607–1775: The Colonial Era 13
   1776–1828: A New Nation 15
   1829–1855: The Jacksonian Era 15
   1856–1878: The Civil War Era 16
   1879–1899: The Gilded Age 17
   1900–1919: The Progressive Era 17
   1920–1939: The Crisis Era 18
   1940–1959: The War Years 19
   1960–1979: The Nationalization Era 19
   1980–2001: The Reagan Era 20
   September 11, 2001–Present: The Era of Security 21
The Development of Academic Criminal Justice and Criminology Programs 21
Summary 24

3   Opportunities and Trends in Criminal Justice and Criminology Employment   26

What's Available? 26
   Law Enforcement 27
      Federal Law Enforcement 27
      State Law Enforcement 28
      County Law Enforcement 28
      Local Law Enforcement 29

   Courts 29
   Corrections 30
   Other Areas 32
  Employment Trends in and Influences on Employment in Criminal Justice and
    Criminology 33
   Terrorism 34
   Technology 34
   Fear of Crime 35
   Sociocultural Changes 36
   Globalism 37
   Private Security 37
  Summary 37

4 Working in Criminal Justice and Criminology 40

  Nature of the Work 40
  Bureaucracies 44
  Politics 45
  Crime and Individuals Who Break the Law 47
  Ethics 49
  Summary 51

PART 2
Preparing and Selling Yourself 55

5 A Self-Assessment to Prepare for a Career in Criminal Justice or Criminology 57

  Self-Assessment 57
  Summary 68

6 Your Criminal Justice and Criminology Education 70

  Maximizing Your Education 71
  Your Coursework 75
  Graduate Studies 77
  Seizing Opportunities 78
  Summary 81

7 Preparing for Employment in Criminal Justice and Criminology 84

  Networking 84
  Locating the Ideal Position 87
  Preparing Your Cover Letter and Resume 88
   Cover Letters 88
   Resumes 89
  Applying for Positions 92
  Interviewing 92
  Summary 96

8 Internships in Criminal Justice and Criminology   98

The Historical Development of Internships 98
"Internships: Otherwise known as..." 99
The Benefits of Internships 101
Expectations of Internships 104
Summary 107

PART 3
Working Toward Justice   109

9 Careers in Law Enforcement   111

Federal Law Enforcement 112
    Career Profiles 112
    Working in Federal Law Enforcement 113
State Law Enforcement 115
Local Law Enforcement 117
Special Jurisdiction Law Enforcement Agencies 120
Recruitment, Selection, and Training 121
Summary 123

10 Working in the Courts   125

Organization of Courts 125
The Courtroom Actors 126
    Judges 127
    Prosecutors 128
    Defense Attorneys 130
    Court Reporters 131
    Clerks of Court 132
    Court Administrators 132
    Bailiffs 133
    Paralegals 133
    Others Who Work in the Courts 134
Summary 134

11 Careers in Corrections   137

The Nature of Working in Corrections 137
Positions Within Institutional Corrections 140
    Wardens 140
    Correctional Officers 141
    Correctional Treatment Specialists 143
    Prerelease Correctional Counselors 143
    Corrections Education Specialists 143
Positions in Community Corrections 144
    Community Supervision Officers 145
    Pretrial Services Officers 147
    Reentry Center Managers 147
Summary 147

12 Working in the Juvenile Justice System 150

Juvenile Involvement in the Justice System 150
Working in the Juvenile Justice System 151
Employment Opportunities within the Juvenile Justice System 153
Summary 157

13 Other Employment Opportunities in Criminal Justice and Criminology 160

Victim Services 160
Private Security 162
Crime Analysis and Mapping 165
Forensic Science 167
Other Crime and Justice-Based Employment Opportunities 169
Encouragement for Career Advancement 170
Summary 172

14 Epilogue 174

Promotions 174
Career Development 178
Summary 180

Appendix A Sample Cover Letter, Resumes, and Follow-up Letter — *181*
Appendix B State Labor Offices — *185*
Appendix C Federal Criminal Justice and Criminology Employment Resources — *188*
Appendix D Careers in Criminal Justice and Criminology — *190*
Appendix E Salaries for Select Criminal Justice and Criminology Positions — *198*
Appendix F Curriculum Vitae Shell — *201*
Index — *202*

Part 1

The Criminal Justice and Criminology Workforce

Chapter 1

An Overview of Careers in Criminal Justice and Criminology

Ronald Burns

Careers in criminal justice and criminology can be described in many terms. Exciting, dangerous, rewarding, challenging, and unpredictable are just a few of the many adjectives that reflect what it is like to work in fields where you help create a safe, secure, and justice-based society. This book explains how one gains employment in the fields, what it is like to work in the fields, and the many opportunities for employment in criminal justice and criminology. It is a tool that should be used to supplement your education and general life experiences. Used properly, the tool can be very effective in helping you reach your professional goals. This opening chapter provides an overview and a foundation that helps readers best utilize this book. Generally, it sets the stage for the chapters that follow, introduces readers to the many rewarding careers in criminal justice and criminology, and prepares them for attaining employment in the fields.

"Graduation Day Trauma"

Today you graduate from college with a degree in criminal justice. You've worked hard to obtain the degree, and your friends and family who came to watch the graduation ceremony are proud of you, as are many other people. You think to yourself, "this is where it all begins." A career, a salary, and most important of all, making your way to the top of the organization with which you'll work.

Suddenly, alarms start going off in your head. You realize that you aren't yet with an organization and haven't done much to begin your career. In fact, tomorrow, the day after graduation, is no longer "summer break." Instead, it's the first day of unemployment as you're no longer a student and are expected to become a bona fide member of the workforce. Sure, you have a college degree, however, you look around and see many others graduating, and realize that many others are graduating in similar ceremonies around the country. And many others graduated prior to them. What makes you different from all others? Why would an agency choose you as an employee over all of the other newly graduated candidates, or other candidates in general? Thinking about the amount of student loans you have accumulated, you begin to break out in a cold sweat and anxiety kicks in. You're experiencing such extreme discomfort on what should be a day of celebration. This book aims to help you avoid such discomfort, and instead allow you to graduate with confidence and a career.

The scenario described above can be prevented through strategic career planning beginning prior to one's anticipated entrance into the workforce. For instance, the individual experiencing "graduation-day trauma" could have taken numerous steps that would have enabled him/her to better enjoy the special day. They could have separated themselves from many others interested in careers in criminal justice and criminology through learning a foreign language, obtaining advanced computer skills, doing an internship or two, assuming leadership positions in various student groups, studying abroad, and many other ways. The goal of this work is to help readers locate and obtain employment positions within the criminal justice system.

Criminal justice is one of the fastest growing fields of study and employment and was recognized by the US Department of Education as being among the "Top Ten" most awarded bachelor's degrees in the United States (e.g., Eren et al., 2019; Sloan & Buchwalter, 2017; Stringer & Murphy, 2020). It is important that those studying criminal justice and criminology be prepared for the workforce. Put simply, graduates beginning careers in policing, courts, corrections, juvenile justice, and other areas must be well-prepared for life after college. Traditional college curriculums provide the knowledge base required to succeed in a criminal justice, criminology, or related career. However, students should also be aware of what jobs are available in these areas, what is required to get a job, and what is expected upon getting one.

This book helps prepare readers/students by providing a directed focus on careers in criminal justice and criminology. Given the increasing popularity of criminal justice and criminology as major areas of academic study and employment, a thorough understanding of how students can progress from student to professional is needed. This book provides information on how students can prepare for and ultimately attain positions in the criminal justice and criminology workforce. The commentary from professionals working within the criminal justice system dispersed throughout the chapters provides readers personal insights regarding careers in criminal justice and criminology. This information helps integrate the academic and practical aspects of working in the fields.

Criminal Justice, Criminology, and the Criminal Justice System

It is likely that readers are familiar with what constitutes the criminal justice system; however, an overview of the field is needed to provide a foundation for career-related advice. The primary components of the criminal justice system are law enforcement, courts, and corrections. There are other areas closely associated with these three components, including juvenile justice, victim services, some nonprofit groups, and private security. Ultimately, it takes the work of many agencies, communities, and people to secure justice.

The term *criminal justice* generally refers to "… the practices and procedures by which individuals who violate the law are identified and held accountable." Related, the *criminal justice system* consists of "The practices of groups within law enforcement, the courts, and corrections designed to bring offenders to justice" (Burns, 2022, 3). We often discuss the criminal justice system as if it is a single entity even though there are many criminal justice systems. The federal government has a criminal justice system, as do all states. These and the criminal justice agencies found at various levels of government are collectively discussed as the *criminal justice system*. The decentralized approach to justice-based practices in the United States means that there is no single agency that controls any primary component of the criminal justice system.

Criminology is a subdiscipline of sociology and involves the scientific study of criminal behavior and the institutions responsible for responding to and preventing crime. It is very closely related to criminal justice, with the primary difference being that criminology is more theory-based and explanatory than criminal justice. The similarities explain why many criminal justice academic programs include criminology courses, and many criminology programs include criminal justice courses. There are, to be sure, differences in the course requirements of both programs, and their histories differ (Oliver, 2016). Some academic programs combine the two areas of study into one department or unit, for instance, going by the title "Department of Criminal Justice and Criminology." The career advice and guidance provided in this book are largely based around criminal justice simply because it is more applied than criminology. Criminology was included in the title and referenced throughout the pages that follow simply because a degree in criminology is often considered to be very similar to a degree in criminal justice. Jobs that require a degree in criminal justice will typically accept criminology degrees, and vice versa, given the similarity between the two. There are, of course, some positions for which a concentration in criminology would seem to be more applicable for employment purposes (e.g., research-based positions). Ultimately, the two areas are closely related enough so that a degree in either area would be applicable for the careers noted in this work.

The similarity between criminal justice and criminology is noted by scholar Freda Adler and colleagues (Adler et al., 2007, 17–18), who noted that "… the two fields are interwoven. Scholars of both disciplines use the same scientific research methods. They have received the same rigorous education, and they pursue the same goals." The authors add that "Both fields rely on the cooperation of many other disciplines, including sociology, psychology, political science, law, economics, management, and education." Others noted that the disciplines often share the same content, faculty members, and research (Oliver, 2016). The similarities between the two fields result in those studying criminal justice or criminology generally vying for the same employment opportunities.

There are many reasons why we should study criminal justice and criminology, including:

- the need to understand how to address crime create a safer society;
- the importance of learning from and addressing our mistakes, and moving forward in a positive direction;
- the fact that crime and justice are, in one way or another, part of our everyday life;
- that fact that there are millions of employment positions within the field; and
- because we find it interesting (Burns, 2022).

Criminal justice and criminology intrigue us. Many people watch movies, listen to podcasts, and/or read about crime and justice. Our fascination with breaking the law and ensuring justice led some people, perhaps you, to study the field. As discussed in Chapter 2, the academic focus on criminal justice and criminology has grown substantially since the 1970s (e.g., Collica-Cox & Furst, 2019; Sloan & Buchwalter, 2017). Many reasons are offered for the growth, including the need to better educate those working in the criminal justice system (e.g., Oliver, 2016). Further, the expansion of the criminal justice system resulting from the "get tough" policies beginning in the 1980s, and media sensationalism of crime and justice contributed to greater interest and job opportunities in the field. As an example, the United States experienced about a 500% increase in the number of people incarcerated over the past four decades (The Sentencing Project, 2021).

Such growth resulted in a substantial increase in employment opportunities. There are nearly 2.5 million government employees working in law enforcement, courts, and corrections (Buehler, 2021). This number excludes the many others who may not directly work in these fields, but contribute much to addressing crime and securing justice.

All signs point to continued growth in the field, given the substantial increases seen in the past several decades. The US Bureau of Justice Statistics noted that the number of full-time employees working in state and local justice systems increased 16% from 2007 to 2017 (Buehler, 2021). Increased globalism, advanced technology and the enhanced use of it, and social unrest are among the many issues that will contribute to continued expansion of the criminal justice system and subsequently additional needs for professionals to work in the field.

What's Ahead?

The chapters that follow are logically divided into three parts that address key areas of employment in criminal justice and criminology. Part 1 provides much foundation building, setting the stage for the sections that follow. The second part of the book covers the preparation needed to become gainfully employed, including coverage of how to identify, prepare for, and secure the job you seek. The third part examines careers in criminal justice and criminology. Specifically, it covers careers in law enforcement, the courts, corrections, juvenile justice, and other areas. This is followed by an epilogue that assists with career development upon getting a job, and helpful job search and related resources provided in the appendices. A more detailed look at each part of the book helps prepare you for what's ahead.

As noted, the first part of the book provides an overview of the criminal justice and criminology workforce. This section includes coverage of (1) the historical development of employment in criminal justice and criminology, (2) the opportunities for employment in criminal justice and criminology, (3) trends and expectations for careers in criminal justice and criminology, and (4) the nature of working in criminal justice and criminology, including issues pertaining to bureaucracy, political influences, dealing with individuals who break the law, and ethics. Understanding past and present developments and trends in criminal justice and criminology employment enables readers to better consider different positions they may wish to consider.

Philosopher George Santayana once noted that "Those who cannot remember the past are condemned to repeat it." Offered in 1905, his words are still relevant. Coverage of early developments in criminal justice and criminology employment opportunities, with a particular concern for the ultimate professionalization of careers in criminal justice and criminology, is important for understanding the current state of the fields. Within the historical coverage provided in Chapter 2 is discussion of the development of the academic study of criminal justice and criminology.

Part 1 also includes an overview of the available employment opportunities in criminal justice and criminology, and an extensive list of opportunities is included in Appendix D. Providing an overview of opportunities and trends pertaining to careers in law enforcement, the courts, and corrections enlightens readers to the wide array of positions in the field. This discussion is followed by coverage of the nature of employment in the criminal justice system, which helps prepare tomorrow's professionals for careers working with individuals who do not always obey laws, rules, and regulations. The nature of working in the field assuredly incorporates the pros and cons of working in bureaucracies and exposure to ideologies that impact one's working environment.

The second part of the book more technically prepares you for entering the criminal justice and criminology workforce. The section begins by challenging readers to closely assess their personal interests, likes/dislikes, and motivations. The assessment is provided for readers to better understand their suitability for employment in criminal justice and criminology and helps them identify what component and/or position best meets their employment-based wants and needs.

The self-assessment is followed by guidance and encouragement for maximizing one's education. Particularly, readers are exposed to the benefits of excelling in their coursework, participating in extracurricular activities (particularly in leadership roles), and taking advantage of opportunities. There are many advantages associated with students maximizing their educational experience to fully enhance their employment marketability.

The final two chapters of Part 2 address preparation for a career in criminal justice and criminology (Chapter 7) and internships (Chapter 8). Chapter 7 covers several topics that are vital to a successful career in criminal justice and criminology. Particularly, it covers identifying the ideal position, preparing cover letters and resumes, the importance of networking, the application process, interviewing, and ethics. Those entering the workforce need to be particularly familiar with the processes involved with transitioning from a student to a member of the workforce. Familiarity with these topics will also help students obtain internships.

The steps involved with identifying, applying, and interviewing for internships are similar to those involved with applying for other employment positions. Internships serve many important purposes, including the opportunity to gain practical experience and sample different career paths. Internships and experiential learning have become increasingly ingrained in higher education and provide numerous benefits for students (e.g., Jones & Bonner, 2016). Although assuming an internship may not be easy for everyone, all who have the opportunity are encouraged to do so.

The third and final part of the book exposes readers to employment opportunities within law enforcement, the courts, corrections, juvenile justice agencies, and related positions. The nature of the work in each of these areas varies, and there are many employment opportunities. Being aware of the nature of the work and opportunities helps students/readers make appropriate employment-based decisions.

Part 3 begins with an examination of careers in law enforcement. Readers are exposed to the types and nature of law enforcement positions at the local, state, and federal levels. Each level of law enforcement provides various positions, and although they generally share the same responsibilities, the work they perform often differs to some extent. Most criminal justice majors express an interest in working in law enforcement, particularly at the federal level (Collica-Fox & Furst, 2019; Stringer & Murphy, 2020).

A Practitioner's View

Dan Cole, Special Agent, Federal Bureau of Investigation

Life as a Special Agent in the FBI is like no other. In my opinion there is no better job in federal service. One of the most unique aspects of life as an FBI Special Agent is its diversity of work. Just a few of the amazing opportunities that have marked my career include investigating complex financial crimes and public corruption; stopping human trafficking; arresting Top Ten murderers, child predators and serial sex offenders; responding to multiple national disasters; interdicting a terrorist bent on killing Americans; stopping adversary nations from stealing our technology; and working alongside US Special Forces and allied nation agencies in a foreign land to halt acts of terror against the civilian population. Among agents, my career is not exceptional. These opportunities are common for most agents.

For those who are interested in serving their country as an FBI Special Agent, I would make a few recommendations. First, stop any recreational drug use. Though the use of recreational narcotics is legal in many states, recent drug use will absolutely derail the application process. Second, seek out leadership opportunities. FBI Special Agents are often thrust into leadership roles, often early in their careers. Young agents often have to make decisions and lead teams during rapidly evolving, high stakes problem sets. Building leadership experience prior to onboarding with the Bureau can build a good foundation for leadership challenges in the future. Third, take your studies seriously and seek out a major that interests you. The FBI does not require applicants with a particular major, but your academic performance in whatever major you choose will be examined. The more interested you are in your major, the better you will likely perform. Fourth, stay in shape. The FBI's physical fitness requirements are rigorous. If you stay in good physical condition as part of your lifestyle, you will find the FBI's fitness standards easier to meet.

(the views and opinions expressed are those of Special Agent Cole and not those of the FBI)

Coverage of working in law enforcement is followed by discussion of working in the court system. The courts provide a safer environment compared to law enforcement and corrections and offer many different employment opportunities. Students may be interested in becoming one of the primary participants in the courts (judges, prosecutors, defense attorneys), or perhaps assuming one of the lesser-known, yet very important roles (e.g., paralegals, court reporters, clerks of court). Among the many attractions to the study of criminal justice are the variety of functions performed by those who work in the field, the variety of positions within each area, and contributions made by the three primary components. Those who work in the system all work toward securing justice, yet their functions and responsibilities can greatly differ. For instance, the role of a paralegal is much different from that of a corrections officer.

Discussion of working in the courts is followed by an examination of careers in correctional agencies. Corrections are viewed in terms of community corrections and institutional corrections, and there are many positions found within each. Working with individuals convicted of a crime can be rewarding and dangerous, among other terms. Research suggests that criminal justice majors rank working in corrections below working in other components in the system (e.g., Stringer & Murphy, 2020); nevertheless, correctional agencies have much to offer those interested in the field, and more specifically, helping others.

As noted, the criminal justice system consists of law enforcement, courts, and corrections. Juveniles are processed in the juvenile justice system, which also provides a wealth of employment options for those interested in helping troubled and at-risk youth. Part 3 also provides coverage of these positions and highlights the differences between working with adults and juveniles. This coverage is followed by discussion of a series of justice-based employment opportunities that are becoming increasingly popular and/or may not be so obvious to criminal justice and criminology students. For instance, readers may be unaware of the variety of employment options in the private security field. Some readers may have the impression that private security primarily consists of being a security officer, when indeed there are many more opportunities in the field. Readers are also be exposed to employment opportunities in crime analysis and mapping, forensics, victim services, and other related areas.

The book concludes with an Epilogue that discusses career development and promotions, and a series of appendices that will help anyone interested in careers and/or internships in criminal justice and criminology. The Epilogue also summarizes the information earlier presented in the book and encourages readers to enjoy and make the most of their chosen career.

Appendix A presents examples of various resumes suitable for employment in criminal justice and criminology. The resumes vary in style, organization, content, and format. A sample cover letter and follow-up letter are also provided. Appendix B contains labor office contacts for each state, and Appendix C directs readers to several helpful online resources created to assist those interested in criminal justice positions at the federal level. The federal government has made things much easier for interested parties to identify and apply for federal-level employment. The information provided in this section highlights those efforts. Appendix D provides an extensive list of positions in criminal justice and criminology, accompanied by a brief description of the associated responsibilities. Finally, Appendix E provides information on select salaries in the criminal justice system, and Appendix F provides an account of the categories of information included on a curriculum vita, which is discussed in Chapter 13.

Summary

The uncertainty and unpredictability of the work encountered by those working within the criminal justice system are part of the attractions to life as an agent of social control. Working within the criminal justice system either as an intern or employee can offer a mixed bag of emotions. For instance, working in the system enables one to get into direct contact with those in need of great assistance. Consider, for instance, the police officer responding to a domestic violence incident. The victim is obviously in need of perhaps physical and psychological assistance. You want to help her improve her situation but you become frustrated when she tells you she loves her abusive husband and won't leave him (despite the fact that he regularly beats her). You feel sorry for her, yet you're angered that she won't leave. As for him, you see he has a substance abuse problem (which contributes to the violence) and want to understand why he beats his wife, yet you can't. You feel for him as he needs much help; however, your disgust with him beating his wife overrides any feelings of sorrow you may have for him.

Bear in mind this mixed bag of emotions stems from one incident. Consider the emotional roller coaster faced by police officers, attorneys, judges, correctional officers, and others who work in the system as they encounter some of the most problematic situations and individuals society has to offer. Despite these challenges, working within the system offers many individuals the opportunity to help others and assist with ensuring a safe society for all. To many who work in the system, the rewards outweigh the costs.

It would serve you well to keep several things in mind as you read this book. First, consider what you can do to best prepare yourself for a career in criminal justice and criminology. Consider avenues through which you can best meet the needs of criminal justice agencies. Second, keep an open mind as you consider employment in different areas. For instance, some students immediately dismiss careers in corrections because they do not wish to be correctional officers. There are, of course, many other opportunities for employment in corrections that do not involve working as a correctional officer. Third, don't underestimate your potential. Obtaining and refining the skill sets needed for employment in many areas of the criminal justice system is mostly a matter of perseverance. Surely, at some point in your life you put your mind to something and achieved what you thought was nearly

There are many positions within criminal justice, and each provides an opportunity to help others and maintain a safe and secure society.
Source: https://pxhere.com/en/photo/493601

impossible. Fourth, remain positive. As you read this book, think of why you *can* obtain a particular career, instead of why you *cannot*. A defeatist attitude breeds defeatist results. Upon doubting your suitability for a preferred position, keep in mind that *somebody* has to fill that role. Why not you? Finally, enjoy the information. Locating and/or learning a career should be exciting.

Discussion Questions

1. What steps can be taken to best prepare for a career in criminal justice and criminology?
2. Why should we study criminal justice and criminology?
3. How is criminal justice different from criminology?
4. Why has the study of criminal justice and criminology expanded so substantially?
5. Do you believe the study of criminal justice and criminology will continue to expand? Why or why not?

Critical Thinking Exercise

Assume you are a criminal justice faculty member meeting with a prospective student. The individual is interested in several areas of study, including criminal justice. What arguments would you make in support of studying criminal justice? What career-related advice would you share?

For Further Examination

Collica-Cox, K., & Furst, G. (2019). It's not the CSI effect: Criminal justice students' choice of major and career goals. *International Journal of Offender Therapy and Comparative Criminology, 63*(11), 2069–2099.

Klutz, D. (2019). *Career guide in criminal justice*. Oxford University Press.

Mijares, T. (2018). *Careers for the criminal justice major*. Charles C. Thomas.

Sloan, J.J., III., & Buchwalter, J.W. (2017). The state of criminal justice bachelor's degree programs in the United States: Institutional, departmental and curricula features. *Journal of Criminal Justice Education, 28*(3), 307–334.

Stringer, E.C., & Murphy, J. (2020). Major decisions and career attractiveness among criminal justice students. *Journal of Criminal Justice Education, 31*(4), 523–541.

References

Adler, F., Mueller, G.O., & Laufer, W.S. (2007). *Criminology* (6th ed.). McGraw-Hill.

Buehler, E.D. (2021). *Justice expenditures and employment in the United States*. U.S. Department of Justice, Bureau of Justice Statistics. NCJ 256093.

Burns, R.G. (2022). *Criminal justice: The system in perspective*. Oxford University Press.

Collica-Cox, K., & Furst, G. (2019). It's not the CSI effect: Criminal justice students' choice of major and career goals. *International Journal of Offender Therapy and Comparative Criminology, 63*(11), 2069–2099.

Eren, C.P., Leyro, S., & Disha, I. (2019). It's personal: The impact of victimization on motivations and career interests among criminal justice majors at diverse urban colleges. *Journal of Criminal Justice Education, 30*(4), 510–535.

Jones, M., & Bonner, H.S. (2016). What should criminal justice interns know? Comparing the opinions of student interns and criminal justice practitioners. *Journal of Criminal Justice Education, 27*(3), 381–409.

Oliver, W.M. (2016). Celebrating 100 years of criminal justice education, 1916–2016. *Journal of Criminal Justice Education, 27*(4), 455–472.

Sloan, J.J., III., & Buchwalter, J.W. (2017). The state of criminal justice bachelor's degree programs in the United States: Institutional, departmental and curricula features. *Journal of Criminal Justice Education, 28*(3), 307–334.

Stringer, E.C., & Murphy, J. (2020). Major decisions and career attractiveness among criminal justice students. *Journal of Criminal Justice Education, 31*(4), 523–541.

The Sentencing Project. (2021). *Trends in U.S. corrections*. Retrieved from www.sentencingproject.org/wp-content/uploads/2021/07/Trends-in-US-Corrections.pdf

Chapter 2

A History of Criminal Justice Focused on Employment and Academic Study

The history of criminal justice and criminology is intertwined to some extent and characterized by innovation, change, brutality, inequality, and intrigue. It is, by historical standards, an exciting account that was largely influenced by the events that shaped the United States. Criminal justice practices have shaped and been shaped by many historical events.

Individuals seeking a career in criminal justice and criminology should be aware of how the system and disciplines evolved. Among other benefits, understanding the past helps prevent repeated mistakes. Recognizing the past also facilitates understanding how current practices emerged and provides a better contextualization of the field. The fact that schools at all levels require history courses as part of their curriculum speaks loudly of the significance of history.

This chapter highlights significant historical events in the development of criminal justice in the United States. In doing so, the chapter is organized into two primary parts: the evolution and development of criminal justice as a practice, with a particular emphasis on the criminal justice workforce, and the development of criminal justice as a field of study. The emphasis in the first part is on criminal justice instead of criminology given the more applied nature of the field. Both parts of the chapter provide a solid foundation of knowledge for anyone seeking a career in criminal justice or criminology.

Why History?

There are many justifications for studying the past. In his work on the role of historical studies in criminal justice curricula, researcher Mark Jones (1994) identified several reasons for teaching criminal justice history: (1) to study the development of current criminal justice components and institutions; (2) to observe the various significant social, economic, political, and/or philosophical forces that have shaped contemporary reactions to deviance; (3) to compare contemporary American criminal justice practices with those of the past and those of both similar and different cultures; and (4) to enable students to place current criminal justice issues in historical context. Unfortunately, many students are deprived of the opportunity to recognize and appreciate the history of criminal justice as the discipline's history is not taught in many academic programs.

Appreciation of how the system can drastically change, sometimes in the matter of a single day, helps us understand the dynamic and vulnerable nature of criminal justice and criminology employment. Examination of the significant historical developments that have shaped criminal justice and criminology in the United States helps readers understand today's criminal justice system. Further, studying the societal events, happenings, and developments that significantly impacted our justice systems facilitates understanding what it would be like to work in criminal justice or criminology.

DOI: 10.4324/9781003360162-3

Recognizing the past is significant for understanding the present and being prepared for the future. Among other effects, understanding how the criminal justice system emerged and changed helps us learn from past mistakes and facilitates understanding what the future may hold. Along these lines, understanding how criminal justice and criminology became academic disciplines, or areas of study, helps readers better understand the more scholarly components of these important fields. Exposing future practitioners to the historical developments in criminal justice and criminology hopefully sharpens their decision-making skills and facilitates sensible policy making. Criminal justice historian John Conley echoes these points in noting that studying history "provides a context for issues and institutions" while offering "a broad foundation for evaluation through comparing and contrasting current issues with past experiences" (Conley, 1993, 904).

The Evolution of Criminal Justice Practices and the Creation of Jobs

Discussing the history of criminal justice practices in the United States in one chapter is a vast undertaking. In other words, there is much to be written about the development of criminal justice practices. This chapter highlights the significant developments, particularly as they relate to employment-related issues. Those interested in more in-depth coverage of the history of criminal justice are encouraged to read the works provided in the *For Further Examination* feature at the end of this chapter.

The roots of American criminal justice practices were established in England, prior to the colonists settling in what is now the United States. To be sure, criminal justice practices in early England are worthy of great discussion; however, the focus here is on American criminal justice.

Historical accounts of any topic are typically organized into particular time periods. Accordingly, the following historical account is adapted from the work of criminal justice historians Willard Oliver and James Hilgenberg, Jr. Oliver and Hilgenberg, in their insightful book *A History of Crime and Criminal Justice in America* (2006, 2018), identify a series of eras of historical developments regarding crime and criminal justice. As noted in this section, employment opportunities were largely impacted by the historical developments. For example, more jobs emerged and the quality of work pertaining to those positions changed as the criminal justice system expanded. The historical account begins with consideration of colonial America and continues to the present.

1607–1775: The Colonial Era

The Colonial Era of criminal justice is divided into the Village Period (1607–1699) and the Town Period (1700–1775) (Oliver & Hilgenberg, 2006). Both periods and the overall era are characterized by a strong reliance on informal social control as opposed to formal social control (e.g., the criminal justice system). Criminal justice practices during the village period in particular were largely influenced by the need to establish and survive in the New World. Much focus was on the recently arrived people who came to America for various reasons, for instance, to avoid religious persecution or to escape biased government treatment based on class. Needless to stay, numerous social, economic, and political factors influenced the settlement of America (Oliver & Hilgenberg, 2006).

The colonists remained under English law; however, the large geographical distance between England and America prevented strict enforcement of those laws. Subsequently, the colonists began creating and shaping their own body of laws and systems of justice. Colonial law at the beginning of the eighteenth century began to more closely resemble English criminal law (Roth, 2005). Fortunately, the crime rate was notably low as there was a strong sense of a need for survival, leaving little time and/or opportunity to engage in crime. The large number of colonists who left England to escape religious persecution were influential in incorporating religion into codified laws (Oliver & Hilgenberg, 2006). Employment positions in criminal justice were relatively scarce, as the country was being established.

Town meetings, church meetings, and families were central to the informal control efforts. There was no criminal justice system at this time (Walker, 1998). Town meetings served the role of courts by settling disputes between individuals and offering punishments and settlements (Nelson, 1981). Families were responsible for controlling the behavior of their children as there was no juvenile justice system at this time. Corporal punishment, including whippings, was a common response to egregious behavior (Walker, 1998). Free from intervention in religious practices, many colonists developed a new set of mores and norms that became part of the law and strictly enforced (Oliver & Hilgenberg, 2006). Accordingly, church members acted in place of courts and issued various types of punishments, including banishment from the congregation and admonition on those engaging in unacceptable behavior (Chapin, 1983).

The tumultuous relationship between the colonists and England was generated by several factors and had notable impacts on the establishment and practices of the American criminal justice system. English authorities demonstrated greater control over the settlers, initially through the magistrates of the courts and the governors of the colonies, and later through military intervention, for instance, with regard to the collection of taxes. Greater assertion of authority generated enhanced interest in independence and revolt by the colonists. The imposition of large taxes upon citizens was perhaps one of the more influential factors leading to revolution and an increase in crime. Extensive black markets emerged and smugglers and pirates more frequently appeared in response to the burden of taxes imposed on the settlers (Oliver & Hilgenberg, 2006). These and related issues prompted movement toward the creation of a criminal justice system, which brought with it new employment opportunities.

The establishment of the United States, particularly its criminal justice system, was assisted by the large numbers of individuals who sought economic, social, and other interests in the New World. As more individuals sought to live in America for various reasons, the population increased and American society became increasingly diverse. Such demographic shifts were impacted by increasing levels of crime in many colonial cities by the 1750s, which overmatched the abilities of the night watchmen and constables (Roth, 2005). Increasing disorder contributed to the establishment and day-to-day practices of the American system of criminal justice (Oliver & Hilgenberg, 2006), and increasing justice-based employment opportunities.

There were no innovative contributions to policing, courts and corrections during this period, as law enforcement agents of this time (e.g., constables, sheriffs, and those staffing watches and wards) were poorly trained and generally ineffective in their duties, and departments were understaffed (Oliver & Hilgenberg, 2006). Constables and night watchmen, where they existed, were often untrained and either elected or drafted into their position (Walker, 1998). There was a notable level of mistrust of law enforcement by the citizens, particularly with regard to tax collection. The mistrust primarily stemmed from law enforcement agents being representatives of the king's government. The judges, or justices of the peace in the courts of this time, were typically laypersons untrained in the law (Friedman, 1993). They became increasingly punitive and tyrannical, and the courts became increasingly ineffective. Citizens fought back against what seemed to be judicial misconduct and the overall ineffectiveness of the courts. Correctional practices continued to incorporate corporal punishment, particularly as displayed in public (Oliver & Hilgenberg, 2006). Incarceration existed, however, its role was minor compared to other forms of punishment. Jails were rarely used to punish individuals deemed guilty of committing a crime (Walker, 1998).

Overall, the criminal justice system during the Colonial period was unable to meet the existing societal demands and changes. Criminal justice practices were not designed at this time to address drastic and volatile social, economic, and political shifts. Further, social control withered as communities grew in size and homogeneous societies became increasingly heterogeneous in their makeup. Criminal justice practices would evolve as settlers gained independence from England and began to shape the United States. Developments during this time set the stage for an expanded criminal justice system; one that currently employs millions of people.

1776–1828: A New Nation

The period immediately following the American Revolution is largely characterized by the need to organize and establish a legitimate society. Such efforts included the establishment of a criminal justice system. Establishing an effective court system was a priority, and efforts were made to improve law enforcement and correctional practices (Oliver & Hilgenberg, 2006).

America consisted of a largely rural population at the turn of the nineteenth century. Nevertheless, crime, particularly property crime, increased slowly during this period. The response to the increase in crime was hampered by overriding concerns to address more pressing issues, such as establishing an agreed-upon structure of government. Changes with regard to policing, courts, and corrections would appear in this period, leading to an expansion in the criminal justice workforce. The newly formed country faced the challenge of designing a criminal justice system, based on the English version, that met the needs of citizens. Among the developments were police powers becoming more limited, and peace officers in the 1820s focusing less on preventing or confronting crime than on public health and municipal regulations. Further, courts were designed to be more effective and controllable, and correctional reforms experimented with the idea of using jails as a form of punishment rather than a means of pretrial detention (Oliver & Hilgenberg, 2006; Roth, 2005).

The Revolution prompted criminal justice reform and perpetuated differences in English and American criminal law (Walker, 1998). For instance, it was during the 1790s when the Attorney General's position and the first federal statute (which defined what crimes constituted a federal offense) were created (Roth, 2005). Further, modern prisons were introduced in the United States in the mid-1820s, an event that would largely shape the future of the American system of criminal justice (Walker, 1998). Accompanying these substantial developments in crime and justice was an increasing number-, and types of employment positions within criminal justice. Employment opportunities expanded both quantitatively and qualitatively. The criminal justice system continued to evolve during the Jacksonian Era.

1829–1855: The Jacksonian Era

The factors underlying the beginning of the Civil War were apparent through much of the Jacksonian Era. The social problems that appeared in the previous period were becoming increasingly recognizable, particularly issues pertaining to slavery and Native Americans. Economic concerns also contributed to social unrest. The industrialized North sought to end slavery, while the agrarian Southerners relied heavily on slave labor. The South fought strongly for states' rights, which contributed to the political dissent of the times (Oliver & Hilgenberg, 2006). Social unrest during this period impacted the increasing crime rates, as riots, violent crime, and unruly behavior by and against Native Americans became increasingly problematic.

Extensive rioting in major cities characterized this time period, and crimes by and against slaves also contributed largely to the pervasive social problems of the time. Criminal justice officials were needed to address the social problems.

The criminal justice system was forced to react to the tumultuous times. The system became increasingly punitive, particularly with regard to slave laws. US police departments, modeled after departments in England, formed during this time to address the unrest. Boston is credited with creating the first American police department; however, it consisted of compiling the services of the constables, the night and day watch personnel, and the sheriffs (Lane, 1971; Walker, 1998). Courts were hearing a greater number of criminal cases, and it was during this time that the United States saw its first prison expansion, as large penitentiaries were increasingly housing individuals convicted of crimes (Oliver & Hilgenberg, 2006). Prison officers and wardens, similar to their counterparts in the courts and policing, were poorly trained and often received their position via political patronage (Walker, 1998).

The Jacksonian period was a time of great change in the implementation and administration of criminal justice. It was not until this time that we saw a system that largely resembles the one we have today. However, the system lacked efficiency and effectiveness, particularly in the largely unsettled western part of the country. Creating and applying tougher laws often generated newer problems instead of addressing existing issues. Police departments, where they existed, too often failed to properly address crime and law violators. Police corruption and political interference hampered many of their efforts. The courts and corrections also failed to properly address the social problems and unrest of the time (Oliver & Hilgenberg, 2006). For example, the establishment of a penal system in the 1820s did little to address increasing crime rates (Roth, 2005), although it and other developments during this period contributed to additional employment opportunities in criminal justice. The expansion of the criminal justice system was increasingly creating a relatively new area of field of employment for many people. The Civil War Era provided additional challenges for the emerging US criminal justice system.

1856–1878: The Civil War Era

The Civil War Era proved to be a significant period in the evolution of the criminal justice system in the United States. The social, political, and economic issues of this very unstable time in US history heavily influenced government responses to crime and the need for justice. Crime rates increased and violent crime became problematic leading up to the Civil War. Violence and crime were largely legitimized during the war; thus, the crime rate dropped while the country fought. Crime rates increased following the war, as displaced war veterans found difficulty adjusting to postwar life, and economic crimes against those in the South and attacks against freed slaves contributed to the problems (Oliver & Hilgenberg, 2006; Roth, 2005).

The progress of the criminal justice system in the Jacksonian period largely ceased once the Civil War began. The country's focus was largely directed toward the war and eventually Reconstruction, leaving little time or resources for other issues. Uniformed police officers patrolled beats in many large cities by the 1860s; however, many police officers left their posts to become soldiers (Oliver & Hilgenberg, 2006; Roth, 2005). Courts began to address war-related issues, and prisons were forced to hold captured soldiers and individuals convicted of crimes. Progress with regard to the criminal justice system continued following the war, particularly during the latter part of Reconstruction. The country was no longer preoccupied with fighting a war and faced many new and unpleasant challenges (Oliver & Hilgenberg, 2006). Despite the impacts of the Civil War, criminal justice practices advanced during this period, as there was a continued need for criminal justice personnel.

1879–1899: The Gilded Age

The Gilded Age brought great hope to Americans who could now redirect their attention from fighting a war toward further establishing the country. Life became increasingly orderly, largely in response to police reform, industrialization, and a more established public school system. Criminologists and other social scientists were increasingly applying scientific techniques to study the causes of crime (Roth, 2005). There was a belief among many citizens that the country provided immense opportunities for individual wealth. However, many individuals struggled to attain the "American Dream," and instead found that only a select group of powerful individuals (e.g., big business owners) prospered and largely controlled society. African American individuals and the growing number of people from other countries struggled both socially and financially, as the rift between race and class persisted (Oliver & Hilgenberg, 2006).

Increased immigration, poverty, and discrimination set the stage for an increase in crime. Again, the criminal justice system was forced to address rising crime rates in response to social unrest. The criminal justice system became increasingly institutionalized as greater numbers of individuals were employed in policing, courts, and corrections during this time (Oliver & Hilgenberg, 2006). For example, the Department of Justice was created at the federal level of government in 1870 (Roth, 2005). Unfortunately, the general public's mistreatment of poor minorities carried over into the system, as police officers continued to protect political interests and courts largely focused on protecting the interests of the elite. Correctional reform was considered; however, prisons nevertheless continued to warehouse the poor. There were several notable developments with regard to juvenile justice toward the end of the Gilded Age, although these efforts largely involved controlling the poor youth who immigrated from other countries, and others who were viewed as threats (Oliver & Hilgenberg, 2006).

Many of the social problems evident in the Gilded Age appear in today's criminal justice system. From a qualitative standpoint, this period helped set the stage for some of the tension and distrust that exists between the public and powerful groups today, including the criminal justice system.

1900–1919: The Progressive Era

The Progressive Era is recognized as a period of significant change in US history. It was a time when many reformers took particular interest in helping law violators, juveniles, prostitutes, individuals living on the streets, and other groups that were and are often brought to the attention of the criminal justice system. Many noncitizens were coming to America in the early 1900s, in turn generating a host of social problems as integration posed many challenges. Socializing these new Americans became part of the charge of progressives, and rehabilitation was viewed as a primary means to controlling those who broke the law (Walker, 1998). Many social service-oriented employment positions emerged to assist the more traditional criminal justice practices.

Crime during this period continued much the same as it did during the Gilded Age. Put simply, it continued to rise. Progressive reforms were requested from the criminal justice system, much like they were requested from the political, social, and economic sectors of society. New laws were passed to address the rising crime rate, and new law enforcement agencies were developed, including state police agencies and the Federal Bureau of Investigation. Progressive changes positively impacted the courts, particularly with regard to the increased use of plea bargaining and indeterminate sentencing, and correctional institutions began incorporating some of the changes proposed during the Gilded Age.

A juvenile justice system, distinct from the (adult) criminal justice system, signified true progressive reform (Oliver & Hilgenberg, 2006) and established new employment opportunities. The criminal justice system gained much independence from political influences during the Progressive Era, and the changes suggested that fighting crime and ensuring justice were headed in a positive direction (Oliver & Hilgenberg, 2006). World War I, however, changed the focus of American society and brought an end to Progressive reform.

1920–1939: The Crisis Era

With the end of World War I (1914–1918) and coming out of a recession, the United States anticipated a promising decade in the 1920s. However, things didn't necessarily go as planned, as the Crisis Era is characterized by several events that changed the face of America. The beginning of the Era saw the effects of the passage of the 18th Amendment in 1919, otherwise known as Prohibition. The latter part of the Era was influenced by the 1929 stock market crash that brought about economic depression. Racial tensions continued during the period, and blacks and other minorities were the first ones to lose jobs as the depression took hold (Oliver & Hilgenberg, 2006). Needless to say, both crime rates and prison populations grew during the 1920s. Overcrowded prisons contributed to tension among the incarcerated and ultimately riots (Roth, 2005). These events, akin to other historical happenings, influenced the quantity and quality of jobs in criminal justice.

Prohibition and the Great Depression combined to generate much crime, and eventually a call for criminal justice reform. Prohibition, for instance, prompted a new criminal class intent on manufacturing, selling, and/or drinking alcohol. It was a time when the Italian Mafia, and organized crime in general, became integrated into American folklore, as organized criminal networks vied for control of the illegal alcohol market (Oliver & Hilgenberg, 2006). Prohibition nullified many of the progressive reforms and generated much crime, including violent crime, as organized crime groups engaged in conflict upon recognizing the potential benefits of distributing illegal alcohol. Unfortunately, the criminal justice system was ill-prepared to address the developments (Oliver & Hilgenberg, 2006; Roth, 2005). In response to their success, organized crime groups became increasingly involved in other areas of vice, including gambling, prostitution, and drugs (Roth, 2005).

Police departments during this period were heavily involved in crime fighting and serving political interests. They were unable to effectively control the problems largely resulting from Prohibition. Police corruption continued at all ranks of departments as organized crime groups would too often pay off police agents to "look the other way" while they would ply their trade. Arrests for Prohibition-related offenses filled the courts and jails. The social problems resulting from the Depression toward the latter part of this period coupled with the struggles stemming from Prohibition and ineffective criminal justice system responses resulted in a public outcry for criminal justice reform.

Public outcry over the ineffectiveness of policing resulted in few reforms during the Crisis Era, largely due to the limited available resources. However, the outcry and exposure of law enforcement's limitations generated interest in policing at all levels of government; interest that would result in significant reform in the decades ahead (particularly the 1960s and 1970s). Similar concerns were recognized in the courts, corrections, and juvenile justice, where reform was needed, but limited resources restricted progress (Oliver & Hilgenberg, 2006). The problems resulting from Prohibition and the Depression would soon be tempered by the repeal of Prohibition in 1933 and the end of the Depression in the late 1930s and early 1940s. The United States, however, would have another crisis to confront: World War II.

1940–1959: The War Years

World War II consumed Americans' interest to the extent that very little criminal justice reform occurred during this period. The United States still experienced struggles with regard to race, class, and gender; however, there was a united effort to fight the war. The wealthy supported the war, minorities and the poor largely fought in the war, and women increasingly assumed the jobs previously performed by males who left to fight the war. Much of the country's energies and focus was on winning the war (Oliver & Hilgenberg, 2006).

Economic prosperity followed the war. In turn, crime rates remained very low in the 1940s and 1950s, and very little criminal or juvenile justice system reform occurred. One could view the postwar period as the calm before the storm, however, as the stage was being set for a tumultuous period of civil unrest, and an expansion in the number of employment opportunities.

1960–1979: The Nationalization Era

The Nationalization Era contrasted the War Years in several ways. Gone were the days of peace, stability, and prosperity. Civil unrest, a baby boom, and political and economic instability largely contributed to riots and general social unrest during this period. Generational differences caused by the postwar baby boom contributed to, among other issues, the civil rights movement, a revitalized feminist movement, and a counterculture that mistrusted government and other institutions. The economy stumbled in the 1960s and ultimately the United States experienced an economic recession largely impacted by an energy crisis in the 1970s (Oliver & Hilgenberg, 2006). Criminal justice historian Samuel Walker called the period from 1960 to 1975 as "the most turbulent in all of American criminal justice history" (Walker, 1998, 180). Individuals employed in the criminal justice system had the extra burden of the public's distrust of authority, particularly in relation to police officers.

The 1960s brought unfulfilled dreams of successful criminal justice reform. The criminal justice system was largely caught off guard however, and somewhat unprepared to address the social upheavals, including unstable race relations, of the time. The Kerner Commission, established to study the causes of the urban disorder, noted that the unequal treatment of Black individuals contributed to the rioting. Employment in criminal justice became increasingly important, controversial, and difficult.

An anti-authority attitude emerged, largely among individuals concerned about equal rights and various other social issues. The collective social problems, and concerns for justice, fairness, and equity in all areas of life heavily impacted those working in the criminal justice system. The role and importance of criminologists expanded, however, as funding for research was allocated to various groups by the government to study crime and responses to it. Nevertheless, criminal justice reform was not immediately evident.

The turbulent 1960s generated a new response to crime beginning in the 1970s. Americans grew increasingly fearful of crime in the 1960s and 1970s, and by 1978, 85% of Americans believed the criminal justice system should become increasingly punitive (Hindelang et al., 1981). A more conservative, "get tough" approach would become the preferred approach to criminal justice. Further, the turbulent Nationalization Era encouraged a directed focus on the criminal justice system, which led to the massive expansion of the system beginning around 1980 (Oliver & Hilgenberg, 2006). The combination of getting tough on crime and expanding the criminal justice system had notable impacts on our modern system of criminal justice. Many new employment positions were created in law enforcement, the legal arena, and corrections.

1980–2001: The Reagan Era

The Reagan Era, according to Oliver and Hilgenberg (2018), began with greater social stability than the Nationalization Era. The election of President Ronald Reagan brought hope that the troubles the country earlier faced would be gone. The economy recovered in the 1980s and prospered in the 1990s. Crime remained a societal concern, particular among inner-city residents who felt the greatest impacts of crime.

A Practitioner's View

Les Smith, Law Enforcement and Criminal Justice Planning

As a police officer, I participated in patrol operations. As a sergeant, lieutenant, and captain, I planned, scheduled, organized, and supervised the activities of the police department; trained sworn staff; developed and implemented departmental policy and programs; and provided administrative and budgetary support. As a criminal justice planner, it was necessary to have a thorough knowledge of criminology, and the criminal justice system including law enforcement, prosecution, courts, corrections, and criminal justice system research, planning and policy development strategies. I currently provide training and technical assistance to organizations related to improving the coordination of the criminal justice system, establishing community justice councils, and establishing policies and programs that help reduce recidivism and control the jail population.

To prepare for your career in criminal justice, you need to bring a critical consciousness and rigor to the world's problems, recognize biases, speak and act with civility, and listen with respect. These traits are needed now more than ever. For example, for future law enforcement officers, engagement with the humanities is essential preparation for working together with people whose world views might differ from their own. Higher levels of education in the community and problem-solving justice are needed. Prevention, intervention, and community research are key components of this strategy and can trace their theoretical roots to community policing, community prosecution, and community courts. Students must prepare to meet these new challenges and plan their careers accordingly.

Two particular factors are representative of criminal justice developments during this period: (1) the government's expanded war on drugs, which largely contributed to rising crime rates and more job opportunities, and (2) the disproportionate numbers of minority males entering the criminal justice system. Large-scale prison expansion began in the 1980s, as warehousing the incarcerated took precedence over rehabilitation, and incapacitation, deterrence, and retribution became the primary goals of criminal sentencing. The widespread introduction of crack cocaine in the 1980s contributed to substantial violence and rising crime rates in many urban areas. Following years of increasing crime rates, the crime rate steadily declined beginning in the early 1990s.

Police departments during this period continued to expand and there was an associated need for additional resources. Many departments changed their philosophical approach to policing from strict crime fighting to a community-oriented approach. Tougher laws were passed and enforced to address all forms of crime, including drug offenses. Courts continued to expand, and the prison boom experienced during this time was unprecedented in US history. Ultimately, there was great optimism that the United States had finally created an efficient and effective justice system that could control crime.

To some extent, working in the criminal justice system differed from the preceding era, when extensive social unrest and numerous social problems strained criminal justice resources. A new era of crime and justice began with the terrorist attacks on the morning of September 11, 2001. Among other effects, the terrorist attacks led to the creation of the Department of Homeland Security (DHS), and many additional employment opportunities in criminal justice.

September 11, 2001–Present: The Era of Security

It is well understood that the terrorist attacks on September 11, 2001, changed the American way of life. From a criminal justice perspective, the attacks signified the beginning of a new era: The Era of Security (Oliver & Hilgenberg, 2018). Police departments were now tasked with the additional burden of closely protecting citizens against terrorist attacks and diligently ensuring homeland protection. The federal government responded in part through creating the DHS. The DHS, a cabinet-level department of the federal government, was created through incorporating various law enforcement groups throughout the federal agencies into one department. The goal was to provide greater cooperation and coordination among federal law enforcement. The agency expanded rapidly, having surpassed the Department of Justice with the largest number of federal law enforcement officers (Brooks, 2022). It currently employs over 66,000 personnel tasked with protecting the country from any potential threats, including terrorist threats, to the homeland (Brooks, 2022).

The Era of Security remains a work in progress. Many issues have and will continue to impact the current and future state of criminal justice and the associated employment opportunities. Continuously incorporating technology into crime fighting and prevention, globalism, and immigration issues are but a few of the challenges faced the criminal justice system. Each challenge faced by the criminal justice system requires the efforts of skilled and talented workers who are prepared for the challenges associated with working in the field. Certainly, much more could be written about the current Era. Nevertheless, the remainder of this work deals in the present and largely reflects the events of this period.

This historical account of criminal justice in the United States helps contextualize criminal justice as an institution, an academic discipline, and an excellent source of employment opportunities. Observing how criminal justice emerged in the United States helps prepare tomorrow's criminal justice professionals for advancing criminal justice practices and identifying employment opportunities and trends. The remainder of this chapter describes the development of criminal justice and criminology as academic disciplines, which also enables tomorrow's criminal justice and criminology professionals to better understand how and why their academic programs emerged.

The Development of Academic Criminal Justice and Criminology Programs

The similarities between criminal justice and criminology highlighted in Chapter 1 are evident in the development of the academic study of the fields. Criminology, which emerged prior to criminal justice studies, is rooted in European scholarship, although scholars in the United States have had significant impacts on the field (e.g., Adler et al., 2007). Criminology is a subdiscipline of sociology, and was historically offered by sociology departments as an area of academic study. Among the early criminologists in the United States were researchers from the University of Chicago School of Sociology, who around 1893 began focusing on deviance and crime in society (Hale, 1998). The study of criminology remains part of some

Much has changed in criminal justice and criminology throughout history, including the number of, and responsibilities associated with employment positions.

Source: https://pxhere.com/en/photo/1356832

sociology programs, although criminology became a stand-alone program in many universities and colleges.

Criminal justice as an academic discipline is more recent than criminology, although some early efforts deemed "criminology" were actually criminal justice. For instance, the roots of criminal justice studies include Berkeley (CA) Police Chief August Vollmer creating an education-based program targeted specifically for criminal justice personnel at the Berkeley Police School in 1916. The school was connected to the University of California, and the program was titled Criminology. It provided "courses on police practices, criminal law, and many of the natural science classes including biology, chemistry, and toxicology" (Oliver, 2016, 455). Beginning in the late 1920s and continuing through the 1930s several colleges and universities created programs focused on the administration of policing and, more generally, criminal justice. Those directing these programs believed that higher education was needed to raise the personnel standards of people working in the field (Southerland et al., 2007).

Criminology programs continued to emerge, and became increasingly based on sociology. The academic study of police sciences also became increasingly popular, as the federal government wished to improve the educational level of police officers (Oliver, 2016). Some police studies programs branched off from the more sociology-based criminology programs, and many eventually broadened their scope to include not only policing, but all aspects of criminal justice. Developments in criminal justice and criminology have contributed to both disciplines no longer being in the shadows of other disciplines.

Following World War II there was a call to better train law enforcement personnel. In 1960, California and New York created formal police officer training programs and initiated the Peace Officer Standards and Training programs that were provided at local colleges and universities. Other states followed, resulting in the great expansion of criminal justice programs between 1960 and 1978 (Foster, 1979; Foster, et al., 2007). Most of these programs were offered at two-year community colleges (Stephens, 1976).

There were 64 colleges and universities offering programs in criminal justice by 1965, with an average of two programs created each year (IACP, 1968; Southerland et al., 2007). The number of criminal justice programs increased dramatically between 1965 and 1978. As of 1970 there were just under 500 degree programs. Such dramatic expansion slowed, however the quality of the education increased, particularly in response to advanced statistical capabilities and the presence of graduate-level studies. By 1990 there were 687 baccalaureate and 157 master's degree programs (Morn, 1995). More recent numbers suggest there were about 670 degree-granting baccalaureate criminal justice programs as of 2016 (Sloan & Buchwalter, 2017), and as of academic year 2021, 42 institutions offered a doctoral degree in criminal justice, criminology, or a closely-related discipline (U.S. News & World Report, 2021).

Higher education has consistently been viewed as a helpful means to attain certain employment positions, and as a means to improve the quality of services within the criminal justice system. Two reports published in 1967 (the US President's Commission on Law Enforcement and Administration of Justice, and the US Task Force on the Police) and one in 1973 (the US National Advisory Commission on Criminal Justice Standards and Goals) emphasized the need for higher levels of education among criminal justice personnel (Southerland et al., 2007). The reports, particularly the President's Commission's, generated a great deal of federal funding and contributed to the passage of the Omnibus Crime Control and Safe Streets Act. Title I of this legislation created the Law Enforcement Assistance Administration and the Law Enforcement Education Program (LEEP), which allocated substantial financial resources toward higher education in criminal justice and prompted the increased number of criminal justice programs during the early 1970s (Foster et al., 2007). In 1969, LEEP was funded for the first time. Congress appropriated $6.5 million that was dispersed to roughly 485 schools. LEEP would ultimately be discontinued during the Carter administration, however, not before providing $303 million in assistance to roughly 316,000 students (Foster et al., 2007; Foster, 1979).

The quality and focus of criminal justice studies have been questioned. For example, criminal justice programs of the 1960s and 1970s assumed competing philosophical approaches, with some programs adopting a more practitioner/professionalism approach, while other programs adopted a more academic study of criminal justice (Morn, 1995). The debate over whether criminal justice studies should focus on theory or practice provided an early and substantial roadblock to the overall development of criminal justice education. Further, the explosive growth in the number of criminal justice programs led to academic institutions, government agencies, and nongovernment organizations to question the quality of the criminal justice programs, the value of the criminal justice major, and the methods by which criminal justice programs would be evaluated by regional higher education accrediting agencies (Southerland, 2007). Many of these debates continue.

Criminal justice professor and historian Willard Oliver succinctly described the history and future of the study of criminal justice in stating:

> Since August Vollmer began the summer program for his Berkeley Police Officers in the summer of 1916, the development of criminal justice education has seen a number of developments over the past 100 years, and there will no doubt continue to (be) further development over the next 100 years.
>
> (Oliver, 2016, 466)

Each development impacts the direction of the fields, and subsequently affects employment opportunities and the nature of the work.

Summary

Shortly following the 2001 terrorist attacks against the United States, criminal justice historian Mitchell Roth noted that "The criminal justice system is changing more quickly than ever before." He added: "What was once a slow evolution based on experimentation and innovation has turned into a dynamic and proactive attempt to contain and suppress criminal behavior that was almost unthinkable in years past" (Roth, 2005, 351). Although offered years ago, his comments still apply. Among other contributions, this chapter helps place the study of criminal justice into perspective. Those entering careers or internships ought to be aware of the origins of the institutions and positions they are about to encounter and the field they are considering.

There are many reasons why students, particularly those entering an internship or the field, should be aware of the historical developments in criminal justice and criminology. For example, in his article on the role of historical studies in criminal justice curricula, researcher Mark Jones (1994, 178) commented on the importance of students being exposed to historical information that serves as a background to current criminal justice policies and responses. He noted that criminal justice students "should learn specifically how historical phenomena, such as progressivism, the Civil War, and the Industrial Revolution, relate both to past and present justice administration and to societal reaction to deviance." Understanding and learning from the past contributes to a more positive future.

Discussion Questions

1. Why is it important to study history?
2. Which era of developments in criminal justice do you believe had the greatest impact on employment in the field? Why?
3. Which three historical events do you believe had the greatest impact on employment in criminal justice?
4. What prompted the academic study of criminal justice?
5. What twenty-first-century events have largely shaped employment in criminal justice and criminology?

Critical Thinking Exercise

For the final in your History class, your teacher asked you to reorganize the historical periods of criminal justice into four eras, and explain how each impacted criminal justice employment opportunities. How would you reorganize the existing eras into four periods? Justify your response.

For Further Examination

Oliver, W.M. (2016) Celebrating 100 years of criminal justice education, 1916–2016. *Journal of Criminal Justice Education*, 27(4), 455–472.

Oliver, W.M., & Hilgenberg, J.F., Jr. (2018). *A history of crime and criminal justice in America* (3rd ed.). Carolina Academic Press.

Roth, M.P. (2018). *A history of crime and the American criminal justice system*. Routledge.

Shelden, R.G., & Vasiliev, P.V. (2018). *Controlling the dangerous classes: A history of criminal justice in America.* Waveland Press.

Thompson, H.A. (2019). The racial history of criminal justice in America. *Du Bois Review, 16*(1), 221–241.

References

Adler, F., Mueller, G.O., & Laufer, W.S. (2007). *Criminology* (6th ed.). McGraw-Hill.

Brooks, C. (2022). *Federal law enforcement officers, 2020 – Statistical tables.* U.S. Department of Justice, Bureau of Justice Statistics. NCJ 304752.

Chapin, B. (1983). *Criminal justice in colonial America, 1606–1660.* University of Georgia Press.

Conley, J.A. (1993). Historical perspective and criminal justice. *Journal of Criminal Justice Education, 4,* 901–912. P. 904.

Foster, J.P. (1979). *Office of criminal justice education and training: An internal report to the administration.* U.S. Department of Justice, Washington, DC: Unpublished manuscript.

Foster, J.P., Magers, J.S., & Mullikin, J. (2007). Observations and reflections on the evolution of crime-related higher education. *Journal of Criminal Justice Education, 18*(1), 123–136.

Friedman, L.M. (1993). *Crime and punishment in American history.* Basic Books.

Hale, D.C. (1998). Criminal justice education: Traditions in transition. *Justice Quarterly, 15,* 385–394.

Hindelang, M.J., Gottfredson, M.R. & T.J. Flanagan. (eds.) (1981). *Sourcebook of criminal justice statistics – 1980.* U.S. Government Printing Office.

International Association of Chiefs of Police (IACP). (1968). *Law enforcement education directory.* IACP.

Jones, M. (1994). Reflections on historical study in criminal justice curricula. *Journal of Criminal Justice Education, 5*(2), 167–187.

Lane, R. (1971). *Policing the city: Boston, 1822–1885.* Atheneum.

Morn, F. (1995). *Academic politics and the history of criminal justice education.* Greenwood Press.

Nelson, W.E. (1981). *Dispute and conflict resolution in Plymouth County, Massachusetts, 1725–1825.* University of North Carolina Press.

Oliver, W.M. (2016) Celebrating 100 years of criminal justice education, 1916–2016. *Journal of Criminal Justice Education, 27*(4), 455–472.

Oliver, W.M. & Hilgenberg, J.F., Jr. (2006). *A history of crime and criminal justice in America.* Allyn & Bacon.

Oliver, W.M., & Hilgenberg, J.F., Jr. (2018). *A history of crime and criminal justice in America* (3rd ed.). Carolina Academic Press.

Roth, M.P. (2005). *Crime and punishment: A history of the criminal justice system.* Wadsworth.

Sloan, J.J., III., & Buchwalter, J.W. (2017). The state of criminal justice bachelor's degree programs in the United States: Institutional, departmental and curricula features. *Journal of Criminal Justice Education, 28*(3), 307–334.

Southerland, M.D., Merlo, A.V., Robinson, L., Benekos, P.J., & Albanese, J.S. (2007). Ensuring quality in criminal justice education: Academic standards and the reemergence of accreditation. *Journal of Criminal Justice Education, 18*(1), 87–105.

Stephens, G. (1976). Criminal justice education: Past, present, and future. *Criminal Justice Review, 1,* 91–120.

Transportation Security Administration. (n.d.). *Leadership and organization.* Retrieved from www.tsa.gov/about/tsa-leadership

U.S. News & World Report. (2021). *Best criminology schools.* Retrieved from www.usnews.com/best-graduate-schools/top-humanities-schools/criminology-rankings

Walker, S. (1998). *Popular justice: A history of American criminal justice* (2nd ed.). Oxford University Press.

Chapter 3

Opportunities and Trends in Criminal Justice and Criminology Employment

One of the more attractive aspects of studying and working in criminal justice or criminology is the wide array of areas, and many positions related to the fields. One could study or work in law enforcement, the courts, or corrections, as a researcher, or in other areas. Many different employment opportunities exist within each component of the criminal justice system. Within corrections, for instance, one could focus on probation, parole, jails, or prisons. Anyone with an interest in helping others, securing a safe society, and seeking justice will certainly find numerous areas of interest within criminal justice and criminology, and in related areas that share many of the same objectives and characteristics.

Contributing to the many employment opportunities in criminal justice and criminology is the fact that the fields are continuously expanding. In addition to the more traditional an employment positions found throughout the criminal justice system (e.g., police officer, an attorney, correctional officer), there are many new areas of employment given the high level of concern for personal safety, advancements in technology, globalism, and homeland security. This chapter introduces readers to the large and varied number of employment opportunities related to criminal justice and criminology. These and many other opportunities are also addressed in Appendix D. Further, the chapter looks at particular trends in the criminal justice and criminology job market, as well as influences on the future of employment with attention to recent developments and projected changes in the fields. The latter part centers on the impacts of terrorism, technology, the fear of crime, sociocultural changes, globalism, and private security. These are by no means the only influences on the future of employment in criminal justice and criminology. They are, however, particularly important ones.

What's Available?

To comprehensively address the employment opportunities available in criminal justice and criminology is beyond the scope of this chapter. Accordingly, this chapter provides a helpful overview of employment opportunities and recent developments and trends pertaining to criminal justice and criminology careers. The goal is to encourage readers to recognize and understand the wide array of employment opportunities that exist in these areas. The information hopefully provides those seeking a career in criminal justice and criminology a better understanding of employment in the fields.

Many students interested in criminal justice and criminology believe that their career options are limited to being a police officer, an attorney, a judge, a researcher, or a prison officer. These are the more commonly known positions in criminal justice and criminology; however, there are many more positions in the fields that often go unnoticed. Keep an open mind as you read this chapter. Investigate the positions and fields that are of interest to you. Research skills are needed to investigate careers and employment positions, just as they are to conduct studies.

The onus is on you to learn about career opportunities. Thoroughly investigating careers and positions could ultimately save you years of aggravation, stress, and resources by preventing you from ending up in a job or career that is not what you thought it would be. Perhaps most importantly, your investigative work should not be done half-heartedly. Do not cut corners when researching careers of interest primarily because you'll only be cheating yourself.

The broad overview of careers in criminal justice and criminology focuses on careers in law enforcement, the courts, and corrections. This material is followed by coverage of careers and positions in other fields.

Law Enforcement

The United States has a decentralized system of policing, meaning that there are law enforcement agencies at various levels of government. Research suggests that the majority of criminal justice majors seek careers in law enforcement (e.g., Barthe et al., 2013), particularly federal law enforcement (Collica-Cox & Furst, 2019). Many students interested in law enforcement are focused on careers in the Federal Bureau of Investigation or local policing. These are certainly admirable career opportunities; however, they are not the only ones. For instance, law enforcement is practiced at the federal, state, county, and local levels, and private security firms provide additional opportunities for those interested in a law enforcement-related position.

Federal Law Enforcement

The executive branch of the federal government consists of 15 departments and 78 independent agencies. The executive branch is accountable for national and homeland security, public safety, and delivering most national services. Law enforcement responsibility at the federal level is currently shared by roughly 65 agencies. Accordingly, the federal government is quite fragmented with regard to jurisdictional authority (Bumgarner et al., 2018).

Federal law enforcement is among the most prestigious positions in criminal justice. Relatively recent concerns and developments in society have notably impacted federal law enforcement and created more and new opportunities for careers in the field. Such concerns include globalism, cybercrime, civil rights violations, white-collar crime, immigration, and terrorism, among others. The terrorist attacks of September 11, 2001, generated a directed focus on revamping and increasing the size of our federal law enforcement agencies. For example, the creation of the Department of Homeland Security (DHS) resulted from the largest government reorganization in 50 years. The Homeland Security Act (the legislation which created the DHS) transferred all or part of 22 existing federal agencies to DHS. In turn the DHS surpassed the Department of Justice (DOJ) as the federal department with the greatest percentage of federal agents with arrest and firearm authority in 2003. More recently, 49% of federal law enforcement officers worked in the DHS, compared to 30% in the DOJ (Brooks, 2022a).

Career opportunities with the DHS include border, airport, seaport, and waterway security; researching and developing security technology; responding to natural disasters or terrorist assaults and threats; analyzing intelligence reports; and many others. The DHS, however, is certainly not the only department at the federal level that offers career opportunities for those interested in criminal justice and criminology. Agencies within the DOJ, for instance, employ attorneys, special agents, engineers, auditors, information technology specialists, criminal investigators, scientists, medical professionals, correctional officers, budget and management specialists, chemists, forensic scientists, management/program analysts, accountants, intelligence research specialists, paralegals, and a host of other professionals. In sum, federal law enforcement positions exist in a variety of areas.

Some careers in federal law enforcement require extensive travel, sometimes on short notice. Relocation is more common in federal law enforcement compared to other levels of law enforcement, primarily due to the nationwide jurisdiction of federal agencies. Additional information regarding federal law enforcement is provided throughout this work, including Chapter 9 and Appendix C.

State Law Enforcement

State police agencies, also referred to as "state police," "state patrol," or "departments of public safety," primarily engage in traffic regulation and criminal investigations. They have geographical jurisdiction over their respective state. Most states have a primary law enforcement agency which may be supplemented by other state agencies that have responsibilities in specific areas such as parks protection, wildlife protection, and alcoholic beverage control. The administrative structure of state police agencies widely varies among the states.

State police officers are sometimes referred to as "State Troopers" or "Highway Patrol Officers." Most full-time sworn personnel are uniformed officers who maintain jurisdiction to arrest law violators statewide and heavily enforce traffic regulations on the state highways. Other state law enforcement agents conduct investigations, engage in court-related duties, and perform administrative and related assignments. They sometimes assist local police agencies, particularly police or sheriff's departments in rural areas. The primary functions performed by state law enforcement agencies include:

- Traffic enforcement and accident investigation on state highways;
- First response and patrol;
- Training academy operations;
- Narcotics/vice enforcement;
- Responding to homeland security threats;
- Fingerprint processing;
- Search and rescue operations; and
- Ballistics/laboratory testing.

Forty-nine of the 50 states in the United States have state-level law enforcement agencies; Hawaii is the exception. Further discussion of the nature of the work provided by state law enforcement is provided in Chapter 9, which addresses law enforcement employment opportunities at all levels.

County Law Enforcement

County-level law enforcement primarily consists of sheriff's departments and county police departments. All states, with the exception of Alaska, Connecticut, and Hawaii, operate sheriffs' offices. There are just under 2,900 sheriff's departments throughout the United States, with roughly 174,000 full-time sworn officers (Brooks, 2022b). Sworn personnel perform duties that closely resemble those found in local police departments. Generally, sheriff's departments perform traditional law enforcement functions, including routine patrol, traffic enforcement, and responding to citizen calls for service. They also often operate jails and assist with court-related duties, including serving legal papers and providing security in courtrooms.

Having jurisdiction over an entire county means sheriff's and county law enforcement agencies are responsible for a much larger geographical area than municipal police. This arrangement contributes to overlap in services and the potential for interagency conflict. This concern, however, is typically addressed by having sheriffs' and county police departments assume responsibility for the unincorporated areas of the county and providing assistance to municipal police when needed. Such an arrangement impacts the general nature of the calls they handle.

Local Law Enforcement

The term "local law enforcement" encompasses many different types of policing and provides the widest variety and largest number of employment opportunities. Many in society are generally familiar with the opportunities and responsibilities of municipal, or city police officers, for instance, as we often encounter officers on patrol. However, one must bear in mind that becoming a police officer does not restrict one to patrol. Larger municipal departments have various divisions that require specific skill sets, including drug task forces, crime prevention units, air patrol, SWAT teams, cybercrime units, canine units, and many others.

The term "local police" also encompasses suburban and rural police departments, in which an officer's general responsibilities may be the same (e.g., serve and protect), yet their day-to-day experiences differ. Rural policing involves more service-oriented tasks and less danger. It may be less exciting than big city policing, however, not all who enter policing are interested in the excitement more often associated with big city police departments. Suburban departments offer a balance between rural and big city policing, as officers in these departments provide much service yet also encounter their share of crime.

Employment opportunities at the rural level are plentiful, as the United States is composed of many rural areas. The Bureau of Justice Statistics reported that just under half (45.5%) of local police departments employed less than ten full-time, sworn officers. Just under three-quarters (73.5%) of departments employed less than 25 officers (Goodison, 2022). Put simply, most departments in the United States are not big city departments. Most officers, however, work in large cities simply because of the higher crime rates and greater populations found in big cities. Accordingly, 62.3% of full-time sworn officers work in departments that employ 100 or more officers (Goodison, 2022). Career opportunities in all levels of law enforcement are discussed further in Chapter 9.

Special jurisdiction police also provide law enforcement services, often at the local level. These agencies provide important services and offer career opportunities, for instance, as campus police, airport police, port police, park police, and other types of law enforcement officers. There are roughly 1,700 special jurisdiction law enforcement agencies, the majority of which maintained jurisdiction over public buildings and facilities (e.g., high schools, colleges, and universities) (Reaves, 2011).

Courts

The United States has a dual court system consisting of state and federal courts. Federal courts process cases that involve violations of federal law and include US District Courts (the trial courts in the federal system), Circuit Courts of Appeals (the appellate courts), and the US Supreme Court, which is the court of last resort. Each state has its own court system, with state laws determining the function, organization, and names of its courts. For discussion purposes, it is best to categorize the different type of state courts into four categories: trial courts of limited jurisdiction, trial courts of general jurisdiction, intermediate appellate courts (although this level is found in only 41 states), and state courts of last resort, or state supreme courts. Criminal cases originating in state courts may also make it to the US Supreme Court.

Courts can be categorized as either state or federal, or according to the types of cases they hear. Trial courts (courts of limited- and general jurisdiction at the state-level, and US District

Courts in the federal system) hear cases of original jurisdiction. Appellate courts (e.g., state intermediate appellate courts, state courts of last resort, US Circuit Courts of Appeals, and the US Supreme Court) have appellate jurisdiction and review trial court proceedings to ensure accuracy and protect constitutional rights. Various employment positions exist throughout all types and levels of courts.

Specific professions and occupations in the courts require employees to spend much time in the courtroom. One will regularly find prosecutors, defense attorneys, judges, bailiffs, court reporters, clerks of court, and other courtroom personnel in courtrooms throughout the US. Judges and attorneys are perhaps the most visible within courtrooms; however, many other individuals contribute to the day-to-day functioning of our courts.

Prosecutors are one of the most powerful actors in our justice systems. They are involved with most steps of criminal case processing and maintain a great deal of discretionary power. Prosecutors are most recognizable in their role as representatives of the government in criminal case processing. Defense attorneys represent individuals accused of committing crime. Their position is not always respected by the public as they're often seen as representing "criminals." However, we must keep in mind that all who enter our courts are innocent until proven guilty.

Judges interpret and apply the law while overseeing the legal proceedings in court. They preside over a wide array of cases and ensure that justice is served and all parties are treated in a fair and just manner. Judicial duties and responsibilities are pretty straightforward at the federal level, given that there is only one federal government. State court judges often only hear particular types of cases (e.g., felony or misdemeanors), and a variety of titles are assigned to these judges. Judicial duties and responsibilities vary by state, and judges may be referred to as "municipal court judges," "county court judges," "magistrates," "justices of the peace," and other titles.

Bear in mind that judges hear cases involving both criminal and civil matters. Many of us all familiar with judges overseeing criminal cases; however, civil court matters also require judicial oversight. For instance, administrative law judges (sometimes referred to as "hearing officers" or "adjudicators") preside over legal matters pertaining to administrative agencies and matters. They may, for instance, assess whether an individual is eligible for worker's compensation benefits. Related to judges and magistrates are arbitrators, mediators, and conciliators. These individuals assist with alternative methods of dispute resolution that, at least initially, do not involve the courts.

Bailiffs provide a uniformed law enforcement presence in the courtroom. Among other things, they ensure that no weapons are brought into the courtroom and are responsible for ensuring the peace while court is in session. Court reporters create transcripts of the courtroom proceedings. Their work is particularly valuable when cases move from trial to appellate courts, as transcripts enable appellate court judges to understand what occurred in the trial court. Clerks of court are accountable for much of the administrative work in the courts. They may prepare the docket of scheduled cases, administer the oath to witnesses and jurors, and perform related administrative duties. Legal assistants, or paralegals, provide research and other forms of assistance to lawyers. Elaboration of careers and positions in the courts is provided in Chapter 10.

Corrections

Correctional agencies offer a variety of employment opportunities at various levels of government. For instance, one could work in community corrections as a community supervision officer. Or, one could work in a correctional institution (e.g., prison or jail), for instance, as a corrections officer, warden, or treatment program facilitator. Working in corrections provides many challenges for employees, including the difficulties associated with supervising individuals who have lost many freedoms. Conversely, working in corrections provides an invaluable opportunity for individuals to help a portion of society that is in great need of assistance.

Employment opportunities in community corrections largely consist of working in a parole or probation agency providing community supervision. Probation and parole agencies employ individuals to perform tasks aside from the traditional practices associated with directly monitoring individuals in the community. For instance, employees within these agencies could administer a residential community center or day-reporting center, or provide some type of treatment for individuals being supervised in the community.

As total institutions, prisons must provide a wide array of services for the incarcerated. They employ many individuals to perform a variety of roles. Jails, another form of institutional corrections, must also provide many services for the incarcerated. Correctional officers and jailers are the most recognizable positions within institutional corrections, although there are many other opportunities within this field, including administrative, clerical, educational, medical, religious, recreational service, maintenance/food service, professional/technical, and treatment-oriented positions (Harr & Hess, 2006).

Working directly with individuals under correctional supervision contributes to many challenges for those working in corrections. Accordingly, careers in corrections sometimes include particular stressors absent from careers in many other fields. The ability to work closely with incarcerated and individuals being supervised in the community, assist others, and help protect society are certainly benefits to careers in corrections. Careers in corrections are generally lower paying compared to careers in other areas of criminal justice and criminology.

The various employment opportunities in criminal justice and criminology can often be described using many diverse terms, including rewarding, dangerous, comfortable, exciting, and unpredictable.
Source: www.pexels.com/photo/man-in-orange-jacket-standing-beside-man-in-black-leather-jacket-6065469/

Chapter 11 provides additional coverage of careers in corrections, and Appendix E includes salaries for employment positions in corrections and other areas criminal justice and criminology.

Other Areas

Policing, courts, and corrections are the primary components of the criminal justice system; however, there are other fields in which those with an interest in criminal justice or criminology may find employment. For instance, juvenile justice systems exist in each state and provide many employment positions for individuals interested in working with troubled youth.

Working with justice-involved and at-risk youth is an important investment in societal well-being. Today's youth are tomorrow's future; thus, it is important that troubled and at-risk children and young adults engage in pro-social behavior. These individuals, however, can be a source of frustration for those working in the field, as some juveniles caught up in the system lack the maturity needed to make rational decisions, while others see their youth as a sign of invincibility. Conversely, working with troubled or at-risk youth can be extremely rewarding. Knowing that your efforts made a difference in someone's life should inspire you to continue making a difference.

Among the career opportunities in juvenile justice are juvenile probation officers, case workers, counselors, educators, intake officers, childcare workers in juvenile detention centers, and group home childcare workers. Chapter 12 expands on employment opportunities in juvenile justice.

The private security industry has grown substantially globally (Provost, 2017). Businesses and citizens are recognizing that they cannot solely rely on law enforcement for protection. Accordingly, citizens and businesses are increasingly taking responsibility for their own protection. Private security services are available to both homeowners and businesses.

While many in the general public may perceive private security as primarily constituting private security officers, the field extends far beyond this position. Private security services are required in all major corporations and are a viable option for employment, yet corporate security is an often overlooked area of study for criminal justice and criminology programs. Individuals with advanced computer skills and a criminal justice or criminology background are becoming increasingly attractive employment targets of many large corporations as technology-based crimes continue to increase. Private security as a career option is further discussed in Chapter 13.

Related, the private investigation field is another often overlooked area of employment for those interested in criminal justice and criminology. Private investigators may be employed to monitor the behaviors of a cheating spouse, track down a lost relative, verify injury in worker compensation cases, and a host of other services. The insurance industry hires many private investigators, for instance, to assist in preventing and identifying various types of fraudulent claims. Private investigators also assist attorneys with case preparation. The flexible hours and autonomy associated with the field are attractive components of working in private investigations.

Assuredly, working directly with youth and adults who break the law is not appealing to everyone. Some students interested in careers in criminal justice or criminology are discouraged to hear that "hands-on" experience is often required or preferred for many high-level positions. Similarly, criminologists may conduct research studies that require direct contact with incarcerated persons. Fortunately for people who may feel discomfort having direct contact with individuals who break the law there are numerous opportunities in criminal justice and criminology that do not necessarily require hands-on experience with individuals caught up in the system. For example, a variety of administrative positions are available in criminal justice. Each state government and many large agencies employ researchers, statisticians, and others to create and evaluate programs, and assess agency performances. Criminal justice administrators perform a vital role in the day-to-day functioning of the criminal justice system. Further, criminologists can certainly use various research methods that do not involve direct contact with the incarcerated individuals they may fear.

There are certainly many employment opportunities in criminal justice, criminology, and related fields. There will be additional areas of employment opportunities as concerns for crime increase and government officials continuously expand efforts directed toward crime control. The onus is on those preparing to enter the field to be aware of relevant trends and use their research skills to identify a suitable area.

Employment Trends in and Influences on Employment in Criminal Justice and Criminology

Imagine you are buying a house. One of the first things you'll likely do is look for a suitable house in your price range. At some point in your decision-making process, you're going to look at housing values in the area. You'll want to know if your house will retain its value when it's time to sell. Wise homebuyers will investigate whether houses in the area have increased or decreased in value over the years. You'll get the house inspected and take numerous other steps to ensure that you make the decision that's best for you. The same level of in-depth research should be conducted when one is searching for a career. Put simply, you'll need to do a thorough investigation to ensure you make appropriate choices.

Understanding trends in criminal justice and criminology and examining the factors likely to have the greatest influence on future employment in the fields are key components of your investigation. Unless something miraculous happens soon, crime will not disappear. In fact, if history repeats itself (as it often does) we can expect that soon the crime rate will again begin a steady upward climb. The crime rate increased steadily between 1960 and 1980, leveled off between 1980s and the early 1990s, and steadily decreased after that. Regardless of actual crime rates, public fear of crime will impact employment opportunities in criminal justice and criminology. For better or for worse, crime and the fear of crime generate employment opportunities in these areas.

The outlook for those interested in a career in law enforcement looks promising. For example, the number of full-time sworn officers in local police departments increased by 11% between 1997 and 2016 (Goodison, 2022), while the number of full-time personnel in sheriffs' offices increased by 39% from 1997 to 2020 (Brooks, 2022b). The US Department of Justice will add to the increase in law enforcement officers, as in 2021 it offered $139 million in grants to law enforcement agencies in efforts to advance community policing (U.S. Department of Justice, 2021).

More law enforcement personnel will likely result in additional employment opportunities in the courts and corrections. The Bureau of Labor Statistics noted that the employment of lawyers is expected to increase by 9% between 2020 and 2030, while employment for probation officers and correctional treatment specialists is anticipated to increase by 4% during the same time period (U.S. Bureau of Labor Statistics, 2021a, 2021b). Several factors largely influence employment opportunities in criminal justice and criminology. Awareness of and familiarity with these factors are important for tomorrow's professionals.

As noted below, several issues will undoubtedly affect the future of employment in criminal justice and criminology. Readers are encouraged to consider these factors as they evaluate potential career opportunities, although it must be remembered that the future is not certain. In other words, those seeking employment in these areas should not expect the fields, and the accompanying employment opportunities, to remain static. Change is imminent. How well individuals prepare for and respond to change will largely dictate their success.

Forecasts of developments in criminal justice and criminology consistently point to several factors as potentially having the greatest impact on change. The onus is on those anticipating employment in the fields to research, recognize, and respond to the changes, especially the most impactful ones. Among the factors expected to continue impacting the fields are terrorism, technological advancements, fear of crime, sociocultural changes, globalism, and private security. Certainly, this list is not comprehensive, as other issues (e.g., economics and political shifts) will impact crime, justice, and ultimately employment opportunities.

Terrorism

Imagine yourself as a New York City Police officer on September 10, 2001. Crime rates are down and life is generally comfortable. Fast forward to September 11, 2001. Life is a chaotic mess. You've lost several good friends, your job responsibilities changed dramatically, and there is a great sense of uncertainty regarding if, when, or where the next deadly attack may occur. The changes you experienced are occurring across the nation, and to some extent, across the globe. Although the attacks occurred at the turn of the century, the effects and threat of similar acts remain today.

It is an understatement to suggest that terrorism has changed society. Following the attacks, societal freedoms were restricted, levels of fear and anxiety pertaining to terrorism increased, and the criminal justice system and criminologists received additional mandates. The presence and threat of terrorist attacks generated extensive career opportunities in a variety of areas for those interested in careers in criminal justice and criminology and altered the focus of many existing positions in the fields.

The United States has a reputation for swiftly and forcefully responding to antisocial behavior. Consider how the United States responded to the terrorist attacks of September 11, 2001. Military action, and the creation of the DHS and other efforts designed to protect the homeland primarily through targeting terrorist activities are examples of the United States responding to threats. Following the attacks, terrorist threats were no longer secondary items of concern for politicians and the general public, as any terrorist threat generated substantial formal social control efforts from various government agencies. Unfortunately, it is unlikely that the threat of terrorism will disappear. Thus, there remains a strong need in the criminal justice system for individuals interested in protecting against terrorist threats.

Technology

As strange as it may seem, we are currently in the infancy of the technological revolution. Computers and technology in general have transformed our lives, including how we work and identify jobs. All signs point to our continued reliance on technology in many facets of our lives, including identifying, researching, and applying for jobs, and working in the criminal justice system.

There is a significant need for tomorrow's professionals to embrace, understand, and incorporate technology, which is not going to disappear from society. In fact, it is going to become increasingly integrated, particularly in the criminal justice system. Technology will influence how those entering the criminal justice system are identified, caught, and processed. It will also influence the nature of crime in society as cybercrime becomes increasingly popular.

The benefits of technological changes are certainly obvious to all of us; however, such changes have also created new avenues for criminal behavior and the need for officials to address high-technology crimes, and others to study them. As such, those seeking careers in law enforcement and the courts must be prepared to work in a justice system that differs to some extent from the one we currently have. Technology has created new careers such as those in cryptology and cyber forensics. Cryptography is the practice of writing or cracking encryption code in efforts to secure information, or to gain access to secured information (Liddle, 2022). Cryptographers may work, for instance, with credit card companies, whose customers rely on the security of their digital transactions. Cyber forensics involves investigative techniques to identify or store evidence on computers. For instance, police investigators may request the assistance of the cyber forensics unit in unlocking a phone or computer and locating hidden information. These and related careers did not exist until high technology increasingly influenced our lives, and it is very likely that we will see more newly developed position in the years ahead.

A Practitioner's View

Harshini Chellasamy, Cybersecurity Consultant

As a cybersecurity consultant specializing in identity and access management (IAM), I work with clients, usually IT or business leaders, to document technical information about their applications, for implementation in an IAM tool. My work helps ensure that the right people in the organization access the right information/systems at the right time, reducing their overall cybersecurity risk. I constantly interact with my team and clients to generate solutions that will improve their organization's cybersecurity capabilities. Networking is a big part of being a cybersecurity consultant; I set aside time to meet new colleagues and connect people together.

Students can best prepare to work in cybersecurity consulting by staying up to date on the latest cybersecurity threats by reading technology news, following government cybersecurity threat updates, and studying IT or cybersecurity online or in school. A great way to familiarize oneself with cybersecurity is by pursuing introductory-level cybersecurity certifications such as Security+ from CompTiA. For those with an interest in Cloud technology, the AWS Cloud Practitioner certification is a great place to start. To become a cybersecurity consultant, having great communication and presentation skills is key; it is also important to be multi-passionate and engage in other extra-curricular activities such as volunteering.

Fear of Crime

Regardless of the extent of crime in society, public concern for crime dictates societal reaction to criminal behavior and, accordingly, employment opportunities in criminal justice and criminology. Interestingly, fear of crime seemingly has relatively little to do with the extent of crime in society. For instance, 37% of Americans noted that they were afraid to walk alone at night within one mile of their home in 2021 (Gallup, 2022) even though crime rates have dropped significantly since the early 1990s.

Nevertheless, politicians typically listen and respond to what the public wants. They must, otherwise they would not get into or remain in office. Getting tough on crime is often politically popular, and politicians may target crime through expanding the criminal justice system if they feel citizens are fearful. One cannot overlook the media's practice of sensationalizing crime (e.g., Wong & Harraway, 2020), which subsequently perpetuates the public's concern. The media, however, are not solely responsible for generating fear of crime. For instance, credit card companies and identity theft groups, in efforts to sell their services, regularly advertise the need for people to protect themselves from victimization. The public's fear of crime provides justification for criminal justice-based responses. Individuals interested in long-lasting and productive careers in criminal justice and criminology would be well-served to keep a finger on the pulse of what scares Americans.

Sociocultural Changes

The future of criminal justice and criminology will undoubtedly be influenced by sociocultural changes, such as demographic shifts and continued concerns about legal and illegal immigration. Significant changes are projected in the demographics of the United States, especially with regard to the percentages of racial and ethnic minorities in society. For instance, the Hispanic population is expected to increase from 18% to 28% of the US population from 2017 to 2060 (U.S. Census, 2018). Ensuring diversity within the criminal justice and criminology workforce will become increasingly important in light of demographic shifts.

The ability to recognize and appreciate cultural diversity is and will continue to be essential for anyone working in the criminal justice system (McNamara & Burns, 2021). Numerous conflicts, including riots, were generated by actions of criminal justice personnel who did not understand or recognize cultural differences. The importance of respect for cultural diversity extends throughout the criminal justice system, for instance, from police officers who must refrain from engaging in racial profiling to judges who must impose bias-free sentences, to correctional officers who must temper the racial tensions often present in prisons.

Immigration issues have consistently generated much public interest. Cities and municipalities battle with culture conflict as, among other concerns, people who come to the United States both legally and illegally assume the jobs that may be sought by nonimmigrants. The controversy largely stems from individuals from other countries being more willing than others to work for less pay. The problems resulting from this division of labor and other cultural conflicts contribute to the criminal justice system further being used to provide social control.

Discussion of immigration requires consideration of the differences between legal and illegal immigration. Individuals illegally entering the country have become the target of much disdain. Criminal justice professionals and criminologists are often asked to "solve problems," for instance, through enforcement efforts or research. Accordingly, they will continue to play an integral role in addressing immigration issues, particularly as they relate to illegal immigration.

There is a demonstrated need for criminologists to address the lack of research regarding immigration and diversity-related issues as they pertain to crime and justice. Substantial evidence indicates that racial and ethnic minorities are overrepresented in the criminal justice system, and at times are treated differently from other groups (e.g., McNamara & Burns, 2021). Better understanding why this is the case, particularly through empirical research, provides a significant step toward addressing the disparities and differential treatment. These are only a few of the social issues likely to impact careers in criminal justice and criminology in the years ahead.

Those considering a career in criminal justice or criminology in particular are strongly encouraged to respect diversity and learn a second language. Anyone considering a career in local law enforcement should consider learning Spanish, or some other second language. They should also consider the demographics of the jurisdiction in which they wish to work, particularly if considering employment at a local-level agency. For instance, those interested in working in a district attorney's office in a jurisdiction populated primarily by Latinx individuals should consider learning to speak Spanish. Doing so improves the criminal justice system and enhances the employee's value to their employer. Being bilingual is financially rewarded in some criminal justice agencies.

Globalism

The globe is shrinking. International commerce, interaction, communication, travel, and exchange are becoming increasingly popular. Accordingly, there will be an increased need for international criminal justice efforts. Criminal justice practices in the United States have historically been confined to specific domestic jurisdictions, and much criminological research lacks an international scope. The study of international crime has increased, although it largely remains limited, and is often focused on homicides and/or only uses official data, which can provide obstacles in cross-country comparisons (LaFree, 2021). It is anticipated that international efforts toward criminal justice and criminological study will be needed on a much larger scale in the future. Currently, there is limited and inconsistent interaction among countries with regard to crime control. It is hoped that this situation will change, and with the change will come new employment opportunities focused on international justice.

In his bestselling book *The World is Flat*, author Thomas L. Friedman (2005) earlier suggested that increased globalization will continue to impact the world in many ways. As such, it is anticipated that crime will continue to develop an international flavor as increasing opportunities for criminal behavior appear. Ultimately, countries will need to establish better and more cooperative efforts with other countries to fight crime, and the expansion in job opportunities will occur across many countries.

International crime fighting provides a vast and underdeveloped area of employment for criminal justice and criminology majors. The field is currently in need of professionals who can clearly establish and implement the most effective ways to address international crime. Assuredly, the need for international crime fighting efforts will increase in the years to come, and those interested in globalism, criminal justice, and criminology are well-positioned to have a significant impact of the future of international justice. Careers in various capacities with INTERPOL, the United Nations, and various nongovernmental organizations that fight for justice are certainly viable options for individuals interested in global justice, as discussed in the final chapter of this book. The uncertainty of the future is such that careers and areas of employment will likely emerge as the need for international justice intensifies.

Private Security

The private security industry is growing at a significant rate. Citizens and businesses are increasingly recognizing the need to assume some level of personal responsibility for crime prevention. The rate at which private security services has increased has notable implications for the criminal justice system. To begin, there will continue to be a demonstrated need for law enforcement agencies to recognize the contributions of the private security sector. Among other issues, there is a need to address the concern regarding the duplication of services provided by private security and public police. Harmonious interaction between the private security industry and public policing agencies is in the best interests of all. Chapters 1 and 13 further discusses the private security industry and opportunities within the field.

Summary

Criminal justice and criminology careers are abundant and will continue to be so as crime persists. Change is imminent and tomorrow's professionals need to be prepared. For instance,

40 years ago not many individuals would have guessed that cybercrime would become a significant concern for the criminal justice system. Understanding what drives crime and responses to it will benefit those interested in careers in criminal justice and criminology. Similar to entrepreneurs, economists, and financial investors who anticipate public demand for goods and services, those interested in careers in criminal justice and criminology are strongly encouraged to anticipate changes in society and capitalize on how they can impact society and establish a long, productive career. This takes effort and initiative.

Many people are unaware of the vast array of opportunities for employment in criminal justice and criminology, and are even less aware of how future trends may impact the fields. Among other contributions, this chapter provided an overview of employment opportunities in criminal justice and criminology and encouraged readers to keep an open mind regarding future changes. It is important to remember that hard work and determination go far toward goal achievement, and tomorrow's workforce needs the ability to think in nontraditional terms. Specifically, those interested in careers in criminal justice or criminology shouldn't solely consider existing employment opportunities to best meet their needs. They should also consider creating positions or opportunities that would contribute to the betterment of criminal justice and criminology. At the very least, this requires forward thinking.

Discussion Questions

1. What level of law enforcement do you believe offers the most appealing careers? Why?
2. What would be the pros and cons of working as a prosecutor? Would the same pros and cons apply to working as a defense attorney?
3. In what area of corrections would you like to work? Community supervision? Institutional corrections? Why?
4. What factors do you believe will have the most significant impact on employment in criminal justice and criminology in the next ten years?
5. What are the primary effects of globalism on careers in criminal justice and criminology? Would you argue that globalism will increase opportunities for employment in the fields? Why or why not?

Critical Thinking Exercise

Create a grid with columns containing the primary components of the criminal justice system, and rows depicting the issues or factors that were noted in the chapter as expected to influence employment in criminal justice. Using the grid, describe how each issue or factor will likely influence each of the major components.

For Further Examination

Disha, I., Eren, C., & Leyro, S. (2021). People you care about in and out of the system: The impact of arrest on criminal justice views, choice of major, and career motivations. *Journal of Criminal Justice Education, 32*(1), 60–89.

Eren, C.P., Leyro, S., & Disha, I. (2019). It's personal: The impact of victimization on motivations and career interests among criminal justice majors at diverse urban colleges. *Journal of Criminal Justice Education, 30*(4), 510–535.

Li, Y., Luo, F., Carey, M.T., & Brown, B. (2021). The desirability of law enforcement careers among college students in a Hispanic community. *Journal of Criminal Justice Education, 32*(2), 234–251.

Stringer, E.C., & Murphy, J. (2020). Major decisions and career attractiveness among criminal justice students. *Journal of Criminal Justice Education, 31*(4), 523–541.

Walters, G.D., & Kremser, J. (2016). Differences in career aspirations, influences, and motives as a function of class standing: An empirical evaluation of undergraduate criminal justice majors. *Journal of Criminal Justice Education, 27*(3), 312–323.

References

Barthe, E.P. Leone, M.C., & Lateano, T.A. (2013). Commercializing success: The impact of popular media on the career decisions and perceptual accuracy of criminal justice students. *Teaching in Higher Education, 18*, 13–26.

Brooks, C. (2022a). *Federal law enforcement officers, 2016 – statistical tables*. U.S. Department of Justice, Bureau of Justice Statistics. NCJ 304752.

Brooks, C. (2022b). *Sheriffs' offices personnel, 2020*. U.S. Department of Justice, Bureau of Justice Statistics. NCJ 305200.

Bumgarner, J., Crawford, C., & Burns, R. (2018). *Federal law enforcement: A primer* (2nd ed.). Carolina Academic Press.

Collica-Cox, K., & Furst, G. (2019). It's not the CSI effect: Criminal justice students' choice of major and career goals. *International Journal of Offender Therapy and Comparative Criminology, 63*(11), 2069–2099.

Friedman, T.L. (2005). *The world is flat: A brief history of the twenty-first century*. Farrar, Straus, and Giroux.

Gallup. (2022). Crime. *Gallup.com*. Retrieved from https://news.gallup.com/poll/1603/crime.aspx

Goodison, S.E. (2022). *Local police departments personnel, 2016*. U.S. Department of Justice, Bureau of Justice Statistics. NCJ 305187.

Harr, J.S., & K.M. Hess (2006). *Careers in criminal justice and related fields: From internship to promotion* (5th ed.). Wadsworth.

LaFree, G. (2021). Progress and obstacles in the internationalization of criminology. *International Criminology, 1*, 58–69.

Liddle, A. (2022). How to become a cryptographer: A complete career guide. *Cybersecurity Guide*. Accessed at: https://cybersecurityguide.org/careers/cryptographer/

McNamara, R., & Burns, R. (2021). *Multiculturalism, crime, and criminal justice* (2nd ed.). Oxford University Press.

Provost, C. (2017). The industry of inequality: Why the world is obsessed with private security. *Theguardian.com*. Retrieved from www.theguardian.com/inequality/2017/may/12/industry-of-inequality-why-world-is-obsessed-with-private-security

Reaves, B.A. (2011). *Census of state and local law enforcement agencies, 2008*. U.S. Department of Justice, Bureau of Justice Statistics. NCJ 233982.

U.S. Bureau of Labor Statistics. (2021a). *Occupational outlook handbook: Lawyers*. Retrieved from www.bls.gov/ooh/legal/lawyers.htm

U.S. Bureau of Labor Statistics. (2021b). *Occupational outlook handbook: Probation officers and correctional treatment specialists*. Retrieved from www.bls.gov/ooh/community-and-social-service/probation-officers-and-correctional-treatment-specialists.htm

U.S. Census. (2018). Hispanic population to reach 111 million by 2060. *U.S.Census.gov*. Retrieved from www.census.gov/library/visualizations/2018/comm/hispanic-projected-pop.html

U.S. Department of Justice. (2021). *Justice Department announces $139 million for law enforcement hiring to advance community policing*. Retrieved from www.justice.gov/opa/pr/justice-department-announces-139-million-law-enforcement-hiring-advance-community-policing

Wong, J.S., & Harraway, V. (2020). Media presentation of homicide: Examining characteristics of sensationalism and fear of victimization and their relation to newspaper article prominence. *Homicide Studies, 24*(4), 333–352.

Chapter 4

Working in Criminal Justice and Criminology

Every field of employment has a distinct "flavor" that characterizes the positions in general and influences those working in the field. For instance, there is a stigma attached with being a medical doctor. Doctors are often perceived as financially comfortable professionals interested in helping others. So, how do we characterize those working in criminal justice and criminology? The answer to this question is complex. For instance, public perceptions of judges and correctional officers likely differ. Nevertheless, there are similarities in being a judge and a correctional officer. For instance, both groups work for the government, both work within bureaucratic structures, and both regularly encounter individuals who have, or have allegedly broken the law.

The varied nature of criminal justice practices results in significant differences among the positions and agencies within the field. There are also many commonalities. This chapter addresses what it is like to work in criminal justice and criminology, including coverage of the challenges, obstacles, and benefits they may encounter. Particularly, this chapter addresses (1) the nature of working within the criminal justice system; (2) the challenges posed by working in bureaucracies; (3) the influence of politics upon criminal justice practices; and (4) what it's like to work on a regular basis dealing with crime and individuals who break the law. The latter part of the chapter addresses ethical considerations.

Nature of the Work

Working in criminal justice and criminology can be challenging. It can also be very rewarding. Take, for instance, the police officer who must arrest parents involved in a domestic abuse incident. The officer is protecting the community by removing the participants. On the other hand, the officer is removing parents from their children and creating an image that may last with the child for a lifetime. The officer is faced with a challenging situation to say the least. Laws will guide the officer's actions, but the use of discretion will certainly be involved.

> ### A Practitioner's View
>
> Bryanna Fox, Associate Professor, University of South Florida
>
> I am a former FBI Special Agent, which is one of the most challenging, exciting, rewarding, enlightening, and unbelievably remarkable jobs in the world. However, it also requires unfettering dedication and responsibility for all those who hold it. Each day as an FBI Agent, you will have a new set of goals and challenges on your plate. Some days you may be writing an affidavit for a search warrant, some you may spend sitting for hours on surveillance, others you may be analyzing years of financial data, and ultimately,

> you may be able to make an arrest and start the wheels of justice turning. All of this is interesting and exhilarating, and while you have some of the best training in the world to guide you, most of the job is self-directed and independent. It is important that anyone interested in working at the FBI knows it is not just a job, it is truly a career and calling, and requires adherence to the highest standards to maintain the reputation as the premier law enforcement agency in the world.
>
> The best advice I can give is to stand out by doing something that you are passionate about and excellent at, and to gain as much life experience handling challenges, overcoming obstacles, and navigating stressful situations prior to applying, as this is what the FBI looks for in their ideal agent. For instance, many people think that becoming a police officer, joining the military, or learning a foreign language are the "best" ways to get into the FBI, but this is not necessarily true. The FBI has thousands of applications from stunningly qualified candidates all over the nation, for just a few open spots at the FBI Academy each year. The best way to get one of those spots is to be truly remarkable at what you do, and that typically comes with doing what you are passionate about and enjoy. I met people in the FBI who were detectives, lawyers, trauma nurses, chemists, accountants, in the special forces, and so much more, and the one unifying trait is that they were all outstanding and some of the best in their field. So working hard, being the best you can at what you love, gaining experience, and staying out of trouble along the way is the best way to prepare yourself to become an FBI Special Agent.

Society relies on criminal justice professionals for effective social control. We look to the system when problems occur. We sometimes criticize law enforcement agencies when a heinous crime occurs and an arrest has not been made. Society sometimes complains when judges do not impose longer sentences for violent crimes, or public defenders help defendants "win" cases on technicalities. Similarly, society questions the effectiveness of correctional agencies, for instance, as many individuals wonder what exactly is accomplished through incarceration, or why there isn't enough punishment associated with regard to community supervision practices.

Criminal justice professionals are often in a no-win situation, primarily because society expects very much from them. Consider that many of us have broken the law at some point in time, yet relatively few of us were probably arrested. Even those who are arrested and processed in the system usually got away with other, undetected, unreported, or unsolved crimes. The criminal justice system is not perfect. It is not designed nor organized to catch all who commit crimes, prosecute all who are arrested, or correct all who have been sentenced. The goal for those working in criminal justice, then, is to do the best they can with what they have; those working in the field can simply hope to make as large a difference as possible. Unfortunately, not everyone is going to be pleased regardless of how successfully we control crime. There will always be people who believe the criminal justice system could do more.

Several research studies examined the reasons why students study criminal justice and criminology, and why they wish to work in the fields. Many of the reasons for studying these areas have to do with the nature of the work. Students sometimes choose criminal justice as a major because they believe the field provides many job opportunities and value the associated job security (Stringer & Murphy, 2020). Criminal justice students are generally motivated by an interest in the fundamentals of public service, and have an interest in protecting people from oppression, ensuring rights, and providing safety through problem-solving (Collica-Cox & Furst, 2019). Students who were victimized by crime are also attracted to the major (Eren et al., 2019), and some chose criminal justice due to their interest in the subject, the relevance of the content to the real world, and the potential for advancing in their careers (Ridener et al., 2020). Ultimately, there are many reasons why people study criminal justice.

The nature of the work within the criminal justice system varies. For instance, there are administrative positions in which professionals are not necessarily involved in direct contact with alleged and convicted law violators. Planners, researchers, crime prevention specialists, some administrators, and others may go their entire careers without working directly with individuals convicted of a crime. Many positions, however, involve some type of regular contact with individuals found guilty of breaking the law, and the accused. As such, the nature of much work in the criminal justice system is not necessarily glamorous, particularly in light of the fact that the reason we have criminal justice systems is to address the problems created by those who break the law. This, of course, does not mean that all caught up in the system are problematic or difficult to work with. Many wonderful people have made mistakes throughout their life. Some get caught and end up in the system, and some do not.

Those preparing for careers in criminal justice and criminology ought to be prepared to see the worst society has to offer. The reason trained personnel are asked to respond to criminal behavior is because most in society cannot, or do not wish to respond to crime and delinquency. Consider a situation involving a man firing a gun on an open street. The individual shot two people, fired at and missed several others, and is reloading his gun. Bystanders generally run *from* the situation. The police run *to* the situation. Upon arrest, those working in the courts must interact with an individual who seemingly has little regard for others, while those working in corrections must interact with the individual (and others like him) on a daily basis. Such a work environment largely differs from, for instance, a tennis instructor working at a country club.

Society expects a great deal from those who work in criminal justice and criminology. Those who work in the system must regularly maintain consideration of ensuring a safe society while respecting individual rights.

Source: www.pexels.com/search/criminal%20justice/

Criminal justice consumes a very large portion of government resources, and the spending continues to increase. In 2017 the United States spent $305 billion for police protection, judicial and legal activities, and corrections at all levels of government. This figure represents a 62% increase and is far more than the $188 billion spent in 1997. The largest portion of justice system expenditures in 2017 was on law enforcement ($149 million), followed by corrections ($89 billion), and judicial and legal functions ($66 billion) (Buehler, 2021). Nevertheless, many working in criminal justice argue that greater resources are needed to more effectively combat crime and secure justice, and many individuals who do not work within the system agree. Overcrowded courthouses, underfunded public defenders' offices, outdated prisons, non-competitive salaries for correctional officers, a lack of adequate funding for rehabilitation services in prisons and jails, and limited law enforcement resources constitute only a small list of areas where greater funding and general reform are arguably needed.

Working in the criminal justice system under these conditions could contribute to employees developing a discouraging outlook on life. Specifically, seeing the worst society has to offer on a regular basis could contribute to the belief that there is more evil than good in society. For instance, police officers face enhanced levels of stress as first responders (e.g., Alpert et al., 2015). Many others who work in the criminal justice system, such as prison officers and community supervision officers, regularly face different types of stress on the job. Unfortunately, some cope with stress through violence and/or alcohol, which contributes to additional problems including those relating to health and family (e.g., Burns, 2022). Many programs exist in various criminal justice agencies to help protect employees from the harmful effects of stress.

Despite these and related potential drawbacks, there are many identifiable benefits to working toward justice. Perhaps the most obvious benefit of working in criminal justice and criminology is the direct opportunity to help those most in need. Individuals who have an intrinsic, or at least cursory interest in helping others will find numerous opportunities and great enjoyment through employment in criminal justice or criminology. For instance, researchers noted that the opportunity to help others was a primary motivator for becoming a police officer (White et al., 2010).

Working in the criminal justice system provides many opportunities to help the accused, the convicted, and society in general. Some employees are motivated for work by the opportunity to correct, or at least help the individuals most in need of assistance. Others who work in criminal justice or criminology may find pleasure and motivation through helping society in general. They appreciate their role as someone who can make the world safer. Others appreciate the opportunity to ensure that justice is done. Young children (and some teens and adults) are often heard saying "This isn't fair" or "That's not right." Working in criminal justice enables you to impose fairness and righteousness, while being rewarded financially and otherwise.

The nature of the work in the criminal justice system or criminology also provides a sense of stability, or security to those who work in the fields. Some employees are comfortable in knowing that they have high levels of job security simply because crime is not soon going to disappear, and the criminal justice system is continuously growing in size and scope. The ever-expanding criminal justice system provides employees vast opportunities for advancement and variety on the job.

Another aspect of working in criminal justice or criminology concerns the irregular working hours associated with some of the positions. Those working in the courts generally work a regular schedule each week; however, law enforcement agents and those working in corrections are often faced with irregular working hours and schedule shifts. While some individuals frown on irregular working hours and prefer greater stability, others prefer the lack of structure and find it enhances one's social and/or family life.

Some individuals who work in criminal justice appreciate the extensive levels of discretion associated with many of the positions. Police officers, attorneys, judges, and many who work in corrections maintain high levels of discretion given the nature of their job responsibilities. Among other benefits, discretion provides workers with a sense of empowerment and provides motivation in many cases. It allows employees to demonstrate their competency and find optimal solutions.

The uncertainty associated with working in criminal justice and criminology is another aspect of the work that is appreciated by many. Some individuals are motivated to work in the fields by the fact that each day will bring about new events, information, and interactions. They may choose to work in the criminal justice system, or study criminal behavior simply because they know that each day, shift, or case will be different from the last.

In sum, the nature of the work found in criminal justice and criminology can be both rewarding and challenging. Working in the system is far from glamorous, although there is an admirable level of respect and reward associated with many of the positions. The bureaucratic nature of many criminal justice jobs is a particularly important aspect of working in the field.

Bureaucracies

Those interested in careers in criminal justice and criminology ought to strongly consider the bureaucratic nature of the agencies with which they seek employment. Too often, employees overwhelmingly let factors such as the nature of the work, salary, and benefits influence their decision to seek or accept employment opportunities. While those factors are certainly significant, the organizational structure and overall administrative practices of the agency, and the field in general, deserve adequate consideration.

Criminal justice agencies are largely influenced by their bureaucratic nature, which involves hierarchical ranking and proscribed rules and regulations that guide agency behavior. The organizational structure and practices of agencies and organizations determine its bureaucratic nature. Many individuals seeking positions concerned with crime and justice will end up in the public sector, primarily because the private sector offers fewer opportunities for employment. In deciding to work in the public or private sector, individuals ought to consider the differences in the bureaucratic nature of public and private agencies, including:

- Public sector employees being more accountable to detailed policies and procedures that regulate much of the day-to-day activities;
- Public sector agencies being primarily concerned with effective and efficient delivery of services, while private sector groups are often concerned with profits; and
- Greater levels of job scrutiny in the public sector (Peat, 2004).

An example of the bureaucratic nature of working in criminal justice is evidenced in the extensive amount of paperwork required by government workers. Report writing has become an increasingly important skill for those in the field.

The research literature contains many accounts of how administrative styles and organizational designs impact criminal justice employee performance. Traditionally, many criminal justice agencies adopted Max Weber's classical, hierarchical design in which control and supervision are provided from the top of the organizational chart. This means that authority flows top-down. Such a structure encompasses a division of labor through which:

- employees have greater levels of specialization,
- promotions are based on skills and merit,

- coded rules and regulations are reviewed and followed by all,
- there is a focus on efficiency and effectiveness, and
- communication must proceed through a chain of command (Weber, 1947/1913).

Such a rigid approach to organization and administration is effective for some individuals in select settings; however, organizational theory has advanced over time and the administrative and organizational approaches assumed by many modern criminal justice agencies stress a greater level of employee autonomy and input than in years prior. Such approaches better empower employees and encourage productivity. The changes emerged, in part, because employees typically do not wish to merely be cogs in a system; instead, they wish to have input and opportunities to offer suggestions.

There is a stigma associated with government work. Specifically, some individuals perceive government workers as lazy, or simply interested in earning a paycheck for doing as little as possible. Some view the government as ineffective and overburdened with bureaucracy which results in limited effectiveness (e.g., Johnson, 2020). To be sure, the stigma is accurate for *some* government employees and agencies. However, the same is true for *some* private agencies and their employees. For instance, it is argued that privatizing prisons would enhance prison effectiveness as private agencies would be less impacted by government bureaucracy. Others argue, however, that government is capable of performing as well, and in some cases better, than private agencies (Kim, 2022).

In his seminal work on bureaucracies and bureaucrats, Michael Lipsky earlier used the term "street-level bureaucrats" to refer to public service workers who interact daily with individuals through their jobs. Included in this group are public lawyers, law enforcement personnel, court officers, community supervision officers, and others employed throughout the criminal justice system. He noted that such employees are often expected to provide a higher-level quality of service than they are capable of providing. For instance, prison rehabilitation programs are often overcrowded, leading to less-than-ideal treatment services. Lipsky highlighted the difficulties with street-level bureaucrats, who often work with limited resources and are expected to administer services to large numbers of clients. The result of such stretched resources is that some individuals receive limited treatment. Unfortunately, the bureaucratic policy of making the most with limited resources restricts effectiveness in services (Lipsky, 1980). Accordingly, the goal of many criminal justice agencies is to seek additional resources while providing the highest-level service possible. Those entering the field ought to be aware of this potential bureaucratic challenge.

Politics

The criminal justice system is intertwined with politics, primarily in response to most criminal justice agencies being part of the judicial or executive branches of government. The nature of public agency resource allocation, political ideology, and the sometimes conflicting or unclear goals of many criminal justice agencies provide many challenges for the effective administration of criminal justice. These and related factors also influence the work environment of employees within the system.

Politics have historically been a part of criminal justice practices. Early correctional institutions and courts were administered by the government and subjected to political influence, and the initial era of policing (i.e., the political era) was characterized by police officers being appointed and notably impacted by government officials (Kelling & Moore, 1991). Efforts have been made to eliminate, or at least minimize the impact of politics on criminal justice agencies, for instance, when civil service regulations concerning hiring, dismissing, and promoting police officers helped remove policing from political influences. It remains, however, that public institutions will maintain at least some level of political influence, as evidenced in the fact that some judges, district attorneys, and sheriffs assume their positions via popular election. Such a process clearly highlights the impact of politics on the personnel working in the criminal justice system and may result in less qualified individuals receiving positions over more qualified candidates. For instance, the sheriff or judge who runs the most effective campaign may win the election even though he or she may not be the most suitable candidate.

The impact of politics on criminal justice agencies is visible in many areas, and there is debate regarding whether or not political influences help or hinder the criminal justice system. For instance, at the federal level the president influences criminal justice practices through nominating Supreme Court justices, fiscal allocations, cabinet appointments, and the like. State-level politics influence the criminal justice system in many ways, for instance, through the governor appointing his or her department heads. At the local level, powerful people holding politically appointed positions undoubtedly influence criminal justice practices, and many department and agency budgets are provided by many elected government officials.

Consider how the government's war on drugs has impacted police practices, court dockets, and prison populations. Government policy may appeal to government officials and the general public, but there is sometimes a disconnect between policy and the criminal justice system's ability to effectively implement the policy. Overburdened police officers; overcrowded courts, jails, and prisons; and overwhelmed community supervision officers are but a few of the impacts of the war on drugs.

Public service agencies are susceptible to changes in government. For example, democrats generally maintain a more liberal view of social issues than republicans, who often maintain a more conservative outlook. Democratic leadership may lead to more corrections-related practices occurring in the community, while republican leadership may lead to the hiring of additional police officers and the construction of new prisons.

Criminal justice agencies rely heavily on the government to provide resources. Accordingly, the ideology of the politicians serving within the various levels of government will impact the extent to which criminal justice agencies are funded. Such ideology and funding obviously impact the size of the workforce, the resources available to criminal justice employees, compensation for employees, employee workload, and the nature of the work performed by the criminal justice system. Politicians, of course, are influenced by a variety of social and economic factors that contribute to their practices and ideology. Factors such as morality, poverty, the media, inflation, unemployment, wars, terrorist threats, and other issues undoubtedly influence their views and reactions to the criminal justice system. As public servants, politicians are also influenced heavily by public opinion and, at least in theory, will react to public concern for particular issues.

Those considering a career in criminal justice ought to strongly consider the political influences upon the criminal justice system, particularly with regard to the areas in which they wish to work. Educating one's self regarding the agendas of political parties is part of professional development. Self-reflection regarding one's ability to work under conditions in which political decisions can have substantial impacts can prevent much frustration.

Management and administrative positions in the criminal justice system are sometimes placed in challenging situations due to political persuasion. Consider the police chief who is being influenced by politicians to have her department crackdown on particular crimes that the chief and the officers believe are relatively insignificant, and doing so would seemingly be a waste of resources and harmful to police-community relations. The police chief would seem weak to the rank and file should she succumbs to the political pressure, yet insubordinate should she not require the officers to act as the politicians suggest. However, it is not simply management that faces such dilemmas. Consider the prosecutor who is tasked with prosecuting cases that she believes are not worthy of substantial attention, yet must do so by political pressure. Or, consider the judge who must, according to sentencing requirements created by elected officials, impose a severe sentence that he believes is not warranted. Dealing with political influences is an important part of many positions in criminal justice. Potentially having to interact with justice-involved individuals is also an important aspect of working in the field

Crime and Individuals Who Break the Law

Recall the trouble-making kid in grade school or high school; the one who was always misbehaving and causing accelerated levels of stress for students and teachers. The one who was regularly given in-school suspension or sent to the principal's office. Imagine assuming a job where your primary goal is to control that kid. Employment in criminal justice may require you to identify individuals doing something wrong, listen to his or her side of the story, and either punish them and/or correct their behavior. The challenge, excitement, authority, responsibility, and unpredictability appeal to some people; however, others may find it unappealing.

Many individuals who work in criminal justice or criminology are attracted to the excitement and unpredictability associated with the fields. As mentioned, the uncertainty of one's day-to-day activities can attract individuals to positions within the system. Those considering a career in the field ought to seriously consider if they can handle such uncertainty and unpredictability, and how they can use these and related aspects of the job for professional development and the betterment of society.

The "clientele" found in the criminal justice system differs from the customers found in most other agencies, businesses, and the like. To deconstruct the term *criminal justice* suggests that we wish to find justice for persons who break the law. In other words, we want to respond in a just manner to those whose behavior is outside of our legal boundaries. Naturally, then, the target individual is more likely to be someone who may have little regard for the law, authority, human life, and/or social responsibility. To many individuals who break the law, criminal justice personnel are the symbolic enemy. To others they are symbolic saviors, doing much needed work that many of us could not, or would not want to do. There is a high level of respect associated with many positions within the criminal justice system.

The individuals who enter the criminal justice system have many unmet needs and problems in life. Some are mixed up in violence, drugs, and/or alcohol, while others have anger issues, limited social skills, learning disabilities, mental illnesses, and other ailments. Some will lie directly to your face. Some have difficulty discerning between reality and fantasy. They may have unmet medical and educational needs. As one might expect, many criminal justice professionals regularly interact with these individuals and address their concerns while ensuring justice.

Popular culture often depicts expert detective work that solves a challenging case, or attorneys who cleverly sway a jury to see things their way. There are also "reality" shows in which police officers respond to challenging cases and offer their insight, or a judge decides a case. Prison movies and television shows highlight life behind bars. These depictions take us inside the criminal justice system, to some extent. The portrayals of criminal justice contain some level of reality. Reality court shows are typically presided over by an arbitrator who is often a former judge, and the decisions are legally binding. Real police officers are depicted on reality police shows. What you see in these shows, however, is a mere glimpse into the criminal justice system. You don't see other aspects of the officer's life, which may be negatively impacted by stress or pressure from the administration. You don't see how judges act when there's not a camera filming in their courtroom. You aren't aware of the pretrial proceedings that impacted the case. In other words, you get a snapshot of some event, but fail to receive contextualization of the material. In other words, you get a glimpse of some event, but fail to receive proper context, including the associated impacts of the events portrayed.

Aside from formal employment in the field, there are many ways to obtain an understanding of what it is like to work with justice-involved persons. To begin, volunteer work or internships within the system provide some understanding of what working in the system is like. Internships (as discussed in Chapter 8) provide excellent opportunities for students to test the waters in a particular agency or position. Volunteer work is always appreciated by criminal justice agencies and provides an effective way to better understand crime and justice, and become familiar with employment in the field. Entry-level positions may not be glamorous, but they often offer an insider's view of crime and justice, and may be an important part of the path to one's ultimate career choice.

Gaining a better understanding of crime and individuals who break the law requires a great deal of effort. Experiencing the system through part-time employment, internships, or volunteer work are very effective means of gaining knowledge. Those anticipating employment in the criminal justice system are also strongly encouraged to consider the academic study of individuals who break the law and the crimes they commit.

Increased knowledge results in better preparation for a career in the field. Speaking with people who work in the field or were involved in the system helps build one's knowledge base. For instance, researchers noted the benefits of having formerly incarcerated persons speak to students and stressed the importance of students having "an understanding of how social factors such as poverty, community violence, gang involvement, and school punishment increase the likelihood of incarceration." They added that "The opportunity to learn firsthand before entering the field can alter existing biases and beliefs, potentially allowing for more educated, empathetic future employees" (Harm & Bell, 2021, 136).

There is considerable discussion regarding who is more aware of crime and individuals caught up in the criminal justice system: academics who study the issues, or practitioners who have firsthand experience. There are strong arguments offered in support of both sides. However, very strong arguments could be made that individuals who have both "book smarts" and practical experience have the widest knowledge base. A combination of both perspectives and cooperative efforts between the groups provides perhaps a robust account of crime and justice (e.g., Carcirieri, 2021). The academic field of convict criminology, in which formerly incarcerated individuals incorporate their personal experiences in the system with academic study, provides an apt example of how the two worlds can combine to offer fruitful insights into the criminal justice system (e.g., Ross & Vianello, 2021).

The are many benefits associated with researching positions and agencies in criminal justice, criminology, and other fields prior to applying for a position. Such research should include a thorough understanding of crime, persons who break the law, and criminal justice based on empirical evaluations and assessments. Most people in society have some perceptions of crime, justice, individuals who break the law, and the work performed in the criminal justice system. However, one would be shortsighted to begin a professional career in a field they have not studied. Many of us invest time researching automobiles, houses, cameras, and other expensive items prior to purchasing them. Why, then, would we not invest substantial resources into investigating key components of our career choices?

The diverse nature of criminal justice and criminology, and the wide array of actions deemed a "crime" results in a need for well-rounded individuals to work in the fields. Among the many qualities, traits, and characteristics sought by criminal justice agencies are a willingness to help others, discipline, the ability to work independently, adherence to rules, an openness to multiculturalism, tolerance for challenges, critical thinking and problem-solving skills, and respectfulness. Those considering careers in criminal justice or criminology ought to assess how well they can meet the needs of the agencies at which they wish to work and address any shortcomings sooner rather than later. Chapter 5 helps with that assessment. Ethically sound, morally strong individuals are always needed and preferred by criminal justice agencies.

Ethics

Ethics can be defined as an individual's principles that impact critical reasoning and assessment on conduct (Bold & Chenoweth, 2008); it is the study of morality. Morals are rules that define appropriate action. Ethics, or a focus on what is considered proper conduct, are of particular interest to criminal justice and criminology given the nature of justice-based work. In other words, ethics and morality are particularly relevant to justice-based practices as criminal justice professionals are often charged with determining right from wrong. An individual's values, standards, and social principles significantly contribute to how well they adhere to the ethical expectations of their professional careers.

Consider the following fictitious account of an intern facing a workplace challenge:

> Caitlin was excited about her upcoming internship with a law firm. She anticipated going to law school (and had already applied to several law schools) and thought that working in a law firm would be a helpful learning experience. She was correct in thinking the internship would be a learning experience, however, what she learned largely differed from what she anticipated.
>
> Caitlin began her internship working closely with Ralph, an attorney who had worked with the firm for five years. She assisted Ralph in preparing criminal cases and on several occasions accompanied him to court. Ralph was very open with Caitlin, primarily through explaining and demonstrating to her what it is like to be a criminal defense attorney. He certainly inspired her to practice law ... at least until Caitlin got to know Ralph's true character.
>
> During the first few weeks of their association, Ralph seemed very professional in the manner in which he went about his work. As they got to know each other better, Ralph opened up a bit with Caitlin, and shared with her some of the unethical "tricks of the trade," as he called them. Their association initially took a negative turn when Ralph showed Caitlin how he defrauded clients by adding billable hours during which he didn't work. He told Caitlin that all defense attorneys do it, and she would too once she began practicing law. Caitlin knew the practice was unethical, unprofessional, and illegal, although she wasn't sure how she should respond to Ralph's behavior.
>
> She initially didn't say anything to anyone, choosing instead to keep quiet out of fear that exposing Ralph's misbehavior might jeopardize her internship and ultimately her career. She feared that she may be dismissed from the internship for speaking out, which would result in her not graduating and potentially not attending law school. The situation worsened when, after weeks of Caitlin hearing and seeing how Ralph falsely billed clients, she suggested that what he was doing was unethical. Ralph responded by telling Caitlin that it was in her best interests to "keep her mouth shut" about what he was doing, or he would "find a way to ensure that she fails the internship and never makes it into the doorway of a law school."
>
> Caitlin was notably distraught about the whole internship and dreaded going to the office. She approached her internship director at school, who explained that what she was feeling was normal and that she did the right thing by telling someone in authority. The

internship director suggested that Caitlin schedule a meeting with the office supervisor, which Caitlin did.

The meeting with the office supervisor went very well. The supervisor told Caitlin that Ralph was going to be investigated. She applauded Caitlin for coming forward with the information and gladly offered to write a letter of recommendation on Caitlin's behalf. She also apologized and transferred Caitlin to work under an ethical attorney. The supervisor also contacted Caitlin's internship director to express her admiration for Caitlin's ethical behavior and overall outstanding work during the internship.

This scenario provides an example of how internships and general work experience can be both educational and uncomfortable. Caitlin was unfortunately exposed to the dark side of criminal justice practices; however, she was able to find out more about herself while testing her ethical preparedness for a career in the field. Working in any field poses particular ethical challenges, and it is hoped that one's education and life experiences prepare them to respond appropriately. Nevertheless, it is impossible to anticipate all ethical dilemmas that may arise.

Dilemmas, whether they be legal, professional, ethical, or moral, sometimes arise in one's personal and professional lives. The term *ethical dilemma* is often used to describe situations in which someone struggles to determine which course of action is most ethical to resolve a sticky situation. Academics have long debated the effectiveness of teaching ethics in a classroom, as there is sometimes no agreement on what constitutes *the* most ethical approach to any challenging situation.

Authors Mary Bold and Lillian Chenoweth (2008) discuss the elements of ethical codes found in many organizations. They noted the great variation among the elements of ethical codes and argued that understanding the expectations of an agency can be challenging and time consuming. Among the more common elements of ethical codes are issues pertaining to:

- Legal requirements, or codes that cite conduct which is mandated by law;
- Confidentiality, or the protection of sensitive information;
- Conflicts of interest, or the balance between one's professional responsibilities and personal gain;
- Accountability, or taking responsibility for one's actions and remaining cognizant of the consequences;
- Conduct, or one's professional and personal behaviors;
- Responsibility to one's profession, or the expectation that one will contribute to the profession, including through one's ethical decision-making;
- Collegiality, or demonstrating collegial relationships with coworkers and clients;
- Cultural competence, or remaining cognizant and tolerant of cultural differences;
- Assumptions, or the awareness of the limitations of assuming anything; and
- Plagiarism, or the unauthorized use of the work of others.

Criminal justice professionals face higher levels of public scrutiny with regard to ethical practices primarily due to the nature of the work. For instance, news outlets occasionally report police officers being arrested. The incident, although a crime, may not be overly harmful. Nevertheless, it makes the news because it involved an officer. The public holds criminal justice professionals to higher standards, thus increasing the significance of ethical practices in the field.

Ethics are important with regard to criminal justice and criminology given the interpersonal interactions that occur in these areas. For instance, workers are less likely to encounter ethical challenges working on a factory line than are probation officers, who may encounter problematic situations on a daily basis. Probation officers are certainly not the only criminal justice officials tasked with regularly making difficult decisions, as many others who work in the system regularly struggle with determining right from wrong.

Researchers offered the C^4 model to assist with ethical decision-making. It involves clarifying, collaborating, considering, and choosing. This model proposes that ethical decision-making is enhanced when one addresses questionable situations through first *clarifying* the situation by considering what, specifically, constitutes the problem in question. *Collaboration* involves working with others (e.g., coworkers, supervisors, internship directors) for consultation, direction, and guidance regarding how to best address the problem. Collaborating with others is helpful in that it may provide additional points of view regarding the questionable actions. *Considering* pertains to one's awareness of the issues and risks involved. For instance, one must consider how their decisions relate to ethical principles that guide their behavior. *Choosing*, the final step, involves selecting the most ethical and appropriate course of action (Bold & Chenoweth, 2008). Caitlin, the subject of the scenario above, certainly proceeded through these steps.

Those encountering ethical challenges should be aware, however, that reporting misconduct maintains the potential for both positive and negative outcomes. For instance, coworkers may ostracize those they believe are a "snitch." Or, one could be considered an "office hero" for identifying the misbehavior. Your training, upbringing, and moral compass will hopefully provide guidance for you to do what is proper, legal, fair, and according to policy.

Summary

This chapter shed light on employment in criminal justice and criminology, with an emphasis on working in the criminal justice system. Working in criminal justice or criminology can be extremely rewarding and difficult in many ways. The nature of much of the work in the criminal justice system can be challenging given the tasks at hand, the backgrounds and behaviors of the individuals with whom criminal justice professionals and criminologists interact, bureaucratic limitations, and political influences. Concerns for ethics abound in criminal justice and criminology. Despite these challenges, working in the fields provides excellent opportunities to serve the community, help troubled individuals, ensure justice, and protect society. It is important for those who wish to work in the fields to gain a thorough understanding of what it is like to work in their area of choice. Those entering the field would be remiss if they did not invest a great deal of research prior to accepting a job.

The complexity of the criminal justice system makes it difficult to succinctly discuss all of the influences of bureaucracy, politics, crime, individuals who break the law, and ethical concerns in one chapter. Further, the nature of the work in the system varies by area, agency, and position, among other factors. In other words, the information found above does not always apply to all positions. Accordingly, there is a strong emphasis on the need to use your research skills. The fields of criminal justice and criminology are always in need of additional creative, forward-thinking, motivated, and adaptable employees. Those who are prepared and have such skills will offer much to the system and society, and undoubtedly have successful careers in the field.

Discussion Questions

1. Compare and contrast what it would be like to work in law enforcement, the courts, and corrections. In which area would you prefer to work? Why?
2. What are some of the benefits and challenges associated with working in a bureaucracy?

3   In what ways does politics influence the criminal justice system?
4   What do you believe has shaped your impressions of employment in the criminal justice system? Do you believe that the source you chose was particularly accurate? Why or why not?
5   Think of a time when you experienced an ethical dilemma. How did you handle the situation? Did you follow the C^4 model?

Critical Thinking Exercise

Create a job description for a police officer, a judge, and a prison officer. Note what skills you believe would be necessary to perform each of the positions, the level of education required, and the tasks associated with the position. Also, note the salary that you believe seems reasonable for each position. Justify your choices.

For Further Examination

Bitton, M.S., & Mashiach, A. (2021). From their angle: A look at the emotional world of defense attorneys who represent sex offenders. *International Journal of Offender Therapy and Comparative Criminology*, 66(13–14), 1347–1365. https://doi.org/10.1177/0306624X21994805

Ko, H. & Memon, A. (2022) Secondary traumatization in criminal justice professions: A literature review. *Psychology, Crime & Law*. DOI:10.1080/1068316X.2021.2018444

Mumford, E.A., Liu, W., & Taylor, B.G. (2021). Profiles of U.S. law enforcement officers' physical, psychological, and behavioral health: Results from a nationally representative survey of officers. *Police Quarterly*, 24(3), 357–381.

Souryal, S.S., & Whitehead, J.T. (2020). *Ethics in criminal justice* (7th ed.). Routledge.

Tomer, E., & Suliman, N. (2021). Prison changed me – and I just work there: Personality changes among prison officers. *The Prison Journal*, 101(2), 166–186.

References

Alpert, G.P., Dunham, R.G., & Stroshine, M.S. (2015). *Policing: Continuity and change* (2nd ed.). Waveland.

Bold, M. & Chenoweth, L. (2008). *Reflections: Preparing for your practicum and internship*. Thomson Delmar Learning.

Buehler, E.D. (2021). *Justice expenditures and employment in the United States, 2017*. U.S. Department of Justice, Bureau of Justice Statistics. NCJ 256093.

Burns, R.G. (2022). *Criminal justice: The system in perspective*. Oxford University Press.

Carcirieri, A.T. (2021). From academic to practitioner: Tips for increasing engagement with your research (essay on best practices). *Journal of Contemporary Criminal Justice*, 37(2), 244–256.

Collica-Cox, K., & Furst, G. (2019). It's not the CSI effect: Criminal justice students' choice of major and career goals. *International Journal of Offender Therapy and Comparative Criminology*, 63(11), 2069–2099.

Eren, C.P., Leyro, S., & Disha, I. (2019). It's personal: The impact of victimization on motivations and career interests among criminal justice majors at diverse urban colleges. *Journal of Criminal Justice Education*, 30(4), 510–535.

Harm, A.L., & Bell, C. (2021). Teaching beyond the textbook: Integrating formerly incarcerated individuals into criminal justice learning environments. *Journal of Criminal Justice Education*, 32(1), 126–142.

Johnson, D.S. (2020). Public versus private employees: A perspective on the characteristic and implications. *FIIB Business Review*, 9(1), 9–14.

Kelling, G.L., & Moore, M.H. (1991). From political to reform to community: The evolving strategy of police. In Greene, J.R. & Mastrofski, S.D. (eds.) *Community policing: Rhetoric or reality?* (pp. 3–25). Praeger.

Kim, D-Y. (2022). Prison privatization: An empirical literature review and path forward. *International Criminal Justice Review*, 32(1), 24–47.

Lipsky, M. (2010/1980). *Street-level bureaucracy: Dilemmas of the individual in public services.* Russel Sage Foundation.

Peat, B. (2004). *From college to career: A guide for criminal justice majors.* Allyn & Bacon

Ridener, R., Kuehn, S. & Scott, P.W. (2020). Why do criminology and criminal justice students choose their major? An examination of parental, personality, and other individual characteristics. *Journal of Criminal Justice Education, 31*(1), 1–22.

Ross, J.I., & Vianello, F. (eds.). (2021). *Convict criminology for the future.* Routledge.

Stringer, E.C., & Murphy, J. (2020). Major decisions and career attractiveness among criminal justice students. *Journal of Criminal Justice Education, 31*(4), 523–541.

Weber, M. (1947/1913). *The theory of social and economic organization.* Free Press.

White, M.D., Cooper, J.A., Saunders, J., & Raganella, A.J. (2010). Motivations for becoming a police officer: Re-assessing officer attitudes and job satisfaction after six years on the street. *Journal of Criminal Justice, 38*, 520–530.

Part 2

Preparing and Selling Yourself

Chapter 5

A Self-Assessment to Prepare for a Career in Criminal Justice or Criminology

Who are you? Such a simple, yet complex question. You could reply to this question by stating your name, or your status as a student, friend, parent, teammate, etc. Or, you could provide an in-depth answer that encompasses much deeper insight regarding, who, specifically, you are. The latter is the goal of this chapter, although the emphasis will be on who you are with particular concern for employment in criminal justice and criminology. This chapter challenges you to consider statements that will contribute to you identifying your suitability for employment in particular areas, and sometimes particular positions, within the fields. Further, you will be asked to consider more general questions about who you are. Your responses can be used to help you assess your strengths and weaknesses, skills and aptitude, and overall suitability for employment in criminal justice and criminology.

The quest to find out who you are begins with a series of statements for consideration. Read the statements and assess your level of agreement or disagreement, and consider the associated feedback. Keep brief notes regarding the feedback you receive. Make a mental, or perhaps written note of both your strengths and things you wish to work on. Be honest with yourself as you proceed through the statements. Doing so will enable you to better present yourself when it comes time to apply or interview for a position and identify areas of weaknesses you can target for improvement.

Self-Assessment

This section is designed to challenge you to examine who you are through assessing your personal interests, likes and dislikes, and motivational factors. Included is a series of statements, each with feedback, designed to help you narrow and ultimately identify an area of employment that's suitable for you.

1 "I'm interested in technology and technological developments"

   Strongly Agree   Agree   Neutral   Disagree   Strongly Disagree

A strong interest in technology and technological developments will likely open up a variety of positions in criminal justice and criminology. Particularly, one with such an interest could work in law enforcement agencies at all levels, including the federal level where counter-terrorism activities incorporate advanced forms of technology, as do crimes such as counterfeiting, identity theft, and fraud. Similarly, state- and local-level law enforcement agencies are and will increasingly be interested in hiring individuals to address electronic crime. An interest in technology (and the accompanying skills) also provides opportunities in various private industries, including private security. All large corporations have security branches/divisions, and part of

DOI: 10.4324/9781003360162-7

that security may entail ensuring the protection of sensitive information. Further, those with an interest in technology should consider, in an entrepreneurial manner, what contributions they can make to the day-to-day operations of the criminal justice system. Consider that it wasn't too long ago that technology was largely absent from justice-based practices. Think about ways in which you can innovatively contribute. Advanced doorbell systems and related technology-based home security devices are fine examples of how creativity and technology can enhance safety.

2   "Financial compensation is important to me"

    Strongly Agree   Agree   Neutral   Disagree   Strongly Disagree

You may wish to reconsider finding employment in criminal justice and criminology if making money is extremely important to you. The pay in many areas of criminal justice and criminology is average, or comparable to many other occupations. Administrators in various agencies, judges, and attorneys are among those who earn the highest salaries. Jailers, correctional officers, and rural law enforcement agents are among the lowest paid positions in the criminal justice system. An account of salaries generally associated with various positions in criminal justice and criminology is provided in Appendix E.

3   "I enjoy working with children and young adults"

    Strongly Agree   Agree   Neutral   Disagree   Strongly Disagree

Those who enjoy working with children seem well-suited to a career in the juvenile justice system. Within the juvenile justice system are positions such as counselor, detention officer, intake and assessment officer, program coordinator, case manager, and related positions. Other positions include school resource officer and various positions within child protective services. Chapter 12 covers employment in the juvenile justice system.

4   "I enjoy working outdoors"

    Strongly Agree   Agree   Neutral   Disagree   Strongly Disagree

Those with an interest in working outdoors should consider positions in law enforcement. Aside from the traditional police officer position, there are multiple opportunities for working outdoors in the criminal justice system, including positions with agencies such as the National Park Service, the Bureau of Land Management, the US Fish and Wildlife Service, and state and local wildlife protection agencies. Wilderness camp counselors, community corrections officers, and environmental protection specialists are also among those who spend substantial time away from the office.

5   "I don't want a job that involves much long distance travel"

    Strongly Agree   Agree   Neutral   Disagree   Strongly Disagree

Most positions within criminal justice and criminology do not involve traveling. Several federal law enforcement positions are the exception, primarily due to the nationwide jurisdiction of federal law enforcement agencies. Transfers and travel requirements are common in this level of law enforcement, particularly for promotion purposes (Yu, 2015). Be aware that travel could be a part of any position, whether it be at the local-, state-, or federal level. Travel requirements and expectations should be discussed during the interview stage prior to accepting a position.

6 "I'm not interested in working overtime"

   Strongly Agree   Agree   Neutral   Disagree   Strongly Disagree

Many employment positions today, both within and outside of the criminal justice system, require some form of overtime. Law enforcement agents, probation/parole officers, correctional officers, and others working in the system must expect to occasionally work overtime. Both public and private attorneys, paralegals, and judges are among those who typically work well over the traditional 40-hour work week. The good news is that overtime provides non-salaried employees an opportunity to boost their income. Those not interested in working overtime should, for instance, seek administrative-type office positions (e.g., in planning and/or research, or as a clerk of court, a court reporter, or a court administrator) where working overtime is less likely to occur than in other areas of employment in the criminal justice system.

7 "I don't work well in groups"

   Strongly Agree   Agree   Neutral   Disagree   Strongly Disagree

Not being able to work well in groups is a deficiency that should likely be addressed prior to entering the workforce. Most positions are going to involve some form of group work, and some positions will involve much group work. It is, after all, the criminal justice *system*. Detectives, special units, judges, district attorneys, public defenders, counselors, and others work in groups on a daily basis. Those interested in avoiding group work ought to consider, among other occupations, rural law enforcement, wildlife and protective services, and private security, although each of these positions is going to involve at least some group interaction.

8 "I want job security"

   Strongly Agree   Agree   Neutral   Disagree   Strongly Disagree

Job security is very important to most people. Knowing that one will be gainfully employed over an extended period of time promotes more effective long-term planning. Fortunately, there is much job security found throughout the criminal justice system. Crime is not going to cease any time soon; thus, there will be a consistent need for those interested in working in criminal justice and criminology. The public sector, where most who work in criminal justice or criminology are employed, provides a greater sense of job security than the private sector, which is more susceptible to profit margins and other economic indicators. Those concerned with job security should generally feel a sense of comfort with any government position; however, they ought to be cognizant of technological changes that could replace their position. For instance, technological advancements may limit, or outdate, the functions performed by court reporters who may be replaced by voice recognition systems and other forms of technology (Williams, 2020).

9   "Opportunities for advancement are important to me"

   Strongly Agree   Agree   Neutral   Disagree   Strongly Disagree

Opportunities for advancement exist throughout the criminal justice system. The extent to which advancement opportunities exist varies by area, agency responsibilities, and the level of agency. Accordingly, it should be the goal of those anticipating employment in criminal justice or criminology to research the various areas and agencies with which they seek employment and assess whether advancement opportunities exist at the time of their employment, or will exist in the near future. This can be done in several ways, including assessing whether or not there is extensive employee turnover, or those in high-ranking positions are close to retirement, or through speaking with current employees. Further, the US Bureau of Labor highlights employment trends in a variety of areas within criminal justice. For instance, it suggested that the 2020–2030 employment change for paralegals, who provide assistance for attorneys (see Chapter 10), will be 12%, which is faster than average (Bureau of Labor Statistics, 2022).

10 "I have difficulty meeting deadlines"

   Strongly Agree   Agree   Neutral   Disagree   Strongly Disagree

Those with difficulties meeting deadlines are going to face challenges in most areas of employment. The ability to be timely and meet deadlines is important for many reasons, not the least of which is that supervisors or colleagues may be dependent on your contribution. Nevertheless, there are positions within criminal justice and criminology that require a limited number of deadlines that must be met. For instance, correctional officers are faced with few deadlines, as are private investigators, security guards, and some law enforcement agents. Detectives do often not work on a schedule that often requires meeting deadlines. Nevertheless, expediency and timeliness in some form or fashion are part of most employment positions both within and outside of criminal justice and criminology.

11 "I have strong interpersonal skills"

   Strongly Agree   Agree   Neutral   Disagree   Strongly Disagree

Strong interpersonal skills are vital in most occupations and professions, particularly within criminal justice and criminology. The ability to effectively interact with others is especially valuable for attorneys, judges, law enforcement agents, mediators, victims' assistance advocates, counselors, probation and parole officers, case managers, crime prevention specialists, researchers, and related positions. Effective interpersonal skills are helpful with regard to interviewing for a position, networking, performing a job, and evaluation purposes. Being able to effectively communicate with others both verbally and nonverbally is a key component of interpersonal skills, and essential for employment in many areas. Criminologists, for instance, may conduct interviews as part of their research practices. In commenting on the importance of communication, McNamara and Burns (2021, 39) noted that "Communication is perhaps the most important, yet often overlooked, aspect of the criminal justice system."

12 "I am tolerant of people who are different from me"

   Strongly Agree   Agree   Neutral   Disagree   Strongly Disagree

Being tolerant of individuals who are different from you culturally, socially, financially, racially, ethnically, and/or physically is particularly important for employment in criminal justice and criminology, and in our increasingly diverse society as well. It is particularly important for individuals who work in these fields to maintain an appreciation for diversity (e.g., McNamara & Burns, 2021). Understanding differences among individuals will, at the very least, make one's job much easier and less stressful. Law enforcement officers, probation and parole officers, case workers, and correctional officers in particular deal directly with individuals caught up in the criminal justice system and, accordingly, should be particularly tolerant of differences.

13 "I have strong writing skills"

   Strongly Agree   Agree   Neutral   Disagree   Strongly Disagree

Strong writing skills are essential in many employment positions in criminal justice and criminology. The ability to write well is vital to developing effective communication skills. Among those who require effective writing skills are police officers, case managers, education specialists, court reporters, paralegals, and attorneys. Criminal justice researchers and administrators should also possess the ability to write effectively. Strong writing skills are important for criminologists, who conduct research, take copious notes, and submit reports. The importance of effective writing and interpersonal skills was noted in a survey of police officer perceptions of the value of higher education. Officers suggested that these two skills were among the most important for students to learn while in school (Edwards, 2019).

14 "I'm not very well organized"

   Strongly Agree   Agree   Neutral   Disagree   Strongly Disagree

Organization is the key to much success in any field, particularly criminal justice and criminology. For instance, given the often large numbers of individuals entering and exiting the criminal justice system, organization is essential. Various positions within criminal justice and criminology require extra consideration of organizational skills. Particularly, attorneys, judges, court administrators, court clerks, laboratory technicians, sheriffs and police chiefs, probation and parole officers, case managers, and community service coordinators should be very well organized. Bear in mind, however, that all positions require at least a modest level of organization and it behooves all who are entering the workforce to enhance their organizational skills. Being organized enables one to be more efficient and effective and is essential for advancement in one's career. Organizational skills are needed by supervisors and line staff. Among the key organizational skills are setting goals, planning, time management, scheduling, delegation, and resource allocation (Atanacio, 2021).

15 "I am a very effective researcher"

   Strongly Agree   Agree   Neutral   Disagree   Strongly Disagree

Research skills are applicable in many areas. Such skills can be used to evaluate jobs, cities, neighborhoods, crime, and so on. Thus, most criminal justice programs at the college- and university-level stress research aptitude. Advanced research skills are applicable in several positions related to criminal justice, including academic criminal justice and criminology, research and planning positions in all areas of the system, paralegals, and private investigations. Attorneys also engage in a substantial amount of research. Criminologists, in particular, regularly engage in research and must have strong research skills.

16 "I don't work well under close supervision"

    Strongly Agree   Agree   Neutral   Disagree   Strongly Disagree

Much has changed in recent history with regard to management practices. Many organizations and agencies are moving away from close supervision of employees toward granting workers more input in decision-making and opportunities guide agency practices. Such participatory management is a break from traditional management practices which often stressed close supervision. If indeed you don't work well under close supervision, it is suggested that you consider a career in policing (primarily due to freedoms often associated with the position), academic criminal justice and criminology, and probation or parole (in which officers are granted much discretion in their day-to-day activities). Judges are also granted a great deal of freedom in how they manage their courts.

17 "I'm interested in an employment position that has much power or authority"

    Strongly Agree   Agree   Neutral   Disagree   Strongly Disagree

Arguably, nobody should seek a position simply for the opportunity to wield power. There should be other factors that influence one's decision to take a job in a particular field. Nevertheless, positions of authority are found throughout the criminal justice system. In fact, the criminal justice system is one of the few areas in which great levels of authority are integrated within some of the entry-level positions. For instance, jailers, and police, probation, corrections, and parole officers maintain a great deal of authority in their jobs. Other positions within the criminal justice system that maintain a notable level of authority include judges, attorneys, and wardens.

18 "I want a job that will reward my creativity"

    Strongly Agree   Agree   Neutral   Disagree   Strongly Disagree

We all seek a position of employment that will best utilize our skills. Accordingly, some of us are creative and would like to be recognized and/or appreciated for our creative contributions. However, not all employees are positioned to be creative, and there are some people who are creative although not rewarded for being so. Among the areas of employment in criminal justice that rewards creativity are victim and witness assistance workers, court mediators, attorneys, researchers, judges, private investigators, community relations officers, and school resource officers.

19 "I'm seeking a position that will provide me an opportunity to help troubled individuals"

    Strongly Agree   Agree   Neutral   Disagree   Strongly Disagree

Opportunities to help troubled individuals are abundant throughout positions in criminal justice and criminology. In fact, such opportunities are what encourage some to seek employment in the field. Among the jobs through which one would be in an ideal position to help others are counselors, psychologists, educators, police officers, corrections officers, defense attorneys, social workers, positions within child protective services, probation and parole officers, and substance abuse counselors. Criminologists contribute through their efforts to better understand the causes of crime, and in doing so advance the field and help keep us safe. Very few fields aside from criminal justice and criminology provide more opportunities to help people.

A Practitioner's View

Lacy Hensley, LMSW, MA, Victim Advocate

As a victim advocate, I have the opportunity to walk side-by-side someone on what is often the worst day of their lives. The magnitude of this gift is not lost on me and is definitely not something I take for granted. Whether it's responding on-scene with the police department or supporting a victim as they navigate the criminal justice system, the most important thing that I can do is meet them where they are. While this looks different for each and every individual, in order to be the best advocate, you must always remember that the survivor is the expert in their journey! You are there to offer support, education, advocacy and resources, but it's up to them to decide what their "new normal" will look like.

One key to preparing to be a victim advocate is to know yourself! You are going to hear a lot of traumatic experiences that people have gone through. In order to be your best, you must find ways to take care of yourself. This is especially true if you yourself have experienced some type of trauma. This will be a continual process of assessing yourself throughout your career. If you set up good boundaries and self-care practices in the beginning it will definitely help you to continue to serve victims well. Another key to preparing to go into the field of victim advocacy is to start volunteering somewhere now! As a criminal justice student, you will be competing with other disciplines such as social work for victim services positions, which are often limited. Therefore, it is crucial to get as much experience as possible as quickly as possible.

Finally, remember that this is a field that exists around crisis and trauma; which is always unpredictable. So you have to be flexible!

20 "I want a job that will help me better protect society"

Strongly Agree   Agree   Neutral   Disagree   Strongly Disagree

It is admirable that some individuals seek a particular job or career primarily based on their motivation to protect society. We should all be so altruistic. Most positions within criminal justice and criminology have the ultimate goal of addressing crime in society and ultimately protecting citizens. Some positions within the field enable individuals to more directly protect society than others. Particularly, those who wish to have the greatest impact on protecting society should consider a career in probation or parole, in law enforcement, in private security, in a prosecutor's office, as a judge, or in most aspects of corrections (particularly, counseling, corrections officers, or education).

21 "Ensuring that criminal justice practices are performed in a fair and just manner is important to me"

Strongly Agree   Agree   Neutral   Disagree   Strongly Disagree

Everyone caught up in the criminal justice system should be treated in a fair and just manner, and the existence of procedural and constitutional law dictates that they are. Some individuals seek employment positions within criminal justice or criminology because they can help ensure that all who enter the system receive a fair deal. For instance, there is certainly a difference between *criminal* justice and criminal *justice*. Individuals interested in helping to ensure that all in the criminal justice system get a fair deal are more interested in criminal *justice*. Among the positions that provide excellent opportunities to ensure the fair and just treatment of all who are exposed to the system are public defenders and other attorneys, judges, correctional officers, corrections classification officers, and case managers. To be sure, this is not a comprehensive list as other positions in the system enable workers to seek fair and just treatment of all.

22 "I want a position that requires no physical activity or danger"

Strongly Agree   Agree   Neutral   Disagree   Strongly Disagree

Some individuals seek particular employment positions simply because the position requires physical activity. Others are deterred by jobs that involve much physical activity. The criminal

Having the word "justice" included in the field in which one is employed places a heavy burden on criminal justice employees. All who work in the system are expected to perform their duties in a fair and just manner.
Source: www.pexels.com/photo/brass-colored-balance-scale-on-a-lawyer-s-table-6077961/

justice system is filled with both types of positions; however, many do not require much physical activity. If you are interested in a position that involves limited physical activity, consider the following: education coordinator, crime and justice researcher, lab technician, dispatcher, court administrator, court clerk, court reporter, intake worker, mediator, and victim and/or witness assistance counselor. Criminologists are also generally not required to engage in physical activity.

Similarly, many jobs in the criminal justice system involve no danger (although interpretations of "danger" vary among individuals). The following positions are among those that are largely "danger-free": court reporters, clerks of court, any administrative position in criminal justice, education coordinators, researchers, counselors, school resource officers (depending on the school), crime prevention specialists, home and business alarm specialists, paralegals, and dispatchers. Criminologists may face some danger if their work involves personal interviews with dangerous or potentially dangerous individuals.

23 "I prefer to work in calm, quiet working conditions"

   Strongly Agree   Agree   Neutral   Disagree   Strongly Disagree

Of particular importance in finding and accepting an employment position is the work environment. Some individuals prefer a chaotic environment, while others prefer a quiet, library-like atmosphere. Yet others may prefer something in-between. Those interested in quiet, calm work conditions ought to consider a position as a laboratory technician, paralegal, criminal justice researcher, planning and policy development specialist, private investigator, insurance examiner, or business/residential security consultant. The work environment for criminologists is often quiet, as they are typically housed in offices. Certainly, there are other positions throughout criminal justice and criminology that provide quiet and calm working conditions. The aforementioned positions are among the more prominent ones.

24 "I don't believe that political interests should directly impact one's field of employment"

   Strongly Agree   Agree   Neutral   Disagree   Strongly Disagree

Political interests imposing into the workplace could provide unwanted stress for some individuals. Many of us appreciate consistency and a shared set of expectations when it comes to our jobs, thus, to have politicians notably impact our day-to-day activities may be too stressful for some. Those who do not believe that politics ought to directly impact the work environment ought to steer clear of sheriff's departments, district attorney offices, and judicial positions, simply because the individuals holding these positions are elected in some instances. Those looking to avoid direct influence by politics should consider careers as a business and/ or residential security consultant, criminologist, court reporter, clerk of court, paralegal, court mediator, security guard, or dispatcher. Chapter 4 addresses the influence of politics upon employment in the criminal justice system.

25 "I'm interested in a career in criminal justice and criminology because I want to know more about crime and individuals who break the law"

   Strongly Agree   Agree   Neutral   Disagree   Strongly Disagree

Most positions within the criminal justice system provide much insight about crime and individuals who break the law. Criminologists learn very much about those individuals engaged in illegal behavior and responses to them. Obviously, some positions provide more information than others. Generally, those analyzing or directly involved with crime and individuals convicted for breaking the law will gain the greatest amount of information in these areas. Among those meeting these criteria are researchers/academics, private investigators, legal aid counselors, paralegals, police officers, probation and parole officers, attorneys, and judges. Prison officers and jailers also learn more about crime and individuals who break the law primarily through their regular interaction with incarcerated persons.

26 "I don't mind a job that involves shift work"

   Strongly Agree   Agree   Neutral   Disagree   Strongly Disagree

Shift work can be difficult for some individuals, particularly as it relates to sleep patterns and family life. The irregular shifts provide additional stress in that there is little consistency regarding one's daily workweek. On the other hand, shift work has little impact on others. In fact, some individuals welcome the varying shifts as it adds to the excitement, or variety of the position. For instance, individuals who work varying shifts get to experience things they otherwise wouldn't have seen (e.g., sunrises, vacated streets, empty stores, and so on). Particular positions within the criminal justice system are more likely than others to involve shift work. Among those positions are police officers, corrections officers, jailers, security personnel, and private investigators. Other positions, such as community supervision officers, may not directly involve shift work, although they do involve irregular working hours.

27 "I am not able to attend a pre-service training academy"

   Strongly Agree   Agree   Neutral   Disagree   Strongly Disagree

Training is a primary component of any position in criminal justice and criminology; however, some positions within the criminal justice system require preservice training in which individuals must spend extended periods of time at an academy. Attendance at a preservice training academy, however, could pose particular challenges. For instance, parents who must attend the academy may not be able to provide childcare while doing so. Fortunately, most positions within criminal justice do not require extended periods of preservice training that could pose particular hardships. Among the positions that may require attendance at a preservice training academy are law enforcement agents, corrections officers, probation and parole officers, and judges. One could also include attorneys with this group as those who wish to practice law must first attend law school. Similarly, college and university professors of criminal justice are expected to spend years in graduate school as part of their training. Criminologists largely get their training through formal education, perhaps supplemented with practical experience. A master's and Ph.D. degree is typically required to become a criminologist.

28 "I can get a job without a college degree"

   Strongly Agree   Agree   Neutral   Disagree   Strongly Disagree

Historically, a college degree was of little value for many positions in the criminal justice system. However, a college degree is becoming increasingly necessary for many positions in the field. Generally, a degree is becoming increasingly necessary for positions and promotions in all areas. Most corrections officers and police officers are required to have a high school diploma as their highest degree; however, others may require officers to have some college hours. About

1% of police departments require a four-year degree (Reaves, 2015). Higher education is not necessarily required for some positions in private security, private investigations, and home or business alarm installation, although technical skills are important. Some positions within the criminal justice system require certification (e.g., paralegals and dispatchers). There are certainly jobs for individuals who do not hold a college degree, although generally, opportunities for advancement and higher-paying positions within the criminal justice system require a degree.

29 "I don't want to live in, or near a large city"

    Strongly Agree   Agree   Neutral   Disagree   Strongly Disagree

The fortunate, yet unfortunate, aspect of not wanting to live near a big city and wishing to work in criminal justice or criminology is that most crime occurs in large cities. Accordingly, many criminal justice agencies and much crime are located in urban areas. Those not wishing to live in an urban area may be free from much of the crime, yet they have fewer opportunities to work in the criminal justice system. Nevertheless, there are certainly positions within criminal justice and criminology that do not require one to live in or near a large city. For instance, one could find employment as a parks and wildlife officer, wilderness camp counselor, or rural police officer. Further, prisons in many states are often located in rural areas (Eason, 2017). Accordingly, many positions within prisons are available to those who do not wish to live near a large city. Criminologists can study crime from various locations, although they are often affiliated with a university, college, or some other institution.

30 "I wish to work in the private sector"

    Strongly Agree   Agree   Neutral   Disagree   Strongly Disagree

Government work is not for everyone. Some individuals do not wish to work for the government, while other individuals are not suitable for working with the government. Fortunately for those individuals there are positions within criminal justice located in the private sector. Some of the primary differences between the public and private sector are the level of job security (a greater level of security in the public sector) and the agency goal (the public sector is often about providing service while the private sector is often concerned with profit). Many of the positions within criminal justice are found within the public sector; however, there are certainly positions within the private sector. Among those positions are any type of position within a private prison, private security officers, home and business alarm specialists, private defense attorneys, private investigators, and personal security specialists.

31 "I don't wish to work directly with individuals who have broken the law"

    Strongly Agree   Agree   Neutral   Disagree   Strongly Disagree

Hoping to avoid direct interaction with persons who have broken the law seems somewhat challenging upon assuming employment in the *criminal* justice system. Nevertheless, there are several positions that do not necessarily require direct contact with suspects or individuals processed within the system. Prominent among those positions are criminologists, administrators in each of the primary areas of criminal justice, home and business alarm specialists, dispatchers, crime prevention specialists, and criminal justice policy analysts. Bear in mind that individuals caught up in the criminal justice system are first and foremost human beings with troubled lives. Many have encountered bad situations that encouraged them to break the law, and are not dangerous people to be around. The very large majority of people caught up in the criminal justice system are not hurtful, hateful people. This issue is further addressed in Chapter 4.

Summary

The self-assessment above was targeted toward areas and employment positions within criminal justice and criminology. Some statements were specifically related to select areas of the criminal justice system, while others were more general in nature. Both types should help you to get a better idea of who you are and what career best suits you. Self-actualization is vital to success in any arena. Understanding your strengths and weaknesses, your abilities and limitations, and your likes and dislikes can help you identify areas of improvement and enable you to better work within your parameters. Be aware that the suggestions for employment in each item are not comprehensive. They are provided as examples.

Below is a series of questions, absent feedback, that will help you better gauge your suitability for employment in criminal justice or criminology. These questions will also help you identify your strengths and weaknesses.

- Is there anything in my background that will prohibit me from working in the criminal justice system?
- Will my health and physical fitness permit me to work in the criminal justice system?
- Do I have the skills necessary to perform the tasks that will be required of me?
- Will my personal values interfere with my job responsibilities?
- Are my long-term goals attainable through working in criminal justice or criminology?
- What positions will interfere with my family life? How will particular careers or jobs affect my social life?
- Economically, is it a good idea to work in criminal justice or criminology?

One final exercise that will serve you well is to make copies of these questions and answer them over time. Perhaps three years from now you'll be considering transferring jobs or going for a promotion. In three years much can change, including your qualifications, and your likes and dislikes. You may find that upon again answering these questions you may be better suited for another area, or another position.

Discussion Questions

1. Consider your strengths and weaknesses as a person. Are your strengths suitable to particular positions in the criminal justice system? Are your weaknesses something you can overcome to be successful working in the criminal justice system?
2. Why would strong writing skills be important for working as a criminologist? How about for a prosecutor or probation officer?
3. Interpersonal skills are particularly important for working in the criminal justice system. How can someone improve on their interpersonal skills?
4. Rank the following according to what you believe is their importance for working in the criminal justice system. Justify your ranking.
   (Rank from 1 to 5, with 1 being the most important, 5 being least important)
   ____ Fairness
   ____ Diversity
   ____ Controlling crime
   ____ Helping others
   ____ Respectfulness

5   What positions within the criminal justice system offer the greatest opportunities to help troubled individuals? Are you interested in a career in these areas?

Critical Thinking Exercise

Create a wish list/personal inventory regarding a career in criminal justice. Use a spreadsheet and create five columns. Document the careers that most interest you in the first column. Include your strengths and weaknesses in the next two columns. Note what job/career-related issues are most important to you in the next column, and use the final column to note what you do not want at all in a job/career. Analyze your results and keep them in mind as you read this book, and research jobs in the field. For instance, consider whether your strengths are suitable for the career you seek, or if a particular job that interests you includes the issues that are most important to you. Save the spreadsheet and update it regularly until you find your dream job.

For Further Examination

Ballaro, J., & Meade, K.R. (2021). Factors determining job satisfaction and dissatisfaction for forensic scientists. *Organizational Development Journal, 39*(2), 37–51.

Lambert, E.G., Keena, L.D., & Morrow, W.J. (2021). Effects of work-family conflict on Southern correctional staff burnout. *Criminal Justice and Behavior, 49*(1), 117–138.

Mack, K., & Rhineberger-Dunn, G. (2022). What matters most? Comparing the impact of individual, job, and organizational factors on job stress and job satisfaction among juvenile justice personnel. *Criminal Justice Studies, 35*(1), 18–37.

Paek, S.Y., Nalla, M.K., Lee, J., & Gurinskaya, A. (2022). The effect of perceived citizen views and supervisor support on private security officers' job satisfaction: The mediating role of self-legitimacy. *Security Journal, 35*, 1047–1065. https://doi.org/10.1057/s41284-021-00313-2

Riedy, S.M., Fekedulegn, D., Vila, B., Andrews, M., & Volanti, J.M. (2021). Shift work and overtime across a career in law enforcement: A 15-year study. *Policing: An International Journal, 44*(2), 200–212.

References

Atanacio, A. (2021, November 5). Top six organizational skills for the workplace. *Forbes.com*. Available at: www.forbes.com/sites/theyec/2021/11/05/top-six-organizational-skills-for-the-workplace/?sh=3097f63c3ff4

Bureau of Labor Statistics. (2022). *Occupational outlook handbook, paralegals and legal assistants*. U.S. Department of Labor. Available at: www.bls.gov/ooh/legal/paralegals-and-legal-assistants.htm

Eason, J.M. (2017, March 12). Why prison building will continue booming in rural America. *TheConversation.com*. Available at: https://theconversation.com/why-prison-building-will-continue-booming-in-rural-america-71920

Edwards, B.D. (2019). Perceived value of higher education among police officers: Comparing county and municipal officers. *Journal of Criminal Justice Education, 30*(4), 606–620.

McNamara, R., & Burns, R. (2021). *Multiculturalism, crime, and criminal justice* (2nd ed.). Oxford University Press.

Reaves, B.A. (2015). *Local police departments, 2013: Personnel, policies, and practices*. U.S. Department of Justice, Bureau of Justice Statistics. NCJ 248677.

Williams, T. (2020, October 1). Will court reporting undergo a pandemic shift? *ABA Journal*. Accessed at: www.abajournal.com/magazine/article/will-covid-19-cause-attorneys-and-courts-to-embrace-ai-enabled-transcription-services-at-the-expense-of-court-reporters

Yu, H.H. (2015). An examination of federal law enforcement: An exploratory analysis of the challenges they face in the work environment. *Feminist Criminology, 10*(3), 259–278.

Chapter 6

Your Criminal Justice and Criminology Education

Congratulations. You're the Chief Operating Officer of your county's Probation and Parole Division. As such, you're very involved and influential in the hiring process. Your name and reputation are associated with each person you hire, thus, you take this aspect of the job very seriously. A colleague who holds the same title and performs the same function in a different county asks you a simple, yet somehow challenging question: "What do you look for in a candidate?" You reflect on the question for a moment, and begin by stating that a college degree is necessary, followed by related field experience. The colleague asks if you consider: (1) the reputation of colleges and universities, (2) the nature and extent of the coursework completed by the candidate, and (3) whether or not they have field experience. This line of questioning causes some deep self-reflection as you have never verbally expressed what, specifically, you look for in a candidate. You simply respond: "I'm looking for the most qualified, well-rounded individuals."

This scenario highlights some of the important, and sometimes nondescript, considerations that are part of the hiring process. A job description will certainly be used to identify suitable candidates, but discretion often comes into play after that. Your response of seeking "the most qualified, well-rounded individuals" is acceptable, but it is vague. It is likely that many candidates will be well qualified, and many may be well rounded. Hopefully, certain job candidates will stand out. This chapter helps you use your educational experience to best differentiate yourself upon applying for positions.

An education consists of knowledge compiled over time and obtained from many sources. It consists of learning skills, gaining knowledge, and developing an understanding of information. Many people believe that educations only emerge from a classroom. An education, however, includes much more. Formal schooling provides a large base of education, but experiences and the basic knowledge absorbed from everyday life fills gaps left by formal education. "Book smart" and "street smart" people differ with regard to their education, yet the both became educated. Although education formally occurs in school, it also develops through knowledge gained from hands-on and general life experiences.

Several highly successful people such as Microsoft founder Bill Gates and Facebook creator Mark Zuckerberg never earned a college degree. Their educations primarily came through life experiences. Sir Richard Branson, an entrepreneur with an estimated net worth of $4.9 billion, dropped out of high school at age 16 (Martin, 2018). He left school because he struggled with dyslexia and wanted to focus on the magazine business he started. Branson likely did not develop his entrepreneurial skills through formal education. Instead, he became increasingly educated as he continuously bought and created new businesses, including an airline, a record label, radio stations, and hotels. He attributed his success to following his passion in life (Connley, 2017). The experiences of Gates, Zuckerberg, and Branson highlight the various paths one can take toward becoming educated. While the education one obtains outside of classrooms (e.g., through internships and life experience) is very important to

DOI: 10.4324/9781003360162-8

career success and addressed throughout this book, this chapter primarily focuses on formal education.

You've likely been told that higher education is the key to success. There is some truth to this statement, although it should be rephrased to read: "Higher education is *one* key to success." Higher education is related to more positive outcomes, including overall happiness in life (Oreopoulos & Salvanes, 2011) and higher income levels (Torpey, 2018). Further, a degree is increasingly becoming a requirement for many positions, both within and in the US outside of the criminal justice system. From 2011 to 2021, the percentage of people over age 24 who earned a bachelor's degree or higher increased by 7.5% from 30.4% to 37.9% (U.S. Census Bureau, 2022). These data suggest that a substantial and increasing portion of people are seeking higher education, which may mean that the quality of one's education takes on additional significance. One must find other avenues to separate themselves from a marketability standpoint as college degrees become increasingly common.

Graduation day in college is very exciting. The ceremony, regalia, and hearing *Pomp and Circumstance* played especially for you and your classmates is a very unique and rewarding experience. Enjoy the day. However, the day will unfortunately come to a close and life beyond college begins. Are you prepared? Have you lined up a job? Do you have a plan? Hopefully, you'll be able to answer "yes" to each of these questions, because you must consider that everyone around you, and those graduating around the country (and globe, for that matter) will become part of your competition in the job market. Further, those already in the workforce may also be seeking the same positions as you, providing additional competition.

This chapter assists and encourages students to maximize their formal education. It provides direction and reasons for doing so and stresses the importance of coursework and taking advantage of opportunities. Primary goals of the chapter are to encourage students to view their educational experience in a more opportunistic manner and highlight the significance of using one's college experience to maximize their marketability.

Maximizing Your Education

You must first ask yourself what you wish to attain by going to college prior to determining how you can maximize your education. Is it the knowledge? Are you most interested in the social aspects? Are you seeking higher education for career purposes or financial reasons? A college education does often result in higher-paying employment positions. The U.S. Bureau of Labor Statistics (2021) found that the median usual weekly earnings for those with a bachelor's degree was $1,334, compared to earnings of $809 for those with a high school diploma as their highest degree. Unemployment rates also differed by education, as the rate for those with a high school degree was 6.2% compared to 3.5% for those with a bachelor's degree. Financial reward, however, should not be the sole reason one seeks higher education.

Many factors other than money attract students to colleges and universities. A solid education, social and professional opportunities, room for personal and professional growth, and the ability to become a more well-rounded individual are among the attractions to higher education. Finding a school that permits you to attain these and related goals and maintaining a personal focus on reaching them are important in finding and succeeding in a career.

Earning a college degree is certainly a significant first step toward landing the position you seek. However, some positions require a bit more than a degree. For instance, criminologists are typically required to have advanced degrees in criminology and/or a field of study centered on human behavior (e.g., psychology). Further, some positions within the criminal justice system require work experience and specific skills in addition to a college degree.

It is often believed that learning occurs only in a formal classroom setting. Instead, learning is a continuous process that occurs both within and outside of classrooms. Accordingly, students should view the college or university experience as a time to broaden one's self. Many people think of the college experience as a means to an end: Earning a degree. While earning a degree is certainly a goal of higher education, it should not be the only goal. Those entering or enrolled in institutions for higher education ought to consider all means through which they can develop and hone skills, network, expose themselves to different aspects of life, and obtain a broad education that best prepares them for life after college. Maximizing one's education means more than simply excelling in coursework. It requires students taking advantage of the many opportunities provided.

It is safe to say that not all institutions of higher education are equal. One merely needs to examine the entrance requirements of various universities to recognize the differences. Put simply, some schools are academically more rigorous than others. Accordingly, some employers may give greater consideration to job candidates who graduate from the more highly ranked schools. This situation creates challenges for individuals considering various colleges and universities, for example, as one assesses whether to study at a less rigorous school (and likely excel academically), or gravitate toward the middle of the pack academically at a more challenging school. There is no easy answer to the question of whether it's better to be a big fish in a little pond, or a little fish in a big pond. Regardless, employers consider many factors in selecting candidates. It would seem that well-round, opportunistic professionals are likely to be chosen over others regardless of the school they attended.

Institutions of higher education vary in ways other than academic rigor. For instance, some provide greater opportunities for networking, and some provide extensive leadership and travel abroad opportunities. Students should select colleges and universities based on academic rigor, opportunities, cost, scholarships and other forms of financial assistance awarded, and other factors. If you're currently enrolled in higher education, consider the strengths of your school. For instance, do the faculty and/or staff make an effort to help you find employment upon graduation? If so, take advantage of that opportunity. Can you travel abroad? Do you have easy access to government agencies that can provide internship or employment opportunities? Taking advantage of these and related opportunities assists with professional growth. The onus is on *you* to consider *your* needs and respond to them.

A historical shortcoming of colleges and universities has been the emphasis on learning content and limited opportunities to apply that knowledge. There are strong arguments on both side of the debate regarding the value of streets smarts vs. book smarts, particularly within criminal justice and criminology. Some individuals believe the time spent in the university could have been better spent working, while others believe the opposite to be true. In response, it would make great sense to have a combination of both the practical and academic sides of criminal justice if one truly wishes to stand out above others. Colleges and universities ensure that students are exposed to and comprehend the substantive content required to become a criminal justice professional. To become increasingly well-rounded and ultimately more attractive to employers, it is suggested that students supplement their education with experience by taking advantage of various opportunities. Many colleges and universities are increasingly encouraging students to become more actively involved in their communities, for instance, through internships, community service, and volunteer work (e.g., Skaggs & Graybeal, 2016). Experiential learning combines the theoretical and applied aspects of criminal justice and criminology.

Students sometimes realize later in their academic careers that they aren't prepared to find a job upon graduation. The most opportunistic time to consider preparation for a career begins prior to entering college. Such preparation includes selecting the appropriate school, choosing an appropriate major, befriending helpful professors, taking relevant classes, locating places of employment, seeking volunteer experiences, successfully completing an internship (or perhaps multiple internships), networking, and various related actions.

Some students fresh out of high school have specific career goals. The same could be said for many college seniors. Some, however, are uncertain as to which field they wish to work in, which could slow them down with regard to career development. On the other hand, it's not a bad idea for one to consider all fields and positions with regard to career options. Fortunately, there are many avenues through which students can prepare themselves for employment upon graduation even if they're uncertain as to what they wish to do.

A Practitioner's View

Adrian Andrews, Vice Chancellor for Public Safety, Texas Christian University

I am the Assistant Vice Chancellor for Public Safety at Texas Christian University (TCU). I supervise the outstanding men and women of the TCU Police Department, the Director of Emergency Management, and the Director of Parking and Transportation. My daily quest is to do everything I can to help make this college campus the safest in the country.

I have served in the capacity of Assistant Vice Chancellor for Public Safety for five years. Before arriving at TCU, I was a Special Agent with the United States Secret Service for more than 28 years. I often tell people "I used to travel the world protecting very important, famous people. Now, I travel to Fort Worth, protect very important, not yet famous people." I used to think being an agent in the United States Secret Service was a dream job. Now, I often think the Secret Service career was preparing me for my "Dream Job."

There are a few things I tell students about how they can best prepare for a successful life: The Vince Lombardi story, two things they must have to be successful, and the need to start making Excellence a habit now. Vince Lombardi was a legendary football coach of the Green Bay Packers. Coach Lombardi who was so successful, the trophy given to the winning team of the Super Bowl is named the Lombardi Trophy. According to my high school and college football coaches, when Lombardi held his first team meeting, he said "Gentlemen, in everything we do, we will strive for perfection. Because we are mere mortals, we will never achieve perfection. But in our relentless pursuit of perfection, we will achieve Excellence." I challenge young people to relentlessly puruse perfection in everything aspect of their lives, knowing that their efforts will result not in a perfect life but one filled with Excellence.

I often tell TCU students there are two things they must have in order to be successful in any line of work. Those two things are a tireless work ethic and a positive attitude. I have worked in the law enforcement for more than 30 years and the most successful and accomplished public servants I worked with were those who worked the hardest (and smartest) and always exhibited a positive attitude.

After applying for the position of Special Agent with the United States Secret Service I discovered that federal investigators went back to every job I had ever worked to interview coworkers and supervisors to inquire about my attendance, work ethic, attitude and initiative. I often tell our student "These are YOUR background years."

The best indicator of what a person will do in the future is what they have done in the past. I implore our students to start their relentless pursuit of perfection now. I tell them that getting in to the habit of performing at a level that is recognized as Excellent at school, at work, and in becoming a better person cannot wait until later. The habit of being Excellent should start now.

Not everyone who goes to college has a clear understanding of their career goals. Some do, although their goals may change over time. One of the primary benefits of the university experience is the opportunity to take a wide array of courses, which exposes students to various fields. Students may start out as an economics major and ultimately switch to criminal justice or criminology after taking an introductory course that attracts their interest. Switching majors is certainly understandable, although at some point a firm decision has to be made. All students should bear in mind that it is not uncommon to obtain employment in areas other than their major. One's major area of concentration in their academic studies does not restrict them from working in other fields.

Regardless of one's major or area of interest, students should broaden themselves by learning a foreign language, obtaining advanced computer skills, conducting volunteer work, assuming leadership roles in student groups, and taking advantage of other opportunities that promote applicable skills and experience. Research suggests that criminal justice practitioners place much value on a strong work ethic, communication skills, solid work habits, and initiative. It is also felt that criminal justice students should be sensitive to and understanding of racial issues (Jones & Bonner, 2016). Colleges and universities are ideal settings to make one's self attractive to employers and become a better person. They provide much more than classroom instruction.

To emphasize the importance of maximizing one's educational experience, consider the following example. Jane attended a school that is academically on par with most other universities. Rafael attended a more academically rigorous university. They both applied for a court administrator's position. Everything being equal at this point, who is more likely to get the job, Jane or Rafael? It would seemingly be Rafael, since he earned his degree from a school that, in theory, is more rigorous.

Let's alter the scenario a bit. Rafael graduated with a 2.6 grade-point-average (GPA), while Jane earned a 3.8 GPA. Rafael was casually involved in two student groups and worked part-time one summer cleaning pools. Jane was the prior president of the criminal justice student group, vice president of the criminal justice honor society, president of her sorority, and worked two summers in a law firm and one summer under the guidance of a municipal judge. She was also active on the debate team and provided volunteer services for battered women and the homeless. Now who would you hire? Jane seems to have the advantage in this altered scenario.

Although Rafael went to the more prestigious school, he arguably failed to maximize his educational experience. Jane, on the other hand, went to the less challenging school, yet made the most of her opportunity. Of course, one could make a strong argument that Rafael is equally or perhaps more suitable for the administrator's position even though his level of involvement was below Jane's. It could be argued that his resume is not as impressive as Jane's, presumably because he was too busy studying and focused on academics to engage in the same type and level of activities. Ultimately, employers are going to seek those who seem most suitable for the job, and the nature of the work and the job requirements. Personal opinions will likely determine the extent to which emphasis is place on book smarts, levels of experience and involvement, leadership roles, and related considerations.

A final note with regard to maximizing one's coursework concerns self-presentation. Presentation is a broad word that encompasses physical appearance, demeanor, verbal and non-verbal skills, and the like. For instance, you may be asked to complete a writing assignment as part of the job interview. Are you confident in your writing skills? You may be asked questions about the importance of cultural diversity in the workplace, ethics, and/or current events. You have knowledge of crime and justice, but are you prepared to answer these questions? Can you effectively express your thoughts in words? In writing? Maximizing your educational experience will prepare you for effectively responding to these and related questions as you begin and proceed through your career.

Formal education provides many benefits for those who work in the criminal justice system and criminology. The means by which we continue to become educated, however, extend beyond the classroom.
Source: https://pixabay.com/photos/graduation-college-graduate-4502796/

Maximizing your education is not always easy. It takes effort, time, and hard work. You will, however, be thankful you did so when applying for employment positions and reflecting upon your college days. One particularly significant way to maximize your education concerns the courses you take and their applicability to life postgraduation.

Your Coursework

Coursework may seem to some students as something that needs to be completed to earn a good grade. However, the courses taken throughout one's college career heavily impact the benefits derived from higher education. Students are required to take specific courses to meet the requirements of their major and perhaps their minor(s). They will also be required to take courses to meet the school's general requirements, including perhaps courses in English, History, and other disciplines. They may have to choose electives to meet a specific number of hours and round out their coursework. Careful selection of the courses one takes is essential for maximizing one's education.

Some of the more popular considerations in student course selection include the time and days courses are offered, the instructor of the course, and fellow student feedback regarding the course. For instance, many students avoid Friday classes, and 8:00 AM courses are often not a top priority of many students. Similarly, students often ask each other if a course is "easy" and ask about the instructor. While such information has some relevance, it may not contribute to a student's overall professional development. For instance, academically "easy" courses help one's GPA; however, students may benefit very little in return. Easy courses do not challenge tomorrow's professionals and may impact professional development. "Cool" professors may be enjoyable in the classroom; however, their ability to teach, challenge, evaluate, and develop professionals is far more important. "Blow off" courses, or those courses that appear to students to be an easy way to earn an "A" for little effort, contribute to "blowing off" a fine opportunity to better yourself.

Students should take elective courses that will benefit them in the long run when meeting the major and university requirements. Those interested in a career in criminal justice or criminology should not take "Introduction to Ceramics" with their electives, unless perhaps they're interested in teaching a ceramics course at a correctional facility. While such courses may be interesting and possibly provide an opportunity to earn a good grade, they offer little toward professional development with regard to a career in criminal justice or criminology. They may, however, contribute to one's overall well-roundedness.

Student coursework should include classes that meet the major and university requirements, supplemented by courses that maximize one's educational experience. Keep in mind that upon graduation all of your fellow graduates will have a degree, as will many others. Your degree can be enhanced in several ways, for instance, by earning a minor and/or a second major. All students should consider completing a minor and/or a second major with the goal of broadening their education and differentiating themselves from their peers. Specialization in a field other than the one in which you majored will provide you greater marketability upon graduation. Some employers may view you as more well-rounded than applicants who didn't broaden their knowledge base.

Choosing a minor can be almost as important as choosing a major for criminal justice and criminology students. Choosing an area in which to minor should include consideration of career aspirations. Disciplines related to criminal justice and criminology include sociology, political science, psychology, foreign languages, social work, public administration, and related disciplines. At some points in their careers, students may be surprised at benefits of having a minor.

Earning a minor is not essential for many employment positions within criminal justice, and not a requirement in various colleges and universities. Further, schools do not offer minors in all areas. For instance, criminal justice and criminology students are often interested in forensics; however, many academic programs are not designed to offer such an education. Forensics is multidisciplinary in nature, and criminal justice and criminology programs often do not have the faculty to teach all courses in the field. In turn, programs either look to other disciplines to assist and make the degree interdisciplinary, or do not offer courses in the area.

To address the lack of directed study in a particular area, students should create their own minor by selecting courses in various disciplines that would contribute to their personal professional development. For instance, students should identify and take courses that are directly related to the study of forensics. Taking courses in chemistry, biology, and related areas would help prepare students for a career in this field, and although the student may not officially have completed a minor, they certainly have an advantage over the students who less thoughtfully chose their electives. Researching the requirements for a minor at other schools assists with creating a directed area of study. Related, one doesn't need formal education to learn. For example, many helpful resources are available outside of formal education that can be used to learn a second language.

The nature and content of student coursework are important for students to develop a solid base of knowledge in a field. Completing relevant courses for a particular job or area enhances one's credentials and helps with resume building, which is an ongoing process. Chapter 7 provides discussion of resumes.

Student coursework is sometimes worthy of inclusion on one's resume, particularly if one has limited information to include. There are benefits of noting relevant coursework on your resume when applying for a job. For instance, which course would be more appealing to an employer seeking a crime prevention specialist: "Fundamentals of Crime Prevention Through Environmental Design" or "Advanced Scuba Diving?" The former would certainly seem more appropriate and should be referenced.

Recent changes in society have contributed to criminal justice employers seeking candidates with specific skill sets and experience. As an example, employers are increasingly seeking bilingual candidates in response to changing demographics in society. Advanced computer skills are also beneficial for some positions, particularly in light of the technological changes impacting crime and justice-based practices. Experience traveling abroad may be of interest to particular employers, including those seeking well-rounded employees who may be able to assist the agency in addressing issues related to globalism. It is imperative that candidates differentiate themselves from others, and doing so requires taking full advantage of the many opportunities presented in institutions of higher education. In some cases, obtaining a graduate degree is an effective way to stand out.

Graduate Studies

Criminal justice professionals sometimes earn an advanced degree, typically a master's in criminal justice or criminology, or they may earn a doctoral degree such as a Ph.D. or Juris Doctorate (J.D.) from a law school. Master's degree often requires 30–36 credit hours, and a thesis and/or passing comprehensive exams. Ph.D. programs are more rigorous than master's programs, particularly in relation to the comprehensive exams and dissertation requirements. A Ph.D. typically takes longer to earn than a master's (the length of time for completion varies by institution and student) and is often required for full-time teaching at the university level, although a Ph.D. is suitable for other positions relating to criminal justice. For instance, statisticians in government agencies are sometimes required to have a Ph.D., and criminologists typically hold a terminal degree. Earning a J.D. typically requires three years of successful training in a law school. Those wishing to practice law will be required to pass the bar exam in the state where they wish to practice.

Graduate studies can facilitate career development in many ways. A master's or Ph.D. in criminal justice, criminology, or related fields can assist with obtaining a position and/or career advancement. It should be noted, however, that graduate degrees are not essential for many positions. Students should consider, among other factors, the field and position in which they wish to work in deciding whether or not to attend graduate school.

Preparing for graduate studies occurs informally throughout one's college career. Academic transcripts, involvement in extracurricular activities, work experience, leadership roles, awards, and related factors are considered for admission to graduate programs. Formally, preparing for graduate school typically begins during the latter part of one's junior year, or early part of one's senior year in college. Of consideration in formally preparing to apply for graduate school are letters of recommendation, writing samples, and taking a prequalifying exam such as the Graduate Record Examination, Law School Admission Test, or some other discipline-specific examination.

Several critical factors should be weighed in choosing a graduate program. Generally, students should consider the quality of graduate programs, the level of funding available for enrollment in the program, the faculty, program size, and the area(s) of specialization offered by the programs. For instance, some graduate programs place a heavy emphasis on theory, while others may emphasize the applied aspects of criminal justice. Assessing overall program quality is often a topic of debate, primarily due to criticisms of the methodologies used in evaluating programs. Nevertheless, there are several evaluations of criminal justice and criminology programs that may help with student decision-making. For example, there is a regular review of criminal justice and criminology graduate programs in the *US News and World Report*, and several researchers have conducted their own assessments of graduate programs (e.g., Davis & Sorensen, 2010).

Students considering graduate school, particularly doctoral programs, should certainly evaluate the opportunities available to them. Students should ask questions such as: "Will the program provide an opportunity to teach, or assist with teaching courses?" "Is funding available?" "Are there employment opportunities both on and off campus?" "Does the faculty provide opportunities for collaborative research?" "Will I be able to take evening classes so I can work during the day?" These are among the more significant questions that should be asked and answered prior to selecting a program. Online programs have become increasingly popular for graduate studies in criminology and criminal justice. Among other benefits, these programs accommodate students who may work full-time or are otherwise restricted from attending in-person classes.

The undergraduate and graduate school experiences differ in many ways. For example, class sizes in graduate programs will generally be smaller, the work will be more academically challenging (e.g., you will read original works instead of interpretations of original works), there will be more interaction with the faculty, reading and writing expectations are greater, there is a greater sense of interest in the material among the students, and students are generally high-achievers. There is also a strong sense of bonding and student interaction in graduate studies, and there is often a higher level of professionalism.

Enrollment in graduate school, similar to enrollment in an undergraduate program, provides an excellent setting to take advantage of resources and opportunities. For instance, graduate students often get to work closely with faculty who can provide excellent mentorship, funding is sometimes available for attending professional meetings or assistantships, and employment opportunities are more widely available than they are for undergraduate students. Networking with classmates, faculty, and representatives from local agencies becomes increasingly important as one enters and proceeds through graduate school.

Those considering graduate studies should not be intimidated by the entrance requirements and program selection processes. For instance, some undergraduate students may not have a particularly high GPA and thus believe that they have little chance of being admitted to a graduate program. While this may be true in some cases, and the students may not be admitted to the more competitive graduate programs, students should consider that GPAs are one of several considerations regarding admission to graduate school. Graduate and law schools consider numerous factors, including one's GPA over their last two years of formal education, volunteer work, work experience, letters of recommendation, and related factors. Further, students interested in graduate school should be comforted by the fact that there are many wonderful programs and schools interested in attracting ambitious students with an interest in the field and advancing their formal education.

Seizing Opportunities

Many individuals reach a point when they reflect on life and wonder what things would have been like if different paths were taken, or different decisions were made. For instance, we may ask: "Should I have gone to college?" "Should I have studied criminal justice?" "Should I have moved to this area of the country?" Hopefully, we are all at least somewhat content with most of the decisions we've made. Anyone who is displeased with their decisions can take solace in the fact that there are steps to address poor decisions. One of those steps involves seizing opportunities. Duly considering all opportunities will likely lead to a greater level of contentment in life and enable you to feel pleased with your responses to the questions asked above.

One's educational experience provides excellent opportunities to seize suitable and appropriate activities that contribute to career development. This advice was shared earlier in this chapter. This section adds to that discussion by encouraging readers to take advantage of specific resources:

- **Career centers** – University and college career centers often provide a wealth of career-related information. The challenge is often getting students to become familiar with their school's career resource center. Students should consider the quality of a school's career center in their decision to select a school. Among the many services provided by career centers are searchable databases containing job listings, assessment services to determine one's suitability for employment in particular fields, career fairs, job preparation skills, and various other services that contribute to career-identification, selection, attainment, and advancement. The services provided by career centers are often free of charge to students (and sometimes alumni); such services are typically costly for those not affiliated with a school.
- **Campus events** – Various on-campus events provide helpful opportunities for career development. Technological advancements have encouraged video conferencing that contributes to student development. Such conferences provide students opportunities for interaction with professionals from across the globe and promote both knowledge and networking opportunities. Aside from video conferences, students are encouraged to listen to invited speakers, attend symposiums/workshops, and take advantage of all professional development-related opportunities. On-campus speakers provide opportunities for networking and more personal interactions with various professionals, while symposiums and workshops enhance various aspects of career development. Colleges and universities sometimes offer graduate and undergraduate research festivals that enable students to share their research with others, learn to present their research in an open forum, and encourage students to conduct research.
- **Professional meeting attendance and participation** – Professional development and career-related opportunities are enhanced through participation in regional, national, and international professional meetings. The Academy of Criminal Justice Sciences and the American Society of Criminology both have annual meetings in which researchers share their work. These meetings are certainly open to students to attend and/or present their work. In fact, both groups encourage student participation in various means (e.g., by providing free student luncheons and offering reduced student registration fees). Further, regional groups throughout the United States provide (and encourage) opportunities for student participation, as do various international groups. Different countries and regions have organizations and associations similar to what is found in the United States, including the European Society of Criminology, which supports educational and justice-based practices related to Europe. Graduate students, especially, are encouraged to make all efforts to attend and participate in professional meetings.
- **Student associations** – Involvement in student associations is helpful for an individual's professional development. Most criminal justice and criminology departments and programs have an organization or group that provides opportunities for their students to engage with others interested in the fields. All schools have at least some opportunities for students to become involved in a group or association. Group-based activities offer opportunities for networking, learning, and overall professional development. Employers

may give special consideration to applicants who demonstrate involvement and participation in campus activities and clubs. They often seek well-rounded leaders who can be comfortable within and adapt to various settings and situations. Further, students are encouraged to seek leadership roles within these associations as employers typically seek employees with demonstrated leadership skills. Students should consider creating a student group if their school doesn't already offer one. Among other benefits, it would demonstrate your initiative and professionalism.

- **Internships** – Internships provide valuable experience and undoubtedly contribute to students maximizing their opportunities for employment. Internships are the topic of Chapter 8, although they are certainly worthy of mention in any discussion of how educational opportunities contribute to career-related success. In short, internships should be viewed as exciting opportunities for personal, professional, and career development. Ideally, students should attempt to complete several internships throughout their academic career.
- **Mentorship** – Of particular interest in selecting an institution for higher learning is the level of mentorship provided by the department faculty. This consideration is particularly important for graduate students given the faculty's increased willingness to work directly with them over undergraduates. Researchers highlighted the six interwoven domains of the mentoring process that are essential for professional development, including teaching, community service, professional development, scholarship, career structuring, and collegial interactions (Ballard et al., 2007). The effects of mentorship on one's professional development are important. Accordingly, students (particularly graduate students) are encouraged to seek suitable and willing faculty members who can effectively guide them with regard to career and professional development.
- **Employment** – For some students, employment while attending school is necessary to pay for the various costs. Being employed, however, often provides more than a financial means toward higher education. Working at a job in your chosen field while attending school provides valuable experience, enhances networking opportunities, and helps contextualize the classroom material. Being able to see the lecture material "come alive" makes learning more enjoyable and promotes comprehension of the material. However, it may be the case that not everyone can find a job in their field. Working in a position outside of one's field of interest is not detrimental to professional development, as such positions enable one to become more well-rounded. Students may wish to consider the extent and nature of employment opportunities when choosing a school. Employers often look favorably upon those who can maintain employment as a student. At the very least, it demonstrates maturity, organizational skills, responsibility, and a solid work ethic.
- **Volunteer** – Volunteer work serves multiple purposes, not the least of which is providing helpful services to agencies, individuals, groups, and/or organizations. Volunteers typically gain helpful experience and often have much flexibility with regard to scheduling. They are often able to set their own hours, which is ideal for students with many obligations. Further, volunteer work enables students to "test the waters" of various fields to get a better understanding of whether or not they wish to pursue a career in a particular area. Unfortunately, many individuals wait for volunteer opportunities to present themselves. This reactive approach is detrimental for career and professional development. Students should be proactive when locating volunteer opportunities and contact agencies of interest to them. If fear of rejection is what restricts you from contacting an agency, consider the worst case scenario: The agency tells you that they don't use volunteers or aren't interested in your services. Proactive efforts will likely pay off in finding an ideal volunteer

opportunity and undoubtedly contribute to career development. Volunteer work can also provide dividends in resume-building, employment and networking opportunities, and identifying individuals to provide letters of recommendation on your behalf. Volunteer work, of course, does not include pay for services.
- **Earn credentials** – Some positions within criminal justice require a master's degree or a Ph.D., while others may require a particular number of credit hours of training in specific areas, or perhaps certification. Training may occur, and certifications awarded in workshops or professional meetings, and may be free of charge.

It is important that those searching for a career in criminal justice or criminology be aware of any licensure, or advanced training requirements related to their chosen field or position. It is equally important for individuals to take advantage of training opportunities to enhance one's ability to perform their job and send a message that the employee is capable, motivated, and interested in advancement.

Stress management expert Ruth White (2022) offered advice for getting the most out of one's college experience and maintaining mental well-being. She suggested:

- Connecting to student groups that focus on the topics you enjoy
- Exploring and utilizing the resources provided by your school
- Using office hours to meet with your professors
- Developing a schedule and sticking to it
- Learning a new language
- Studying abroad
- Being prepared
- Building your resume
- Being assertive
- Living a healthy lifestyle
- Having fun

These suggestions are noted throughout this book, and all facilitate professional and career development in many ways. They emphasize the importance of seizing opportunities.

An area of caution when taking advantage of all that is offered is overextending or overburdening one's self. Taking advantage of all appropriate or suitable opportunities does not necessarily mean that one needs to delve deeply into each opportunity that appears. Instead, individuals should effectively filter their activities and involvement to ensure that they aren't overwhelmed, or overextended. Carefully selecting and following through on appropriate opportunities often requires careful consideration of multiple factors, not the least of which is the expected outcome of how taking advantage of an opportunity may affect other aspects of one's daily life. Academic studies should take priority over all extracurricular activities.

Summary

Graduating from college and entering the workforce does not, by any means, signify the conclusion of one's learning experience. Learning is a continuous process that occurs both in and out of the academic setting. It occurs constantly and everywhere. Decisions made throughout life have career-related impacts.

College should be enjoyable, productive, and exciting. It is a time for growth and development. Maximizing one's education, carefully selecting coursework, and taking advantage of opportunities facilitate career and professional development, and help prevent uncomfortable reflections later in life when one considers what they *could* or *should* have done.

Students are strongly encouraged to become civically and/or professionally involved in their discipline, on their campus, and in their communities. Doing so promotes networking opportunities, broadens one's knowledge base, demonstrates initiative and motivation, and helps build a resume. Those seeking careers in criminal justice or criminology should consistently consider the career-related impacts of what they're doing (or not doing) both in and outside the classroom. They should do this while being careful not to overextend themselves.

Much of this chapter focused on preparing for employment and careers via opportunities provided by educational institutions. Also of significance in career development are the specific steps involved in locating, and applying and interviewing for employment positions. These and other topics are discussed in Chapter 7.

Discussion Questions

1 What do you believe are the best steps you can take to maximize your formal education?
2 In what disciplines other than criminal justice or criminology should you take classes to best prepare you for a career in law enforcement, courts, and corrections? Explain your choices for each component.
3 What are the career-related benefits of joining extracurricular groups, such as a student criminology group?
4 Have you considered going to graduate school to further your education? If so, why? If not, why not?
5 How do people become more educated outside of formal education?

Critical Thinking Exercise

Familiarity with job advertisements assists with career preparation. Examine job announcements for positions as a juvenile detention officer, private security officer, and community supervision officer. Job announcements can be found on various websites using a simple search for "jobs in criminal justice" or the like. Do you notice any similarities or differences between the ads? Note what steps can be taken by students to best prepare for each of these positions.

For Further Examination

Ahlin, E.M., & Atkin-Plunk, C. (2020). From supporting role to front stage: Shining a spotlight on the programmatic features and experiences of master's degree programs in criminology and criminal justice. *Journal of Criminal Justice Education, 31*(4), 563–579.

Baxter, D.N., & Ely, K. (2020). Research in action: Student perceptions of active learning in criminal justice research courses. *Journal of Criminal Justice Education, 31*(1), 141–154.

Haisley, P., Grandorff, C., Agbonlahor, O., Mendez, S. L., & Hansen, M. (2021). Why study abroad: Differences in motivation between US and international students. *Journal of Global Education and Research, 5*(2), 185–201.

Hummer, D., & Byrne, J. (2021). Rethinking criminal justice education: Applying experience credits towards CJ degree completion – generates dollars, but does it make sense? *Journal of Criminal Justice Education, 32*(4), 415–445.

Smith, H.P. (2021). The role of virtual reality in criminal justice pedagogy: An examination of mental illness occurring in corrections. *Journal of Criminal Justice Education, 32*(2), 252–271.

References

Ballard, JD., Klein, M.C., & Dean, A. (2007). Mentoring for success in criminal justice and criminology: Teaching professional socialization in graduate programs. *Journal of Criminal Justice Education*, *18*(2), 283–297.

Connley, C. (2017, November 29). Richard Branson says the key to success isn't a university degree. *CNBC.com*. Available at: www.cnbc.com/2017/11/29/richard-branson-says-the-key-to-success-isnt-a-university-degree.html

Davis, J., & Sorensen, J. (2010). Doctoral programs in criminal justice and criminology: A meta-analysis of program ranking. *Southwest Journal of Criminal Justice*, *7*(1), 6–23.

Jones, M., & Bonner, H.S. (2016). What should criminal justice interns know? Comparing the opinions of student interns and criminal justice practitioners. *Journal of Criminal Justice Education*, *27*(3), 381–409.

Martin, E. (2018, December 15). Self-made billionaire Richard Branson says he regrets this money mistake. *CNBC.com*. Available at: www.yahoo.com/now/self-made-billionaire-richard-branson-140000906.html

Oreopoulos, P., & Salvanes, K.G. (2011). Priceless: The nonpecuniary benefits of schooling. *Journal of Economic Perspectives*, *25*(1), 159–184.

Skaggs, S.L., & Graybeal, L. (2016). Service-learning and experiential learning in criminal justice education: An exploratory examination of faculty perspectives. *Journal of Criminal Justice Education*, *30*(2), 296–312.

Torpey, E. (2018). Measuring the value of education. *Career outlook,* U.S. Bureau of Labor Statistics. Available at: www.bls.gov/careeroutlook/2018/data-on-display/education-pays.htm

U.S. Bureau of Labor Statistics. (2021). *Education pays.* Available at: www.bls.gov/emp/chart-unemployment-earnings-education.htm

U.S. Census Bureau. (2022, February 24). *Census Bureau releases new educational attainment data.* Available at: www.census.gov/newsroom/press-releases/2022/educational-attainment.html

White, R.C. (2022). 11 ways to get the most out of the college experience. *PsychologyToday.com*. Available at: www.psychologytoday.com/us/blog/culture-in-mind/201406/11-ways-get-the-most-out-the-college-experience

Chapter 7

Preparing for Employment in Criminal Justice and Criminology

American inventor and educator Alexander Graham Bell once said: "Before anything else, preparation is the key to success." Accordingly, one's level of success in a career in criminal justice and criminology is related to the amount of preparation she or he puts forth prior to entering the field. One's personal character is consistently under development, and throughout life individuals acquire and refine skills required for employment in the fields. Strategically preparing for employment in criminal justice and criminology largely begins in young adulthood, for instance, in high school. The high school experience helps set the stage for later developments, including the possibility of enrolling in institutions of higher education and earning employment positions. Preparation continues through adulthood as one acquires knowledge and skills, and hones their skills and abilities.

This chapter addresses the critical components of strategically preparing for employment in criminal justice and criminology. Emphasis is placed on seeking, preparing, and applying for positions in the fields. Particularly, the topics discussed include networking, locating positions in the field, resume preparation, identifying employment opportunities, and applying and preparing for positions. Put simply, the chapter examines strategies designed to help readers enhance their abilities to earn the positions they seek. Coverage begins with consideration of the importance of networking.

Networking

One of the most effective ways to locate and land a position in any field is networking. This involves meeting new people, or utilizing the ones you know, to obtain information about specific employment positions, the job market, and/or careers in general. Some estimates suggest around 70% of all jobs are not posted publicly to job sites, and personal and professional connections are used to fill up to 80% of employment positions (Fisher, 2020). Needless to say, networking is a particularly important aspect of one's job search. While the unlevel playing field associated with using personal contacts may not seem just or fair to some individuals, it remains that getting a job often involves who you know and what you know.

We often hear the term "network of friends," which conjures the image of a relatively tight group of individuals who share similar interests and spend much time together. The individuals in the network typically assist one another, whether it be sharing notes in school, providing a ride to work, or exchanging information about particular opportunities (e.g., job openings). The concept of "strength in numbers" undoubtedly applies when one is seeking employment opportunities, as wider networks logically should relate to more resources. Both the size and quality of networks are important.

Preparing for employment is a long, continuous process. A significant part of that process involves the people you know and those with whom you associate. When you were

DOI: 10.4324/9781003360162-9

younger your parents or caregivers probably told you to stay away from particular individuals they thought would negatively influence you. The statement "I don't want you playing with that kid" has been heard in the homes of many children. The directive was subscribing to Sutherland's differential association theory and preparing you for adulthood, including your career.

Edwin Sutherland (1939) published the book *Principles of Criminology* in 1939 in which he provided a formalized presentation of his differential association theory. In basic terms, differential association theory holds that criminal behavior is largely influenced by interaction with criminal lifestyles, while conformity is influenced by exposure to conformist living. In other words, behavior, as it pertains to crime, is largely influenced by socialization. One could easily apply Sutherland's theory to job searching, as socialization and the influences of those with whom one interacts often have career and employment-related impacts.

Research suggests people are often uncomfortable with or are unsure of how to contact others as part of their job search (e.g., Wanberg et al., 2012). The university setting provides numerous opportunities for networking. Particularly, one's classmates, fellow students in a dormitory, work contacts, school career center, and instructors provide excellent networking opportunities. One should always consider the individuals with whom they interact as potential contributors to one's professional development, as shallow as it may seem. What may seem like a racquetball partner at the time may ultimately be a vital source of information or connection for an excellent job. Faculty members, who often write student letters of recommendation, are typically a very valuable source of employment-related information and key components for student networking. Further, professional organizations, student groups, and intramural activities provide excellent opportunities for networking, particularly as one assumes leadership roles.

A Practitioner's View

Glenn Master, Director of Asset Protection/Security, McLane Company

The supply chain is a global environment that incorporates manufacturing, distribution and transportation under one umbrella. Essentially, it's a true end-to-end network of touch points where goods and commodities flow freely. As business has evolved into Ecommerce, the supply chain has evolved as well. This has created a wide variety of exposures where both theft and loss can take place. Companies now realize the importance of having an internal group of subject matter experts that are well versed in physical security, investigation techniques, and asset protection strategies.

My recommendation for anyone seeking a career in this growing field is to prepare themselves prior to entering the workforce. Having a solid understanding of Business 101, especially at a global level is essential. I often recommend reading the Wall Street Journal daily, which will provide them with a wealth of business acumen. Another critical area for success in the private sector is networking. I can't stress enough the importance of having a strong group of contacts both in law enforcement and with peers in other companies. Growing one's network should start early and continue throughout their career.

Other opportunities on campus include personally speaking with invited lecturers and other guests. For instance, students should consider introducing themselves and staying after class when their instructor invites a guest speaker of interest. This time could be used for formal introductions and the exchange of contact information. Similarly, one could use their class assignments as networking opportunities. For instance, students are sometimes required to do a police ride-along or interview someone in criminal justice or criminology as part of their coursework. These and related assignments could be successfully completed and simultaneously viewed as excellent opportunities to expand one's group of contacts in the field.

Networking begins prior to one's career and continues through retirement; it is a continuous process. Networking efforts can contribute to obtaining an initial position, promotions, or getting a new job. It becomes easier to network with other professionals upon being employed. Networking efforts also occur outside of one's field, places of employment, and school. The interdisciplinary nature of criminal justice and criminology, and the employment opportunities within dictate that networking efforts will expand beyond the fields, for instance, to include social work, psychology, counseling, and related areas. Family members, friends, neighbors, teammates, fellow group members, and many others also serve as social networks.

Effective organization of key contacts obtained through networking efforts is essential for career development. Depending on the extent of one's networking efforts and level of success, it may be necessary to document, in an organized and effective manner, the individuals with whom one has made contact. Those seeking, beginning, or in the midst of a career are encouraged to maintain a file with information pertaining to the contacts they've made, including the contact's title, agency of employment, and access information. One never knows if or when a contact from the past may be able to provide critical career-related assistance. Depending on the nature of the interaction and how helpful you believe the resource may be in the future, you may wish to consider contacting the individual at some later point simply to maintain the relationship.

Networking efforts are enhanced as one "sees and is seen." Compare the active student who has taken heed of the aforementioned suggestions to the student who spends most of their time in a dorm room playing video games. Which one do you believe is more likely to benefit from networking? Particularly, interacting with extensive numbers of individuals (both in and outside of the workplace and school) facilitates networking efforts. Such interaction is enhanced through asking questions of the individuals with whom one encounters. Individuals often enjoy speaking about themselves and their work. Effective networking involves asking questions and considering each interaction an opportunistic, learning experience. Investing in others has the potential for many career-related benefits.

An article by Anthony DeRosa (2021) in the *Wall Street Journal* emphasized the importance of networking as part of one's job search. He noted that it is "one of the most powerful" acts job seekers can take, adding that networking can be awkward, and requires some "courage, initiative, and self-discipline." Overcoming these challenges may be necessary, as the benefits of connecting with others are well-documented. The author provided four tips for networking:

1   Start with friends and people familiar to you
2   Locate people with similar jobs to the one you seek
3   Force yourself to move out of your comfort zone
4   Keep in mind that people genuinely enjoy your interest in them

Networking has evolved with advancements in technology and the proliferation of social media. LinkedIn is the world's largest social network for professionals and others to connect, learn, share, and generally engage with each other. It and other social media sites enable the employed and job seekers to engage with one another, identify job opportunities, post one's credentials, and generally learn more about jobs, fields, and careers. LinkedIn users create a profile and begin establishing contacts and networks that can be particularly valuable for beginning a career, advancement in one's career, or career changes. The use of social media in this capacity is a primary means to find employment and enhance one's professional development.

Handshake is another effective resource for locating and applying for positions. Handshake is more directly targeted toward college students, and boasts having a network of over 10 million active student users, over 1,400 college and university partners, and over 650 employers (Handshake.com, 2022). Those seeking a career in criminal justice and criminology are strongly encouraged to use social networking resources such as LinkedIn and Handshake as part of their job search.

Locating the Ideal Position

Job searches begin with locating and applying for positions. There are many ways to locate positions, and technological advancements have made the job search much easier than in the past. Research skills and familiarity with technology greatly assist with finding employment.

Locating employment opportunities involves much effort and preparation. Knowing where and how to search for positions requires much prep work. Students are strongly encouraged to use their school-based resources to identify positions, including career centers, faculty, and career counselors. Career fairs hosted both on and off campus also assist with identifying positions and interacting with recruiters.

Locating positions may be as simple as visiting the website of agencies to see if they are hiring. Perusing agency websites is helpful for many reasons, as are online employment-based services such as:

- Glassdoor.com
- Indeed.com
- LinkedIn.com
- SimplyHired.com
- ZipRecruiter.com

These resources provide information for careers in many areas, including criminal justice and criminology. Those interested in a career in the federal government are encouraged to visit the US Office of Personnel Management's website **USAJOBS.gov**. This site provides information on the federal-level openings and enables users to search for positions. It is the primary means through which applicants identify and apply for positions in the federal government.

Trade journals, government newsletters and bulletins, and government employment offices are also effective sources of identifying jobs. Appendix B provides a list of state agencies that can be helpful during a job search. Some people locate employment positions through an advocate or a placement agency, which charge a fee for essentially doing the job search for (or with) you.

Time and place should also be considerations in determining whether or not to apply for a position. With regard to the former, applicants should be aware of the time lag between applying for a position and ultimately getting hired. If applying for multiple positions, you may be faced with having to accept or decline a position while your application at a different agency is being considered. There is no simple solution to this dilemma, as it is up to you to weigh all of the variables and make what you believe is the most appropriate choice.

With regard to place, geographic location should be considered. Will the position you're considering force you to relocate? Will you have to travel very far to get to your job? Will you be able to work from home at times? One must factor in the cost of travel to and from work, with special consideration of time and money. Do you have the resources to travel a long distance? These and other questions should be considered when deciding on whether or not to apply for a position.

There are, of course, many other considerations with regard to applying for a position. Aside from interest in the position, field, and/or agency, one should consider the benefits and salary associated with the position, as well as the potential for personal growth and advancement. Salaries are not often posted to job advertisements, even though pay is particularly important to those in the job market (Burns & Kinkade, 2008). Speaking with someone in the field and researching positions provide some expectations regarding salary. Appendix E provides information regarding salaries in criminal justice and criminology.

Ultimately, there are many ways to search for a job, and some are more effective than others. Job searches, of course, are of little value if one isn't able to effectively demonstrate their many fine qualities and suitability for employment.

Preparing Your Cover Letter and Resume

It is said that you can never make a second first impression. If this is true, your cover letter and resume are perhaps the most important documents in your job search. Together, they are critical to landing an interview and provide a crucial first impression absent face-to-face interaction. Along with your application for employment, cover letters and resumes provide an initial opportunity to display one's experience, strengths, and accomplishments. Constructing cover letters and resumes involves careful organization and emphasizing your abilities to match an employer's requirements.

Your cover letter and resume need to be powerful, concise, and professional. This is your primary chance to "sell yourself," and you need to do it quickly, properly, and effectively. Indeed.com reported that employers spend an average of six to seven seconds looking at resumes, although the time varies by companies (Indeed.com, 2021). Your task is to sell yourself as powerfully and succinctly as possible.

Cover Letters

A cover letter should accompany a resume, unless instructed to do otherwise. Much like a resume, a cover letter makes a first impression, conveys one's interest in a position, highlights one's competencies, and comments on one's overall level of professionalism. Important considerations in drafting and submitting a cover letter include directing the information to a specific individual whenever possible. Generic salutations may result in application packets being misplaced. Applicants should note their interest in a particular position in the cover letter and should feel free to identify the individual who suggested the submission of their application packet to help establish an association with the reader.

Cover letters should be brief, directed, and arguably no more than a single page, simply because employers likely have to review numerous applications and may not give each application due consideration. Cover letters should demonstrate the applicant has researched the position and agency and be tailored to the particular position for which one is applying. They should explain why the applicant is deserving of the job, and how they will contribute if given the position. Applicants should not restate their entire resume in the cover letter. Instead, the letter should highlight key qualifications for the position. The final part of a cover letter should express appreciation for the employer's consideration of the submitted materials and inquire about the next step in the process (e.g., will you follow up with a phone call or wait to hear from them?).

Perhaps most important, cover letters (similar to all other documents submitted) should be professionally written. Grammatical errors, typos, spelling errors, and other blemishes are unacceptable in any written communication. A lack of professionalism in any aspect could very easily eliminate a candidate from consideration.

Closely following all instructions is also required. For instance, include references if requested, and submit your materials in the appropriate manner (e.g., via electronically and using particular software). Place yourself in the position of the employer considering your application. Would you give much consideration to someone who makes errors in their cover letter or can't follow the initial directions?

Individuals applying for multiple positions may find it easier to use a form letter that generally applies to many positions. Doing so may save time; however, it is important that cover letters (and resumes) be developed and directed toward specific agencies, people, and positions. Among other things, generic cover letters suggest to employers that the applicant is applying for multiple positions and is not invested enough in the position to create a specific and individualized letter.

Cover letters can quickly differentiate applicants and may immediately generate positive or negative impressions. Various online tools and resources are available to assist with writing cover letters. Visit the sites to learn more about cover letters in efforts to identify the content, style, and format that best suits you and the positions for which you are applying. A sample cover letter is provided in Appendix A.

The application process can be lengthy, particularly with certain positions and agencies. For instance, the application process for federal law enforcement agencies can take many months, and many criminal justice agencies require extensive background investigations that take time. Accordingly, applicants should have a plan to remain productive in their career development while the hiring process is completed. Again, effective preparation is vital for job searches.

Resumes

The term *resume*, in French, means brief history. Your resume is an account of your accomplishments and suitability for an employment position. Resumes are generally organized according to one of several standard formats and provide a synopsis of information rather than full descriptions or lengthy explanations. The following elements should be included in a resume:

- **Contact Information**: Your contact information should be prominently displayed at the top of your resume. Use an email address that is solely devoted to employment-related issues and ensure that your address is not offensive or descriptive. You may also wish to include your LinkedIn URL profile with your contact information.
- **Employment Objective**: State the type of position you are seeking. It should include a definition of the job title as well as the skills you would utilize within that position. This statement should be customized for each employer to best meet their needs.
- **Employment History**: List job titles and a brief description of the positions held. Share your most recent positions first and show specific length of tenure at each job. Include specific details and quantifiable results.
- **Education/Certifications**: List schools attended, degrees earned, and date bestowed. Include any relevant certifications and/or licenses. You should only include high school-related information if it is your highest level of education. Students attending college should include that education instead of high school.
- **Honors/Awards**: List professional and personal awards received. Employers often view awards as insight into one's job performance and character.
- **Skills**: Including skills on a resume is recommended, particularly if the skills relate to the position for which you're applying. Sharing your skills may distinguish you from other applicants. Specific skills may include computer software expertise or the ability to speak a second language.

- **Affiliations**: Noting one's affiliations on a resume is recommended. Reference should be made to active memberships, and leadership roles in social clubs, professional associations, and similar groups.
- **References**: Including references on one's resume is helpful; however, the job application requirements often dictate if and how references are to be submitted. Applicants should be sure to list name and contact information for any references (as directed). One could include the statement "References provided upon request" on their resume if preferred. It is strongly suggested that you contact your references before including them on your resume. Ask their permission to use them as a reference and share your interests about careers and the job search. Keep in mind that they may be commenting to potential employers about you, and they will be better prepared with helpful information.

Space limitations, directives from the job advertisement, and your credentials will guide the extent to which these areas are included on your resume. For instance, you may have limited work experience, yet an abundance of skills related to the position. In this case, you would emphasize the skills area of your resume. Seeking guidance from a career counselor or professional to create and regularly update your resume is encouraged.

Unless requested to do so, resumes should never include personal information such as marital status, age, height, weight or physical shortcomings or disabilities. Resumes should always include truthful information. Presenting yourself in the best light is acceptable and expected; however, exaggeration is not. In developing a resume, applicants should use action words such as "optimized," "motivated," "balanced," and "initiated" to fully express their qualifications. A quick search online can help you identify words and terms that will help you "speak resume."

The format of one's resume is relevant to the likelihood of making an impactful first impression and getting an interview. Resumes are typically printed in an easy-to-read font (e.g., Times New Roman) on white or light-colored professional weight paper, although electronic submission has become the norm. Depending on the field, applicants may be more or less creative in the design of their resume. For instance, resumes submitted for positions in graphic design may allow for a more inventive format than for resumes submitted for administrative personnel positions. Your resume should be no more than two pages; however, a one-page resume is ideal as sometimes "less is more." Employers may not get to reading multiple pages. Perhaps most important of all in constructing a resume is honesty. Never lie on your resume as doing so is unethical, unprofessional, and unacceptable.

There are several styles to choose from in developing a resume. Among the more commonly used styles are the chronological and functional resumes. The historical or chronological resume style is the most traditional and recognized by experts to be the most effective. This style presents information in reverse chronological order, beginning with one's most recent work experiences first and proceeding back in time. This style is easy to read and is most familiar to employers. This format is best if you've spent substantial time with a previous employer, are seeking a position in the same field, have worked for reputable companies or agencies, or show notable growth in responsibilities.

The functional style of resume, also known as the "skill-based format," emphasizes abilities and experiences pertaining to the job for which one is applying. This approach emphasizes one's strengths with regard to particular skills, maximizes limited work experience, and minimizes unrelated work experiences and employment gaps. This style is best suited for those who (1) are seeking a job in a new field, (2) have been unemployed for over three months, (3) wish to highlight particular accomplishments on their last job, and/or (4) are competing with younger applicants. Examples of both the chronological and functional resume are provided in Appendix A.

Employers are increasingly requiring applicants to submit all materials electronically. This may occur in the form of an established electronic submission process or simply sending an email attachment. Regardless, make sure that you closely follow all directions regarding the submission process.

Technology is increasingly being used to scan resumes prior to anyone actually viewing them. Ninety-nine percent of large companies, and an increasing number of other companies use resume scanning, or applicant tracking programs to reduce the burden on hiring managers tasked with reviewing many resumes (Smith, 2021). Formatting your resume appropriately and including keywords helps ensure that your resume gets past the initial scanning. With regard to the former, format your resume appropriately by following the guidelines for submission. This can be done, for instance, by ensuring that the page layout and software used are acceptable, and avoiding the use of acronyms, which may offer no helpful information to a computer. Computers search for keywords as part of the scanning process; thus, you should edit your resume to include key terms used in the job post (Smith, 2021).

Finally, the need for carefully proofreading the application materials cannot be overstated. Continuously proofread your work, and have others review it. Spelling and grammatical errors are an obvious sign of carelessness and could quickly eliminate an opportunity to interview. Researchers noted that "compared to error-free resumes, hiring penalties are being inflicted for both error-laden resumes (18.5 percent points lower interview probability) and resumes with fewer errors (7.3 percent points lower interview probability)" (Sterkens et al., 2021, 1). Applicants should not simply rely on their computer's spellchecking function for spelling accuracy, simply because this function may not catch all misspellings. For instance, the word "for" could slide by mistyped as "four." The error would not be highlighted by the spellchecking function. A thorough proofreading, however, would identify the error.

Your resume is indeed your brief history. Your task is to condense that history into a concise document that impresses those who read it. It is not uncommon for young adults and others beginning their career to lack information that can be shared on a resume. It is understood that much of a resume concerns work history, and those lacking that history may have to emphasize other qualifications. Employers generally understand that some people lack significant work experience and may overlook that limitation depending on the job and other qualifications.

Resumes are constant works in progress. Information regarding new jobs, degrees, skills acquired, and related accomplishments often replaces previous content. Updating your resume involves merging the new with the old, and at some point you will likely extend far beyond one-page's worth of information. It is strongly recommended that you create a "me" file that contains all of your resume-worthy accomplishments. This is a master resume that serves as a database of information that you may include in different versions of your resume. Select content from the master file to tailor your resume to the job you seek. For instance, an earlier job that you no longer keep on your most recent resume may be helpful when applying for a new position. Instead of trying to remember or recreate the details of the previous position, you would simply pull it from the "me" file. Organizational skills, research skills, determination, and perseverance are necessary to find the career you seek.

Applying for an academic position requires you to submit a curriculum vitae. A vitae is similar to a resume, although it focuses primarily on one's scholarly accomplishments. It includes categories such as scholarship, teaching, service, volunteer work, and other areas associated with an academic position. Individuals seeking to become a criminologist should strongly consider preparing both a resume and vitae. Additional information about positions in academia is provided in Chapter 13, and Appendix F provides a list of the categories included in a curriculum vitae.

Applying for Positions

Preparing and applying for employment are notably time-consuming. The identification of a potential place of employment is followed by the application process, which is hopefully followed by an interview (and perhaps multiple interviews), testing, and potentially other methods of evaluation. Hiring for some positions requires much more consideration and evaluation than others.

Applicants should pay particular attention to the requirements of the application process, as failure to meet the requirements could result in disqualification. For instance, applicants may be required to drop off their resume, visit the site to complete an application, submit the application online, or meet with a representative to submit their credentials. While this requirement may seem menial to some applicants, it is undoubtedly part of the assessment practices. Again, if you can't meet the initial requirement, why would an employer believe you would be a suitable candidate?

Becoming familiar with job advertisements should be part of your career preparation. Consider the following requirements for a Police Trainee and eventually Officer position with the Fort Worth Police Department.

The qualification and requirements for this position are clearly defined, leaving potential applicants with a clear account of what is expected. Notice the applicant requirements, special notes, and opportunities for additional exam points. These are the primary areas of consideration with regard to the construction of your resume and cover letter. The department is telling you what they want. Your job with the application process is to demonstrate that you have what they want.

A key component of career preparation is ensuring that your social media, and general online presence does portray you in a negative or suggestive manner. This can begin with a simple Google search of your name. Are you pleased with the results that directly pertain to you? If not, contact the source and see about having inappropriate content removed. Prepare to justify or explain the content if attempts to remove it fail, as employers are increasingly going online to screen applicants. Their efforts extend beyond simply conducting a Google search, for instance, as cybervetting applicants have become more common. Cybervetting involves using information technologies to screen social media and applicants (Jacobson & Gruzd, 2020). Keeping social media accounts private or carefully monitoring one's accounts is strongly recommended. Ensure that you thoroughly filter your online presence. Keep in mind that criminal justice agencies may have highly skilled investigators who will likely find any available unflattering content.

Interviewing

Interviews provide applicants an opportunity to personally interact with potential employers and demonstrate their worthiness and suitability. Interviews provide candidates a chance to elaborate and expand on the information provided in the application packet and their resume and demonstrate one's interpersonal skills and overall level of professionalism. They also enable opportunities to get a feel for what it is like to work at the agency. Interviewing is a two-way street in which both parties evaluate each other.

Turning off or setting phones to cause no distractions and being punctual are required for interviews. Interviewees should dress professionally and arrive alone to the interview. A firm handshake that demonstrates confidence should be offered during the introduction, and interviewees should have researched the agency and position in preparation. They should be prepared to answer and offer relevant questions. Some other general guidance for the interviewing process include:

TEST DATES:	
January 9-13 and January 17-18, 2023	

Multiple testing times will be offered each day.

LOCATION:
Bob Bolen Public Safety Bldg, 505 W. Felix, St., Fort Worth, TX. 76115

Must provide a valid email address and phone number to receive test notifications.

SPECIAL NOTE: To be selected for a Police Academy Training Class, applicants must successfully pass a written or electronic exam, a physical assessment test, a polygraph examination, an interview board, a medical examination, a psychological examination and an extensive background check.

Following the exam, if you receive a passing score, your name will be added to the Police Trainee Program Eligibility List, from which participants will be selected for the Police Training Academy. This list will be valid for one year or until the list is exhausted, whichever comes first.

THE CITY OF FORT WORTH
POLICE TRAINEE PROGRAM NEEDS YOU!

Earn $3,337 per month (while in Police Academy Training)
Earn $5,549 per month ($66,593 annually upon graduation)
amounts stated above are approximate

APPLY TODAY!
Applications accepted: October 1, through October 31, 2022.
https://police.fortworthtexas.gov/Recruiting/

APPLICANT REQUIREMENTS:

EDUCATION: High school diploma; (or GED Certificate, plus 12 semester hours, with a "C" average, from an accredited college or university).

CITIZENSHIP: Must be a U. S. Citizen at the time of application. **(Must be able to read and write the English Language).**

AGE: 20 – 44 years of age; (Must be 20 years of age and not be 45 years of age by the date of your assigned entry-level test/civil service examination (January 9-13 and 17-18, 2023).

LICENSE: Must present a valid and current driver's license and possess an acceptable driving record.

ADDITIONAL EXAM POINTS: Additional points up to a maximum of five (5) cumulative points shall be added to a **passing exam** score as follows:

CADETS: Two (2) points for graduates of the Fort Worth Police Department's Cadet Program.

EDUCATION: Five (5) points for Bachelor's degree (or higher). Education will be verified by Human Resources after the exam.

VETERAN: Five (5) points for military veteran candidates with Honorable Discharge per DD-214. *In order to receive veteran points, you must email your DD214 showing character of service (Member 4 or equivalent) to CCCTesting@fortworthtexas.gov no later than 9:00 a.m., Sunday, January 8, 2023. Please include your name and best contact number in the email. DD214s will not be accepted on the day of the examination.*

Once your information has been properly submitted online, please expect a call and email from the Fort Worth Police - Background Unit
Email: backgroundunit@fortworthtexas.gov

PLEASE BE ADVISED: The Civil Service Police Trainee exam will be a **live in-person** exam. Qualified applicants will be required to report in person on their assigned date and time. During this testing cyle, each qualified applicant can take the Police Trainee exam once.

This job ad highlights the primary considerations of departments seeking officers. Interested applicants are strongly encouraged to closely consider each aspect noted in the ad.

- Speaking clearly
- Being courteous
- Using appropriate eye contact and smiling
- Maintaining good body posture
- Being honest, friendly, and professional
- Thanking the interviewer for meeting

Being aware of any cultural differences between you and the interviewer(s), for instance, with regard to shaking hands and eye contact, would also enhance the interview. Cultural differences among job candidates and interviewers can contribute to misunderstandings that subsequently result in poor applicant evaluations (Manroop et al., 2013). Further researching the agency and its personnel prior to the interview may alert the interviewee of potential cultural differences.

Some things that should *not* be done for an interview include:

- Being late
- Wearing tight, dirty, or revealing clothing
- Mumbling
- Being rude or disrespectful
- Avoiding eye contact
- Slouching
- Interacting on one's phone
- Frowning or smirking at inappropriate times
- Being hostile or argumentative
- Lying
- Leaving without saying "thank you" and "goodbye."

This, of course, is not a comprehensive account of thing to avoid on an interview.

As noted, technology is increasingly influencing the hiring and job search process. It's possible that you may be interviewed via phone or teleconferencing. Regardless of format, preparation is a key to success. Ensure that your phone is fully charged, and you are located in a quiet area for phone interviews. Conference calls are sometimes awkward, particularly when multiple parties speak, so be sure to practice and become comfortable with the technology.

Interviewing via teleconferencing has become increasingly popular, as it saves time and resources. Also become familiar with the various platforms prior to your interview. Ensure that your computer is fully charged, you are located in a quiet place with no distractions, and all software updates have been installed prior to the online interview. Be wary of the lighting in the area where you will interview, and choose a professional background that will accompany your professional appearance and demeanor.

Interviews can be somewhat stressful, especially if the applicant is unprepared. Preparation is essential for effective interviewing. Demonstrating that you've researched the agency, position, and person(s) with whom you're interviewing generally makes a good impression with the interviewer. It is important that all information shared is truthful. Impression management is acceptable during interviews, as interviewees should try to appear in a particularly positive light. Outright lying, even though it occurs relatively frequently (Weiss & Feldman, 2006), is unacceptable.

A critical aspect of most interviews occurs when the interviewer(s) ask the interviewee if they have any questions. Interviewees should have questions prepared and should seek elaboration as needed on information shared during the interview. Interviewees might ask about travel requirements associated with the position, the next step in the hiring process, benefits, training opportunities and requirements, the work hours for the position, and related

Interviewing is one of many steps involved with securing employment in criminal justice or criminology. Securing employment, in turn, is one of many steps involved with one's overall career and professional development.
Source: https://pxhere.com/en/photo/758357

questions. Salary-related questions can be awkward during the initial interview. Ideally, the employer would state the salary, or a salary range. Or, the interviewee may be asked what salary they seek. Effectively researching the agency and position, including salaries, prior to the interview prepares you to effectively respond.

Interviewees should always submit a "thank you" note shortly after meeting with a potential employer. The note should be short and error-free and reinforce your strong qualifications for the position. Referencing some information from the interview in the letter typically has a positive impact on potential employers. The follow-up enables the individual to recall your interview and demonstrates to them that you're attentive, appreciative, and interested in the position. It also better familiarizes them with you as they consider candidates. A sample follow-up letter is provided in Appendix A.

Each interview is a learning experience. Critically evaluate how you responded during the interview and make notes in order to better prepare for the next interview. The career centers at some schools offer students the opportunity to conduct a mock interview, which may or not be videotaped, followed by an assessment. Students should certainly take advantage of this opportunity as it will help them identify their strengths and weaknesses, including habits or behaviors that appear when one is interviewing yet go unnoticed by the interviewee. Undergoing additional interviews, particularly those in which you are critiqued, improves one's interviewing skills.

Depending on the nature of the position, the interviewing process may be followed by a series of evaluations, including physical agility tests, written examinations, psychological evaluations, oral examinations, background investigations, and/or a polygraph examination. Identifying and attaining a job are very time-consuming and involve much preparation. Strategically preparing for a career in criminal justice or criminology is not, however, beyond the capabilities of anyone. Applicants should not be discouraged by lengthy application processes, particularly if they truly want the position.

Summary

There is a strong perception in society that "work" does not begin until one secures a job. In contrast, much work is needed prior to securing a job. The efforts required for effective career preparation should be viewed as investments that should pay dividends. Typically, what you get out of the process depends on what you put into it. Cutting corners, taking shortcuts, and investing anything less than full effort only affect you.

Career development has been a lifelong process. For these and other reasons it is important that those seeking a career or internship in criminal justice or criminology carefully plan and give great attention to detail beginning with the job search and continuing through all phases of the selection process. Effectively networking, locating positions, constructing a resume, applying for positions, and interviewing are all parts of the learning experience and career development. Just as you would practice playing an instrument in attempts to reach perfection, you must also practice and invest resources in career development.

Discussion Questions

1 Discuss the benefits of networking. What are the best methods to network?
2 How would you research a career as a paralegal? How would this research help you with the application and interview processes?
3 Which type of resume would be most appropriate for someone with limited work experience? Which type would be best for someone with much work experience?
4 How could you best prepare yourself for an interview?
5 What steps have you taken to prepare yourself for employment in criminal justice or criminology? What steps remain?

Critical Thinking Exercise

Create a checklist of all that is needed to prepare for a career in criminal justice. Select the career you seek, or any other one that interests you. Within the checklist, note all the steps required to prepare for the position. For instance, you likely should note the need to create a resume and develop interviewing skills. Next, note what actions you have taken to meet each step, and what actions remain. It may help to find a job advertisement for the position.

For Further Examination

Mengel, F. (2020). Gender differences in networking. *The Economic Journal, 130*(630), 1842–1873.
Radatz, D.L., & Slakoff, D.C (2022). A practical guide to the criminology and criminal justice job market for doctoral candidates: Pre-market preparation through offers and negotiations. *Journal of Criminal Justice Education, 33*(3), 368–387. DOI:10.1080/10511253.2021.1966061
Rios, J.A., Ling, G., Pugh, R. Becker, D., & Bacall, A. (2020). Identifying critical 21st century skills for workplace success: A content analysis of job advertisements. *Educational Researcher, 49*(2), 80–89.

Rossler, M.T., & Scheer, C. (2020). Student perceptions of employer use of social media in selection decisions: Comparing criminal justice majors to non-majors. *Journal of Criminal Justice Education*, *31*(1), 43–62.

Sterkens, P., Caers, R., De Couck, M., Geamanu, M., Van Driessche, V., & Baert, S. (2021). Costly mistakes: Why and when spelling errors in resumes jeopardise interview chances. IZA Discussion Paper No. 14614, Available at SSRN: https://ssrn.com/abstract=3900876 or http://dx.doi.org/10.2139/ssrn.3900876

References

Burns, R.G., & Kinkade, P. (2008). Finding fit: The nature of a successful faculty employment search in criminal justice. *Journal of Criminal Justice*, *36*, 372–378.

DeRosa, A. (2021, June 29). Where to search for jobs: Finding your next opportunity. *Wall Street Journal*. Available at: www.wsj.com/articles/where-to-search-for-jobs-finding-your-next-opportunity-11605109352

Fisher, J.F. (2020, February 14). How to get a job often comes down to one elite personal asset, and many people still don't realize it. *CNBC.com*. Available at: www.cnbc.com/2019/12/27/how-to-get-a-job-often-comes-down-to-one-elite-personal-asset.html

Handshake.com. (2022). We are driven. Available at: https://joinhandshake.com/about/

Indeed.com. (2021, June 3). How long do hiring managers look at a resume? Available at: www.indeed.com/career-advice/resumes-cover-letters/how-long-do-employers-look-at-resumes

Jacobson, J., & Gruzd, A. (2020). Cybervetting job applicants on social media: The new normal? *Ethics and Information Technology*, *22*, 175–195.

Manroop, L., Boekhorst, J.A., & Harrison, J.A. (2013). The influence of cross-cultural differences on job interview selection decisions. *The International Journal of Human Resource Management*, *24*(18), 3512–3533.

Smith, M. (2021, August 4). 99% of large companies use resume-scanning software – how to make sure yours beats the bots. *CNBC.com*. Available at: www.cnbc.com/2021/08/04/how-to-write-a-resume-that-will-beat-applicant-tracking-systems.html

Sterkens, P., Caers, R., De Couck, M., Geamanu, M., Van Driessche, V., & Baert, S. (2021). Costly mistakes: Why and when spelling errors in resumes jeopardise interview chances. IZA Discussion Paper No. 14614, Available at SSRN: https://ssrn.com/abstract=3900876 or http://dx.doi.org/10.2139/ssrn.3900876

Sutherland, E.H. (1939). *Principles of criminology* (3rd ed.). Lippincott.

Wanberg, C. Basbug, G.,Van Hooft, E.A.J., & Samtani, A. (2012). Navigating the black hole: Explicating layers of job search context and adaptational responses. *Personnel Psychology*, *65*(4), 887–926.

Weiss, B., & Feldman, R.S. (2006). Looking good and lying to do it: Deception as an impression management strategy in job interviews. *Journal of Applied Social Psychology*, *36*(4), 1070–1086.

Chapter 8

Internships in Criminal Justice and Criminology

Students are sometimes anxious upon considering an internship. Such anxiety often stems from the many uncertainties surrounding the internship experience. For instance, there may be uncertainty regarding what constitutes an internship, how they will be accepted into the workplace, and/or their ability to perform adequately. There may be similar levels of anxiety on behalf of internship providers, for instance, with regard to placing the intern, how well the intern will fit into the workplace culture, and various privacy-related issues. This chapter alleviates uncertainties through examining the fundamentals of internships.

Effective Internship directors prepare interns for placement in the field. Preparation includes clearly explaining the internship requirements (e.g., the number of hours to be completed, the number and nature of assignments, and so on), the expectations of working in the field, and the goals and benefits of an internship. Perhaps most important, students should be made aware of why they're expected to gain field experience. Effective preparation for an internship also includes internship directors identifying and working closely with internship providers, for instance, as all internship sites should be closely evaluated to ensure that interns are productive and learning.

This chapter discusses the fundamentals of internships, particularly those within criminal justice and criminology. It begins with examination of the history of internships, followed by consideration of how internships relate to experiential, applied, and service learning. These terms are often used interchangeably; however, there are differences between them. The chapter continues with discussion of the benefits of interning and concludes with coverage of the expectations of the internship experience. Understanding what constitutes and is needed for an effective internship contributes to maximizing this important aspect of career development.

The Historical Development of Internships

A brief historical account of internships, with an emphasis on criminal justice and criminology, helps readers better understand the fundamentals of internships in general. Recognizing the origins and short history of internships in criminal justice and criminology, among other things, helps set the stage for understanding the significance of this form of experiential learning.

Although internships are common components of many criminal justice programs today, the origins of internships in general are traced to the Middle Ages, when inexperienced apprentices worked closely with more experienced mentors in learning various skills and trades. For instance, knights and blacksmiths learned the skills of their trade through apprenticeships, while children worked for little or no money to learn various trades from master craftsmen during the periods of industrialism (Sgroi & Ryniker, 2002). More recently, internships have become ingrained in certification and training programs in many areas, including law enforcement and law.

DOI: 10.4324/9781003360162-10

While it is assumed that early criminal justice practitioners shadowed and learned from experienced personnel, internships in criminal justice formally began in 1968 when the Law Enforcement Assistance Administration made federal funds available to compensate students who wished to learn from hands-on experience (Gordon & McBride, 2012). Such funding was phased out in 1980; however, internships became increasingly ingrained in many criminal justice and criminology agencies and academic programs.

Prior to the formal introduction of criminal justice internships in colleges and universities, many students studying the disciplines were working in the field. Accordingly, they had less of a need for formal experience than students today. Many students earn their high school diploma or college degree prior to working in criminal justice (Parilla & Smith-Cunnien, 1997). Internships have become the most often used form of experiential learning in criminal justice and criminology programs primarily because they provide students the opportunity to apply the information learned in their coursework. Roughly 58% of criminal justice bachelor's degree programs in the United States require an internship or a capstone experience (Sloan & Buchwalter, 2017).

Looking back helps us move forward. Internships and other forms of experiential learning have gained popularity as many students prefer to graduate from college with a degree *and* work experience. This contributes to the desires of many employers who prefer employees that have a formal education and experience.

"Internships: Otherwise known as..."

The term "internship" is often used interchangeably with "fieldwork," "practicum," "experiential learning," "service learning," "externship," and "cooperative education." Although there are subtle differences among some of these terms, they all share the expectations that students and others will engage in some form of employment or service, expand their knowledge base, develop both personally and professionally, and acquire and/or hone particular skills.

Experiential learning has become increasingly common in institutions of higher education (e.g., Skaggs & Graybeal, 2019). However, there is often uncertainty regarding what constitutes experiential learning. Researchers Celia Sgroi and Margaret Ryniker (2002, 188) noted that "Experiential learning is by its very nature a form of active learning, in which the student takes significant responsibility in the learning process." It is based on the belief that students must be active participants for effective learning to occur. Ideally, active participation is accompanied by formal classroom training with regard to professional development. Experiential learning in criminal justice, which can include field trips, service-learning, research projects, guest speakers, and internships, was perceived by students as significantly beneficial both professionally and academically (Belisle et al., 2020; George et al., 2015).

The many benefits of experiential learning include (e.g., Belisle et al., 2020):

- Increased student engagement
- Challenging and possibly changing student perceptions of crime and justice
- The improvement of career skills and overall career readiness
- Influencing career goals in criminal justice and criminology
- Reinforcing what was taught in the classroom
- Increased critical thinking skills
- Increased levels of student empathy

Internships certainly meet the definition of experiential learning primarily through providing students the opportunity to gain field experience. Students engaged in an internship are required to step outside the classroom and gain work-related experience. The same can be said for students engaging in externships, fieldwork, or a practicum. Generally, these terms refer to the same type of experiential learning.

Cooperative education programs (sometimes referred to a "co-ops" or "work experience education") differ from internships in that co-ops generally involve more structured work experiences. Particularly, students in co-op programs work a semester and take classes the following semester. In other words, work and schooling are technically exclusive. This approach to co-ops, or learning outside the classroom, has increasingly shifted toward the internship model in which work experience and schooling are closely intertwined. Some agencies and universities still subscribe to the traditional co-op model, and some continue to refer to co-ops as what is technically an internship.

Service learning programs are also quite similar to internships, although they require that some type of service be provided to the community and the service be connected to course objectives. Such service comes without pay and typically provides many of the same benefits of an internship experience. Service learning, however, results in students being required to directly provide services to the community, which ultimately benefits the community, the agency or group for which one is working, and the college or university. Colleges and universities benefit, for instance, as their reputations are enhanced through providing higher levels of community service.

Researchers tested the effects of experiential learning in the form of a jail visit, guest speaker, and a documentary and found that students benefitted from the experiences in several ways. Among the benefits were students becoming better able to connect concepts taught in class (including theories), gaining a greater sense of empathy, and finding assistance with career-related decisions. The experiences also influenced some students to assist with correctional reform efforts (Belisle et al., 2020). Internships also provide these and other benefits.

A Practitioner's View

Christopher A. Curtis, Assistant Federal Public Defender

I served as an Assistant Federal Public Defender (AFPD) for almost 20 years. I became an AFPD after serving three years as an Assistant District Attorney in Parker County, Texas, for three-and-a-half years and serving as an Assistant US Attorney for almost ten years.

AFPDs are appointed to represent indigent defendants charged with a federal crime in federal court. Most individuals charged with a crime in federal court do not have the financial ability to hire their own attorney. Once appointed on a federal criminal case, the AFPD is responsible for representing the client in all proceedings in US District Court, which is the trial court in the federal judicial system. The AFPD is also responsible for handling the case on appeal if the client is convicted.

The duties of an AFPD include appearing with the defendant at his or her initial appearance, arguing for conditions of release pending trial, filing pretrial motions, trying the case to a jury, and arguing on behalf of the defendant at the sentencing hearing. If the case is appealed, the AFPD is responsible for filing an appeal brief and arguing the case before the Circuit Court of Appeals. The AFPD is also responsible for filing a petition for certiorari to the US Supreme Court. Almost every day for an AFPD is exciting and rewarding, involving interviewing new clients and appearing in court, reviewing evidence and interviewing witnesses, preparing cases for trial, preparing for sentencing hearings, and handling cases throughout the appellate process. AFPDs often visit jails and federal holding facilities, meeting with their clients. They also spend much time in federal court, appearing in court several times a week. AFPDs also spend a lot of time drafting written motions and legal briefs.

For anyone desiring to become an AFPD, I would recommend taking as many criminal law and criminal procedure classes as possible as an undergraduate school. Of course, a law degree and bar license are required in this field. I also recommend that law students take as many criminal law and criminal procedure classes as possible and sign up for criminal law clinics. Finally, I recommend participating in an internship program with a state public defender office as well as with a federal public defender office. Upon graduation from law school, I recommend seeking employment in any state public defender office and using that experience to eventually apply with a federal public defender office.

The Benefits of Internships

Internship courses are found in many criminal justice programs, and the courses may be offered as a requirement or an elective. The number of required hours in the field varies, as does the extent to which students meet in the classroom for discussion. Regardless of how internships are offered, it remains that the internship experience enables students to better comprehend, appreciate, and relate to the content of their coursework. Further, internships:

- facilitate self-directed learning skills that will benefit individuals throughout their careers;
- increase one's knowledge of criminal justice and criminology;
- encourage the development of particular skill sets;
- enable students to assess whether or not they wish to work in a particular position, or in criminal justice or criminology in general;
- enhance networking opportunities;
- build self-confidence and self-esteem;
- expose students to life in the workplace and occupational socialization; and
- promote overall professional and career development.

Classroom instruction in criminal justice and criminology is, among other things, designed to educate, promote leadership, and prepare individuals for professional careers. Formal education should include introduction to the practical side of life, with the goal of exposing students to real-world applications of what is learned in the classroom.

Self-directed learning, particularly as it exists in internships, involves individuals acting in a highly autonomous manner. Academia is sometimes criticized for discouraging critical thinking in students, particularly when students are asked to simply repeat facts shared in the classroom. Being able to learn through experience supplements the "nuts and bolts" of academic learning by enabling students to assess various areas of employment, experience various aspects of the workforce, learn at their own pace, and move toward areas that interest them. Everyone learns differently. Some students excel in the classroom, but lack the skills associated with applying that knowledge. Others may be less "book smart," yet are more practical and better suited to adjust to the workforce. Internships identify strengths and weaknesses by removing students from the classroom and letting them "test the waters."

Criminal justice and criminology students receive much coursework that covers the particular components of the system, theories of crime, means of measuring crime, and various related aspects of crime and justice. Classroom-based education sometimes lacks direct preparation for working in the field. The debate regarding whether the benefits of higher education outweigh field experience demonstrates that there is indeed a difference between academia and the real world. Practitioners sometimes feel that the knowledge acquired in college is superficial and largely inapplicable to real-world experiences. Academics sometimes believe that practitioners' views lack theoretical and empirical grounding. Combining real-world experience with formal education helps bridge the gap, increases one's knowledge of crime and justice, and enables students to make more informed decisions.

Students are often encouraged to ask the question: "Why?" They are trained to not simply accept information at face value. Instead, students are encouraged to understand the underlying factors, influences, or explanations behind various phenomena. Adopting such an approach will serve students well throughout their professional career, as one become more invested in their work when they truly recognize its value.

Of equal importance to understanding "why?" is understanding "how?" Understanding "how" is standard practice in some academic disciplines, particularly the hard sciences. For instance, chemistry students mix chemicals in a lab to better understand *how* chemicals interact. Biology students cut things open to better understand *how* organisms function. The social sciences, including criminal justice and criminology, are more generally concerned with understanding *why*. The distinction between *why* and *how* is important given that employers are not always concerned with *why*, and often want results, which are typically based on *how* to do things. Understanding both is necessary in many aspects. For instance, we must understand *why* racial profiling occurs and *how* we can eliminate it.

Criminal justice and criminology programs provide students particular skills applicable to working in the field. For instance, research methods courses are required in an estimated 75% of criminal justice programs (Sloan & Buchwalter, 2017). Yet, there's much more that can be done to prepare students for the criminal justice and criminology workforce. For example, crime mapping and advanced computer skills are becoming increasingly attractive to employers, as is the ability to speak a second language. Internships provide students the opportunity to develop and hone particular skills that may not be offered in a classroom, yet are particularly relevant to working in the field.

Among other benefits, internships enable students to assess whether or not they wish to work in a certain agency, a particular area of criminal justice or criminology, or in the fields in general. What may sound like an exciting job or career may ultimately result in frustration, anxiety, and/or discouragement. The opportunity to "test the waters" in a particular agency or area serves a valuable purpose and can lead to more effective career development.

Students sheltered by college life can benefit by exposure to life in the workplace through an internship. For instance, internships provide opportunities for students to directly view the practices of bureaucracies and the influences of government and office politics. Networking opportunities, enhanced employment opportunities, and the development of particular career-related skills are among the many benefits of students being in the workforce. Enhanced responsibilities and the opportunity to befriend and interact with individuals who maintain similar, career-related interests are also among the benefits. Students also benefit by the opportunity to work with individuals from diverse backgrounds and cultures. The value of an internship is further noted in research examining how police officers valued higher education for officers. Results from a survey of county and municipal officers found that they believe higher education ought to include more hands-on experience, for instance, in the form of internships (Edwards, 2019).

Most of what is experienced during an internship provides a learning opportunity and undoubtedly contributes to professional development. For instance, interns will be better prepared for the workforce simply through overcoming the initial shock of entering the workforce during their internship experience. They may build self-confidence and self-assurance in various aspects of job searching and in various aspects of their job performance. Even "busy-work" (e.g., extensive filing or data entry) during the course of an internship can be a learning experience, for example, as interns may consider whether or not to suggest to their internship supervisor that their services be better utilized, or when they realize that they do not wish to perform busywork in their career.

Internships provide benefits in numerous ways and to different groups. Interns are not the only ones who benefit from internships. Employers and schools also benefit from student internships. Consequently, internships, if done correctly, can be viewed as "win–win–win" opportunities. In fields such as criminal justice and criminology, one could also include clients as benefactors of internships, particularly in cases where student labor contributes to enhanced client services and attention.

Colleges and universities benefit from student internships in several ways. Student placement upon graduation is enhanced through internships, and faculty can establish and maintain productive relations with community agencies through working with representatives from the community via internships. Such relations can benefit the school and faculty member in several ways, including the identification of individuals who may serve as invited speakers on campus or research opportunities. Internships enable faculty members to keep abreast of changes in the community and field and assist academic departments in their efforts to recruit students. Promoting the opportunity for students to engage in the classroom and obtain work experience is often a selling point for schools.

Agencies and organizations also benefit from internships in multiple ways. Perhaps the most obvious benefit to agencies is the (typically) free labor provided by interns. Agencies and organizations, however, gain more from interns than labor. Internships enable agencies to recruit and screen prospective employees over an extended period of time, which can be beneficial in fields such as corrections where staff turnover is a concern (Bayers et al., 2005).

Internships are very helpful avenues to gain experience, obtain employment, and acquire skills. They provide both the intern and agencies important opportunities for evaluation.
Source: https://pxhere.com/en/photo/1432545

Also, interns are sometimes able to bring to the agency fresh ideas or perspectives on particular issues and may provide particular skills that meet agency needs (e.g., knowledge of select computer programs, the ability to speak a second language, social media skills, and so on). Further, an agency or group can enhance its image or reputation on campus and in the community as interns share their positive experiences with others.

Despite the many benefits associated with internships, there are also some concerns with placing students in the field. For instance, ineffective, disinterested, and/or lazy interns provide challenges for internship directors and internship agencies. Accordingly, some criminal justice and criminology programs attempt to ensure the success of their interns through having students meet particular requirements prior to being permitted to intern (e.g., a particular GPA and/or upper-level standing). Most criminal justice programs require student interns to be in the major, have either a junior or senior standing, or have earned a particular GPA (Stichman & Farkas, 2005). Unethical interns pose particular problems for agencies and schools alike. Clear expectations of the internship requirements and accountability provided by both the agency and school should address any negative aspects of an internship.

Expectations of Internships

Establishing clear expectations and holding interns accountable for their actions contribute to the overall effectiveness of internship experiences. To begin, there are expectations on behalf of the college or university requiring or offering the internship opportunity. There are also expectations on behalf of the organization or group providing the internship. Students also maintain their own set of expectations for the internship. Combined, much can be and is expected from an internship.

The requirements and nature of internship courses provided by universities and colleges across the country vary. In response, researchers surveyed 99 criminal justice programs nationwide to better understand the organization, application, implementation, and evaluation of their internship course. Among other findings, the researchers found that most interns did not meet as a group (54.1% of programs surveyed), roughly half of the programs required outside readings, and most (57.8%) internship coordinators/supervisors conducted on-site visits of interns. They also found that students could earn three hours of semester credit most often through completing 120–150 internship hours; six hours of credit typically required 240–300 hours per semester (Stichman & Farkas, 2005). Internships are often unpaid, which poses particular challenges for those who need to earn an income while attending school, and transportation issues sometimes pose challenges.

Preparation involves the process by which students arrange an internship. Initially, students should consult with their internship director for assistance with the guidelines. Some internship programs require students to complete their work at specific places of employment, while other programs may have a list of agencies from which students can select an internship site, or may encourage students to find a place on their own. Encouraging students to find an internship placement on their own facilitates professional development by preparing students for locating future employment opportunities and taking initiative in securing a position. Students, however, may be unsure about how to do this.

The global pandemic surrounding COVID-19 beginning in 2020 posed significant challenges with regard to internships. Requirements and the need for social distancing and quarantining eliminated many internship opportunities. Some fortunate students were able to obtain virtual internships, although there were relatively few opportunities. Akin to many other groups in society, criminal justice and criminology programs that require internships of their students had to make adjustments and did so for instance through permitting students to take a different course in the major to substitute for the internship course, or providing a capstone-like course that did not include experiential learning.

Preparation also involves agency expectations of interns. Students may be apprehensive entering a position with limited skills and largely unfamiliar with agency practices or expectations, and/or they may be unsure whether they can effectively balance work and school. Interns may be uncertain as to how or if they will be accepted into the organizational culture. While such feelings are understandable and in many cases expected, it is important for interns to keep things in perspective. Working closely with their faculty and internship site supervisors helps address these and related concerns.

Uncertainties regarding the internship workload and work-related expectations should be tempered by the fact that agencies utilizing interns are often aware that some level of training is needed for interns. Part of the learning experience associated with internships involves navigating the workplace culture. Students may question whether or not coworkers will welcome them into the workforce. While it would be refreshing to believe that all interns are welcomed by all employees, such is not the case. Some individuals in the workforce view interns as a threat to their job, while others view student workers as "lowly interns." Such treatment (should it occur) may provide some level of discomfort; however, it could be viewed as preparation for one's career, as not everyone in the workforce openly welcomes new employees. Interns are strongly encouraged to discuss notably negative treatment with their internship supervisor. It is hoped, however, that the intern will be valued and viewed as a significant contributor to agency objectives.

Fitting in with the organizational culture may or may not happen, just as it may or may not happen for those employed full time in the agency. If fitting in socially with the agency or organizational culture is important to you, consider becoming more involved in the workplace culture, for instance, through participating in out-of-office activities such as agency luncheons or events. These and related efforts also contribute to networking.

Interns should not enter their position with the expectation that everything will be exciting and glamorous, nor should they expect the worst. To be sure, there may be some busywork involved in an internship. Internships, however, should include more than busywork. Interns are strongly encouraged to respectfully share their concern to their internship director and/or agency supervisor(s) if they feel they're being misled or misused. Sharing legitimate concerns has numerous benefits, not the least of which include the student demonstrating initiative, attempting to maximize the educational experience associated with internships, and possibly being freed from the negative experience.

Generally, the expectations of an internship consist of knowledge acquisition, knowledge application, skills development, personal development, and professional development. There is certainly some overlap among these goals, for instance, as professional development generally requires knowledge acquisition. Nevertheless, each goal is facilitated and certainly attainable through working in the field.

One of the primary benefits of doing an internship is the knowledge attained via the experience. This knowledge contributes to each student's well-roundedness, makes each student a more attractive option for full-time employment at the internship site, assists with student coursework, and may open up avenues for future employment opportunities in other areas within the field. Students should identify and select internships that will enable them to learn and develop. Finding an internship that is simply "easy" is discouraged.

Part of the learning associated with one's internship experience includes skills development. Interns bring certain skills to their internship and hopefully gain many more upon completion. They should expect to develop particular skills as part of their experience. Writing reports, learning new computer programs, and effectively navigating office politics are among the skills that may be developed and honed through an internship. Practical applications facilitate skill development. A sports analogy highlights the significance of fieldwork: One can read books on how to accurately hit a tennis ball; however, hitting effective shots requires one to actually hit tennis balls. Similar to on-the-court training in tennis, internships provide students the opportunity to learn through doing.

Internships also provide opportunities for professional development with regard to addressing unethical behaviors. Interns are typically new to the agency and may be unaware of what constitutes acceptable behavior. Further, they may feel powerless to expose unethical practice. For instance, interns may not understand what constitutes an appropriate level of force in restraining a suspect, and how they should react if they perceive misbehavior in the form of too much force. Research in this area found that over half (55%) of the interns surveyed reported observing at least one incident they suspected to be unethical. The greatest percentage of observed misconduct involved unprofessional comments or behaviors in a private setting (36% of respondents observed such behaviors), while 21% reported that an officer told the intern not to share something they heard or observed on the job. Further, 2% of respondents observed illegal behavior during their internship, and another 3% suspected they observed illegal behavior (Jordan et al., 2007).

The researchers also assessed intern responses to these situations. Only about three-quarters (74.3%) of interns reported or discussed the observed or suspected misbehavior with anyone, and the greatest percentage informally discussed any misbehavior they witnessed with family members or friends (39%) or another student (35%). Interns formally reported the misconduct they observed to an agency official (5%) slightly more often than they reported the behavior to their internship directors (4%) (Jordan et al., 2007). Policies should be in place to guide interns who witness inappropriate or questionable practices, and, at the very least, interns should discuss any troubling situation with the appropriate authorities. It may be the case that the student's internship director and site supervisor need to meet and discuss the issue, or law enforcement or human resources personnel from the agency need to become involved. Regardless, it will be a learning experience.

Internships provide excellent opportunities to grow both personally and professionally. Interns will encounter particular experiences unlike those in the classroom, or even on a university setting. They may encounter ethical dilemmas, which may be troubling yet will help them grow. Further, they may be expected to perform duties that they didn't believe they could or would do. For instance, part of the internship experience may involve interviews with potentially dangerous persons or counseling clients. Effective internships include challenges for interns; challenges that provide opportunities for assessment and facilitate professional development. Such challenges and internships in general can contribute to students changing their views toward crime, justice, and individuals in the criminal justice system.

Students are encouraged to find out as much as possible about their anticipated internship position prior to accepting it. Such information is provided by the internship agency, although one's internship director and fellow students who previously interned at the site may also be able to provide information (e.g., how the agency treats interns). Understanding as much as possible reduces the likelihood of any surprises upon accepting a position and contributes to one's overall success. Of particular importance in assessing the nature of an internship position are the agency's goals, the duties one will be expected to perform, and the hours the intern will be needed.

Creating a list of expected outcomes assists with having an effective internship. Do you wish to acquire particular skills? Are you seeking extensive networking opportunities? Do you want to learn how to engage in legal research, or effectively interview people on probation? Will you seek letters of recommendation from your internship supervisors? The answers to these and/or similar questions may be on the list. The list should be updated and evaluated as one progresses through their internship, and changes should be made as one's goals and/or objectives shift. Interns should thoroughly assess whether or not their expectations were met following the internship experience and determine how or why they did or didn't meet specific goals.

Perhaps most important of all, interns should expect to have a positive experience. Research suggests that student interns are able to reach their goals and rate their experiences positively. They view internships as an important contributor to their crime and justice-based education (Murphy et al., 2013). Entering an internship with a positive attitude, a clear set of expectations, and overall professionalism contributes greatly to a successful internship, which subsequently contributes to career development.

Summary

The college experience is a time to grow, mature, and develop in many facets. Hands-on involvement in situations unique to you, and engaging in practical experiences facilitates growth, maturation, and development. This chapter addressed the role of internships in criminal justice and criminology career development, beginning with the origins of internships. Such information, among other benefits, helps readers/students better understand the utility of internships, how they originated, and why they are important.

Internships are as aspect of experiential learning, and sometimes referred to as "practicums," "co-ops," and related terms. Regardless of the term used, any student involvement in the criminal justice or criminology workforce or community service provides numerous benefits to various parties, including clients, agencies, the community, schools, and interns. Among the benefits to these groups are knowledge acquisition, skills development, professional development, personal development, enhanced recruitment efforts, and assistance with meeting goals.

Students should enter the internship experience with a set of personal expectations and be cognizant of the expectations of their school and the agency at which they wish to intern. Although there will likely be no financial rewards stemming from an internship, the many other benefits of this type of experiential learning will very likely pay dividends throughout one's professional career.

Discussion Questions

1. What are the origins of criminal justice internships?
2. What would be your ideal internship? Be sure to note the agency, responsibilities, and overall benefits.
3. Discuss the benefits of completing an internship in criminal justice. What are the drawbacks?
4. What do you believe would be the most difficult aspects of doing an internship? How would you address those challenges?
5. Do you believe all criminal justice students should be required to complete an internship as part of their academic studies? Why or why not?

Critical Thinking Exercise

Assume you are the assistant police chief in a medium-sized police department. You decided that the department should take three interns from the local university each semester. You propose the idea to the chief, who asks you to write up a report outlining the pros and cons, the resources involved, and how to proceed with making this happen. Write the report using much detail in efforts to convince the chief.

For Further Examination

Belisle, L., Boppre, B., Keen, J., & Salisbury, E.J. (2020). Bringing course material to life through experiential learning: Impacts on students' learning and perceptions in a corrections course. *Journal of Criminal Justice Education, 31*(2), 161–186.

Crandall, K.L., Buckwalter, M.A., & Witkoski, M. (2021). Show and tell: An examination of experiential learning opportunities in criminal justice courses. *Journal of Criminal Justice Education, 32*(2), 155–170.

Jones, M., & Bonner, H.S. (2016). What should criminal justice interns know? Comparing the opinions of student interns and criminal justice practitioners. *Journal of Criminal Justice Education, 27*(3), 381–409.

Skaggs, S.L., & Graybeal, L. (2019). Service-learning and experiential learning in criminal justice education: An exploratory examination of faculty perspectives. *Journal of Criminal Justice Education, 30*(2), 296–312.

Williams, T., Pryce, D.K., Clark, T., & Wilfong, H. (2020). The benefits of criminal justice internships at a Historically Black University: An analysis of site supervisors' evaluations of interns' professional development. *Journal of Criminal Justice Education, 31*(1), 124–140.

References

Bayers, G.J., Berry, P.E., & Smith-Mahdi, J. (2005, November/December). A descriptive study of student appraisals of the benefits of a criminal justice internship. *American Jails*, 26–30, 32, 34–36.

Belisle, L. Boppre, B., Keen J., & Salisbury, E.J. (2020). Bringing course material to life through experiential learning: Impacts on students' learning and perceptions in a corrections course. *Journal of Criminal Justice Education, 31*(2), 161–186.

Edwards, B.D. (2019). Perceived value of higher education among police officers: Comparing county and municipal officers. *Journal of Criminal Justice Education, 30*(4), 606–620.

George, M., Lim, H., Lucas, S., & Meadows, R. (2015). Learning by doing: Experiential learning in criminal justice. *Journal of Criminal Justice Education, 26*(4), 471–492.

Gordon, G.R., & McBride, R.B. (2012). *Criminal justice internships: Theory into practice* (7th ed.). Anderson.

Jordan, W.T., Burns, R.G., Bedard, L.E., & Barringer, T.A. (2007). Criminal justice interns' observations of misconduct: An exploratory study. *Journal of Criminal Justice Education, 18*, 298–310.

Murphy, D., Merritt, W., & Gibbons, S. (2013). Student and supervisor perspectives on the benefits of criminal justice internships. *Journal of Criminal Justice Education, 24*(2), 235–250.

Parilla, P.F. & Smith-Cunnien, S.L. (1997). Criminal justice internships: Integrating the academic with the experiential. *Journal of Criminal Justice Education, 8*(2), 225–241.

Sgroi, C.A. & Ryniker, M. (2002). Preparing for the real world: A prelude to fieldwork experience. *Journal of Criminal Justice Education, 13*(1), 187–200.

Skaggs, S.L., & Graybeal, L. (2019). Service-learning and experiential learning in criminal justice education: An exploratory examination of faculty perspectives. *Journal of Criminal Justice Education, 30*(2), 296–312.

Sloan, J.J., III., & Buchwalter, J.W. (2017). The state of criminal justice bachelor's degree programs in the United States: Institutional, departmental and curricula features. *Journal of Criminal Justice Education, 28*(3), 307–334.

Stichman, A.J., & Farkas, M.A. (2005). The pedagogical use of internships in criminal justice programs: A nationwide study. *Journal of Criminal Justice Education, 16*(1), 145–179.

Part 3

Working Toward Justice

Chapter 9

Careers in Law Enforcement

Many people associate a career in criminal justice with law enforcement. It is often perceived that criminal justice majors will become law enforcement officers. Certainly, some criminal justice or criminology majors will become officers and have wonderful careers; however, many will assume careers in other areas, including the many different areas of law enforcement. Law enforcement is a popular option upon graduating with a criminal justice degree. The enhanced emphasis on homeland security witnessed in the United States following the terrorist attacks of September 11, 2001 resulted in law enforcement in general becoming an increasingly popular career choice. On the other hand, several disturbing incidents involving the police, including the George Floyd incident in Minneapolis during 2020, have made a policing career less desirable for some.

Careers in law enforcement are attractive for many reasons. They can be exciting, rewarding, and enjoyable. For instance, some people seek careers in law enforcement due to the variety and spontaneity and/or the opportunities to help others and society in general. An often overlooked aspect of a career in law enforcement is the opportunity to work in a variety of areas, or perhaps to specialize in a particular area (e.g., vice work, white-collar crimes, crime scene investigation, canine units, and so on).

The duties, responsibilities, and nature of law enforcement positions vary by the positions and levels within law enforcement agencies. For example, the nature of the work associated with street patrol is much different from the work performed by most federal agents. Accordingly, the following discussion is organized based on the level of law enforcement and, in some places, positions within those levels.

The decentralized organizational structure of law enforcement in the United States results in a great disbursement of responsibilities, various jurisdictions, and differing levels of authority. For example, the duties and responsibilities of various state law enforcement agents are somewhat different from what is expected from municipal police officers. Regardless of the level of law enforcement, it remains that law enforcement officers are charged with enforcing social control. The approaches taken by law enforcement agents to provide social control are influenced by a variety of factors, including the level of law enforcement at which they work, the agency at which they work, and their role within a particular agency.

The following discussion of careers in law enforcement is organized according to the three primary levels of law enforcement (federal, state, and local) and briefly addresses special jurisdiction agencies. Coverage centers on the nature of the work associated with employment at these levels, and the opportunities available. This is followed by an examination of law enforcement recruitment, selection, and hiring practices.

DOI: 10.4324/9781003360162-12

Federal Law Enforcement

The organization of federal law enforcement agencies is much easier to comprehend than the organization of state and local agencies, primarily because there is only one federal government. However, the varied nature and specialization of federal law enforcement sometimes results in hampered cooperation among agencies, limited interaction with state and local enforcement officers, and difficulty in precisely describing the many career and internship opportunities available at this level.

The federal government is the United States' largest employer with over two million employees working both domestically and abroad in a wide array of occupations. Federal law enforcement agents work in many federal departments, independent agencies, and subagencies. Many students considering a career in federal law enforcement focus primarily on the most popular agencies, particularly the Federal Bureau of Investigation (FBI) (Howard et al., 2011). There are, of course, many other federal agencies with law enforcement responsibilities, and, accordingly, there are a variety of career tracks within federal law enforcement.

Careers in federal law enforcement are particularly attractive to many criminal justice students (Collica-Cox & Furst, 2019; Stringer & Murphy, 2020). Among the more appealing aspects of the work are the prestige, compensation, and general perceptions of the responsibilities of federal law enforcement (Mijares, 2018). Discussion of career profiles in federal law enforcement and the agencies that employ federal law enforcement personnel provides guidance for those seeking a career in the field.

Career Profiles

Federal agents provide a wide array of services and are responsible for many duties. The Bureau of Justice Statistics noted that federal law enforcement officers, as their primary function, most often engaged in criminal investigation, followed by corrections, police response and patrol, court operations, noncriminal investigation/enforcement, and security and protection (Brooks, 2022). Former federal agent Thomas Ackerman (2006) categorized the career profiles of federal law enforcement positions in his book *Federal Law Enforcement Careers*. Particularly, Ackerman described and categorized careers as follows:

- **Criminal investigators** are among the best trained and most respected law enforcement officers in the world. They collect and examine evidence associated with federal offenses, serve subpoenas, engage in surveillance operations, interrogate suspects, assist US Attorneys in prosecuting crimes, and perform related tasks. They also assist law enforcement agencies at all levels and provide security for high-ranking government personnel and foreign dignitaries.
- **Intelligence analysts** collect, analyze, interpret, and disseminate crime and related data that pertain to national security. Their work may relate to drug trafficking, organized crime, white-collar crime, transportation security, and terrorism. Generally, these individuals perform the vital task of "data crunching" and information dissemination.
- **Uniformed law enforcement officers** ensure compliance with and enforce the law. Their functions are quite similar to local police in that they preserve the peace; protect civil rights; patrol; prevent, detect, and investigate crimes; arrest violators; assist individuals in emergency situations; engage in traffic control; perform search and rescue operations; and perform related duties. They work in a wide array of settings, including at courthouses, national borders, airports, hospitals, historic landmarks, national parks, power plants, and other areas requiring federal protection.

- **Law enforcement technicians and specialists** perform specialized missions that vary among agencies. The varied nature of the work performed by technicians and specialists dictates that individuals in these positions have expertise in particular areas that contribute to performing law enforcement functions. These positions are mostly found in the largest federal law enforcement agencies. The areas of specialization associated with these positions include examining fingerprints, operating aircraft, analyzing evidence, identifying handwriting, taking surveillance photographs, and determining the cause and origins of explosions and fires.
- **General and compliance investigators** inspect and investigate activities pertaining to federal laws and regulations. Their efforts typically serve as the basis for administrative sanctions, judgments, or penalties. Most of their actions are regulatory in nature; however, they sometimes work with the US Attorney's Office in criminal cases or incidents requiring civil action. The nature of their work varies widely.
- **Compliance inspectors and specialists** perform functions similar to general and compliance investigators; however, the emphasis of the former is on inspections as opposed to investigations. Compliance inspectors enforce laws, regulations, and activities under the jurisdiction of the federal government. Inspectors are highly specialized and may be involved in site inspections at mining shafts, inspecting establishments that produce tobacco and alcohol, enforcing marine safety regulations and laws, performing deportation proceedings, and ensuring compliance with wildlife laws.
- **Security specialists** perform a wide array of tasks, with the primary goal of identifying and protecting federal government assets and employees. Physical security specialists protect physical assets, while personnel security specialists analyze the character and suitability of particular individuals with concern for access to classified or other sensitive information, materials, or locations.
- **Communications and electronics personnel** provide support operations at every level of law enforcement, including the federal level where telecommunications specialists, dispatchers, and computer database systems operators assist investigators and others.

The nature of the work associated with these positions certainly varies given the wide array of responsibilities associated with each.

Working in Federal Law Enforcement

Federal law enforcement agencies are spread throughout the United States. There is often much prestige associated with working as a federal agent, and the training and resources are superior to most other agencies worldwide. Nevertheless, there is also an increased likelihood that one will have to relocate to another city or state during their career in federal law enforcement (Yu, 2020), and changing political leaders can disrupt the agencies in which they are employed.

A Department of Justice (DOJ) report provides insight on the federal law enforcement workforce. It noted that there were roughly 137,000 full-time federal law enforcement officers authorized to carry a firearm and/or make an arrest in 2020. Most worked in either the Department of Homeland Security (DHS; 49%) or the DOJ (30%). The US Customs and Border Protection (CBP) by far employed the largest number of individuals, followed by the Federal Bureau of Prisons, and the US Immigration and Customs Enforcement (ICE). About 15% of federal officers were women, and just over one-third of federal officers were members of an ethnic or racial minority group (Brooks, 2022). An overview of some prominent agencies within the DOJ and DHS sheds light on the varied work of federal law enforcement agencies.

The DHS houses several of the largest federal law enforcement agencies, including CBP, ICE, and the US Secret Service. CBP is charged with preventing terrorism, the importation of illegal drugs, illegal entries into the United States, and resources harmful to agriculture from entering ports of entry to the United States. ICE is generally charged with identifying and removing vulnerabilities with regard to US borders, the economy, the transportation sector, and the overall infrastructure of the United States. The US Secret Service is tasked with investigating and addressing crimes primarily related to finances, counterfeiting, and computer fraud. It serves the dual purpose of protecting dignitaries. There are, of course, other agencies within the DHS that assume law enforcement responsibilities, including the Cybersecurity and Infrastructure Security Agency and the Transportation Security Administration. The DHS also houses the Federal Law Enforcement Training Center, which trains federal agents.

The DOJ also houses several prominent federal law enforcement agencies, including the FBI, the Drug Enforcement Administration (DEA), the US Marshals Service, and the Bureau of Alcohol, Tobacco, Firearms and Explosives (ATF). The most popular among this group is the FBI, which has many responsibilities, including protecting the United States from terrorist attacks, foreign intelligence efforts, protecting civil rights, and combating corruption, cybercrime, violent crime, white-collar crime, and organized crime. The DEA investigates major narcotics violations, enforces regulations pertaining to the manufacture and dispensing of controlled substances, and performs other duties with the goal of preventing and controlling drug trafficking. As one of the oldest federal law enforcement agencies, the US Marshals perform a variety of law enforcement functions. Primarily, they maintain custody and transport all individuals arrested by federal agencies, have jurisdiction over federal fugitive matters, manage the Federal Witness Security and Asset Forfeiture programs, and provide security for federal judicial facilities and personnel. The ATF is generally charged with enforcing federal laws pertaining to alcohol, tobacco, firearms, explosives, and arson. The DOJ also includes the US Attorney General's office.

There are agencies with law enforcement responsibilities at the federal level housed outside of the DHS and DOJ. Combined, they provide a wide array of services.

The discussion above highlights the functions of the more prominent agencies. Among the other federal agencies with greater than 1,000 federal law enforcement officers are:

- **The US Postal Inspection Service**, whose officers are responsible for criminal investigations covering over 200 federal laws pertaining to the postal system.
- **The Internal Revenue Service**, whose officers are tasked with enforcing the Nation's tax laws.
- **The National Park Service**, whose Park Rangers and Park Police provide law enforcement services in national parks and at historic sites.
- **The US Capitol Police**, whose officers provide police services for the US Capitol grounds and buildings.
- **The Department of State's Bureau of Diplomatic Security**, whose officers serve the primary function of protecting visiting dignitaries. These officers also investigate passport and visa fraud, and threats against foreign missions in the United States, foreign dignitaries, or federal employees.

Among the federal agencies employing fewer than 1,000 federal law enforcement officers are:

- **The Pentagon Force Protection Agency** within the Department of Defense, whose officers provide law enforcement and security at the Pentagon.
- **The US Mint**, whose officers provide police services for US Mint facilities.

- **The Bureau of Engraving and Printing**, which is tasked with providing police services for the bureau's facilities, including sites where stamps, currency, securities, and other official US documents are produced.
- **The Environmental Protection Agency**, which investigates and responds to violations of environmental laws.
- **The Food and Drug Administration**, whose officers investigate violations of the Federal Food, Drug, and Cosmetic Act and related public health laws.

Federal law enforcement positions are also available in the federal offices of inspector general found throughout federal agencies. Offices of inspector general prevent and detect fraud, abuse, and waste as they relate to federal programs, employees, and operations. They also investigate criminal violations.

Job seekers interested in a career in federal law enforcement (or any federal-level career) are encouraged to become familiar with the US Office of Personnel Management's USAJOBS.gov website. The site is operated by the federal government and lists all employment position openings. It allows users to search and apply for federal law enforcement positions. Upon being hired, training for most federal law enforcement agents will occur at the Federal Law Enforcement Training Center. This is typically followed by agency-specific training. Appendix C provides additional guidance for locating and applying for federal law enforcement positions.

The outlook for employment in federal law enforcement is positive given societal concern for homeland security and the notable emphasis on drug and human trafficking, cybercrime, and immigration. These and other issues such as globalism and advancements in technology will very likely contribute to growth in many federal law enforcement agencies.

State Law Enforcement

State police agencies emerged to address the increasing frequency and seriousness of social order problems. Industrialization and the facilitation of transportation earlier in US history created a gap in policing as crime increased and moved away from large cities (Johnson, 1981). Since that time, the roles and functions of state law enforcement continuously evolved as state law enforcement agencies attempted to keep pace with societal changes, particularly as they related to law enforcement concerns. State law enforcement agencies have jurisdiction over their respective states.

Variations among state law enforcement agencies result in differing organizational designs and agency functions. There is a general perception among those in society that state law enforcement agencies solely engage in highway patrol. While highway patrol is certainly a priority, it is not the only function of state police. State law enforcement personnel engage in a variety of law enforcement duties other than highway patrol. For instance, they may also conduct investigations, protect natural resources, and provide training for local-level law enforcement agencies. They are generally more specialized than local law enforcement agencies, yet less specialized than federal ones.

State agencies have jurisdiction over the entire state, and each state government regulates its own law enforcement agencies. Hawaii is the only state without a state law enforcement agency. The organization of each state agency differs, as does the emphasis states place on particular functions. For instance, Florida has a large coast and, accordingly, directs many resources to coastal enforcement efforts. States without as much coastline obviously place less of an emphasis on marine patrol. Related, some states have more highways and thus state law enforcement agencies devote more resources to highway patrol. In light of this, states vary in their organizational approach to state law enforcement, with some being more centralized, and

The field of law enforcement provides many employment opportunities in different areas, yet each area works toward the same goal.
Source: www.pexels.com/photo/agents-working-in-solving-a-case-6069237/

others adopting a more decentralized approach. Centralized agencies combine the various law enforcement functions in one agency (e.g., a state department of public safety). Decentralized approaches have specialized units that are more autonomous (e.g., a state highway patrol department).

State law enforcement agencies are typically categorized according to state bureaus of investigations and state agencies with general law enforcement powers. The responsibilities of state police officers, also known as state troopers in some states, resemble those of local-level police officers and sheriffs' deputies. State law enforcement officers are generally tasked with ensuring public safety and patrolling state and interstate highways. Their tasks are generally summarized as:

- Traffic regulation on state roads and highways
- Driver's license renewals and automobile inspections
- Collecting, assessing, and sharing crime data
- Criminal investigations
- Crime lab services
- Emergency management services
- Counterterrorism and intelligence-gathering practices
- Protecting natural resources
- Training and cooperating with other law enforcement agencies (Burns, 2022).

State bureaus of investigations investigate the cases assigned to them and typically report to the state attorney general. They are plainclothes agents who often investigate both criminal and civil cases throughout the state. They provide technical support to the local-level law enforcement agencies and assist with investigations of serious crimes.

States have also created a variety of specific-jurisdiction investigative units that are typically narrow in focus and investigate specific types of crimes and regulatory violations. Examples of these limited-jurisdiction organizations include alcohol and beverage control units, gaming or gambling units, state fire marshals, and environmental conservation officers. For instance, environmental conservation officers operate at the local, county, and state levels and typically work outside for long and irregular hours. They often work independently and usually carry a firearm. Sometimes referred to as game wardens and fish and wildlife management officers, they investigate complaints and attempt to deter environmental law-related crimes and violations. They sometimes perform public service duties, for instance, through educating the public regarding environmental protection. Some jurisdictions require conservation officers to live within the geographical limits of the area they patrol, and the officers are typically supplied with all-terrain vehicles, boats, snowmobiles, binoculars, radios, cameras, and other equipment to facilitate working in nature.

State law enforcement agencies benefit from the size of their jurisdiction and the scope of their work. Particularly, they draw a larger and more qualified pool of applicants statewide and are better funded and trained than many of their counterparts at local agencies. The narrow scope of crimes upon which particular state law enforcement agencies focus, and the increased specialization of the agencies are also viewed as benefits. Such specificity, however, can also be viewed as a limitation for those who enjoy variety. Another concern is the distant relationship many state agencies have with the general public. Local officers more often directly interact with the public.

The nature of the work associated with state law enforcement agencies could be considered a compilation of what exists in federal- and local-level law enforcement. For instance, local law enforcement agencies largely focus on crime fighting and interacting with the general public. Federal agencies primarily engage in investigative work, with some agencies providing traditional police services (e.g., the US Park Police). State agencies provide a more balanced combination of both.

The Bureau of Justice Statistics reported that in 2018 there were roughly 93,000 full-time employees in state law enforcement agencies. This includes about 60,500 sworn officers, and 32,300 civilians who provide a variety of support services (Gardner & Scott, 2022). The number of sworn employees increased by about 10% from 1997 to 2016 (Hyland, 2018), which is promising for those interested in careers in state law enforcement.

As law enforcement in general continues to expand, one can expect continued expansion in the state-level law enforcement agencies. Retirements, expansion, and the need to replace state-level law enforcement officers who leave for federal positions or work in the private sector will contribute to enhanced prospects of employment in state-level law enforcement.

Local Law Enforcement

The term "local law enforcement" refers to local police departments, sheriffs' offices, departments with special jurisdiction, and other agencies such as Constable's offices. These agencies maintain jurisdiction of local areas and are often required to work cooperatively as crime crosses jurisdictional boundaries. The nature of the work at the local level of law enforcement is what most people associate with the term "police work." It primarily entails maintaining order, providing services to individuals, and enforcing laws. Local law enforcement agents are typically required to be generalists, although there are several positions within these agencies that require specialization in particular areas.

The following discussion largely focuses on police officers given the large number of individuals interested in those positions and the large number of available positions. Further, the focus of the discussion is directed toward police officer positions primarily because one typically must serve some time in this position prior to assuming other roles within a department. However, not all who work in state and local law enforcement must be a sworn officer, as there were roughly 426,700 full-time civilians (or over one-third of all who worked in these law enforcement agencies) employed in departments in 2018. The number of full-time civilians employed in state and local law enforcement agencies increased by roughly 58,000, an increase of about 16%, between 2008 and 2018 (Gardner & Scott, 2022).

Positions in local law enforcement are numerous and provide excellent career opportunities for those interested in a career in criminal justice and criminology. For example, in 2018 there were roughly 17,500 local law enforcement agencies that employed roughly 717,000 full-time sworn personnel, or those with general arrest powers (Gardner & Scott, 2022).

There is a significant difference in the nature of the work associated with policing in large and small cities. These differences become apparent in the nature of the work performed. Generally, big city police officers are more actively involved in crime fighting and order maintenance than are their counterparts who work in smaller cities, where providing service to the public may consume most of their active time. Officers who serve medium-sized cities (e.g., those found in the suburbs) experience somewhat of a balance between the two, engaging in a fair share of all three major components of police work: crime fighting, providing service, and order maintenance.

Patrol is often referred to as the backbone of policing. Officers on patrol actively engage the community through various means, most often through the use of an automobile. Mounted patrol, motorcycle patrol, foot patrol, and bike patrol are among the other means by which officers patrol. The varied nature of patrol work opens opportunities for individuals with special skills or affinities, such as being able to ride horseback or handle canines. Among other benefits, patrols enable police to quickly respond to calls, identify and deter criminal behavior, and better interact with the public.

While on patrol, law enforcement officers often provide services to the public. For instance, officers may assist motorists in need of assistance or provide directions or guidance. Officers in smaller departments working in less populated, close-knit communities have more downtime and are more familiar with the people they serve. Providing service helps departments build strong ties to the community; it encourages positive police–community relations.

Larger cities are typically more specialized when it comes to public demands for specific services. For instance, one is more likely to see a "traffic response team" or a similar group that specializes in accident control in large cities, where accidents are more likely to occur. Officers in larger cities are more likely to request that motorists locked out of their car call a locksmith than in smaller cities, where the officers may be more willing to help the motorist get his/her keys out of the car. Big city officers must prioritize how they use their time, and addressing crime is more important than unlocking cars. Those interested in a career in local law enforcement should consider the extent to which they wish to provide service to the public or fight crime when choosing an agency.

Local-level law enforcement officers are far more likely than their counterparts at the state and federal levels to engage in order maintenance. The size of the city in which one works largely impacts the extent to which an officer is expected to maintain order. Officers provide order maintenance, for example, during festivals, parades, sporting events, and the like. Among other benefits, a law enforcement presence during these and related events deters antisocial behavior and permits immediate assistance as needed. Order maintenance is also evident in regular, everyday police work, for instance, as municipal officers walk beats on congested city streets.

> **A Practitioner's View**
>
> Dale Smith, Corporal, Coppell Police Department
>
> As a corporal in the patrol division of a suburban police department, I split my time between patrol duties and administrative tasks. While on patrol, I enforce traffic laws, investigate suspicious persons, and answer calls for service. When I'm in the office I approve reports, arrests, and timesheets, and help develop younger officers. It's a fun and unique position that allows me to participate in the supervisor arena while not being tied down to a desk all day.
>
> I wholeheartedly believe students can best prepare for a career in law enforcement by developing their writing and people skills. The police academy and field training will teach officers all the finer details of police work such as laws, tactics, and procedures. But learning to interact with people of all backgrounds in a respectful and genuine manner is an absolute necessity in today's society. Couple that with the ability to write a thorough, well-written report and students will be well on their way to a long, meaningful law enforcement career.

Crime fighting, or law enforcement, is the most recognizable component of local-level police work. The image of police officers as strictly crime fighters is perpetuated by popular culture and contributes to the societal perception that police work regularly consists of dangerous practices. Officers and deputies do indeed encounter dangerous situations; however, the extent to which they face danger varies according to a variety of factors, not the least of which involves the size of the city in which they work, and the crime rate. Larger cities generally have higher crime rates compared to smaller ones. Officers rarely face life-threatening situations, although every encounter between the police and the public maintains the potential threat of danger.

Local-level law enforcement officers face particular challenges when fighting crime and enforcing the law. For instance, as the gatekeepers to the criminal justice system, they sometimes work directly with dangerous individuals under threatening situations. They see society at its worst. They are charged with expediently getting to the situations from which most of us run from. They see the direct results of child abuse and other forms of domestic violence, dead bodies, neglect, and drug addiction. They must understand how to properly assist, coerce, and/or arrest the mentally ill and the drug-impaired. They deal with the stress associated with irregular working hours, the potential for danger, and being expected to have the correct answers for every problematic situation. These are but a few of the challenges associated with the job.

Conversely, police work can be very rewarding, both figuratively and literally. Police officers are attracted to the position for many reasons, including the desire to stop criminal behavior and help others in the community. They also appreciate the excitement and challenges of the work, and the variety of responsibilities involved (Clinkinbeard et al., 2021). Not many jobs other than law enforcement provide workers such accessibility to troubled individuals, and excellent opportunities to make a difference in society. The vast array of local law enforcement agencies across the world provide welcomed opportunities for officers to work anywhere, and for officers to be promoted or work in various aspects of law enforcement. The high level of job security associated with local law enforcement positions also attracts applicants.

To be sure, there are many positions in local law enforcement other than patrol officers. The following highlights other positions at this level of law enforcement.

- Canine Officer – Handlers are sworn officers responsible for the proper use and care of a police canine. They must take care of the canine, keep updated with regard to training, and be prepared to respond to a variety of calls for service.
- Chief of Police – Oversees the day-to-day operations of their police department. They are responsible for a wide array of duties, most of which involve various forms of administration.
- Crime Prevention Specialist – Performs public service functions providing crime prevention programs and building citizen and law enforcement awareness. They perform public relations, administrative and operational duties, and other tasks related to stopping crime before it occurs.
- Crime Scene Investigator – Responsible for the collection of evidence at crime scenes and preservation of evidence for processing. They may have to testify in court proceedings.
- Deputy Sheriff – Uniformed law enforcement position similar to police officers and state troopers but with court and corrections responsibilities. They have county-wide jurisdiction.
- Dispatcher – Responsible for the reception and dispatch of emergency and routine calls to patrol units. They also perform record checks, maintain computerized and written reports, and operate sophisticated computer equipment.
- Police Training Officer – Develops, implements, and provides training programs in law enforcement academies. They ensure consistency with development needs for the law enforcement profession and teach, update, and revise courses with concern for currency and relevance to policing.

Appendix D describes various positions throughout law enforcement.

Special Jurisdiction Law Enforcement Agencies

Various special jurisdiction law enforcement agencies operate at the state and local levels. These agencies have special enforcement or investigative responsibilities, maintain jurisdiction over particular areas, and provide additional employment opportunities for those seeking a career in law enforcement. These agencies provide law enforcement services related to:

- Public buildings/facilities, including colleges and universities, public schools, government buildings, public housing/health facilities, and the courts.
- Natural resources/parks and recreation, including parks and other recreational areas. They may address fish and wildlife issues, environmental laws, water resources, sanitation laws, and forest resources.
- Transportation systems/facilities, including mass transit systems, railroads, airports, port facilities, commercial vehicles, bridges, and tunnels.
- Criminal investigations at the county, city, and state levels.
- Special enforcement, including alcohol enforcement, agricultural law enforcement, gaming/racing enforcement, and drug enforcement.

Most special jurisdiction law enforcement agencies secure public buildings/facilities, particularly as they relate to colleges and universities. Special jurisdiction agencies provide additional career opportunities in law enforcement and offer the opportunity to specialize in a particular area of enforcement.

This chapter by no means comprehensively addresses the positions in law enforcement. Missing, for instance, is coverage of intelligence analysts in law enforcement agencies at all levels. Departments are increasingly relying on intelligence and data to guide their practices. Intelligence analysis positions have long existed in various state and federal law enforcement agencies, and beginning in the 1990s local law began to increasingly use data and intelligence to more effectively fight crime (Burcher & Whelan, 2018). A career in intelligence analysis involves using information to identify threats, patterns, and trends with regard to criminal behavior, and offering guidance for responses based on assessments of intelligence. There are various levels and scopes of intelligence and data analysis positions. For instance, intelligence gathering and data analyses at the federal level may be much broader in scope, perhaps on an international level. Or, one could collect, assess, and apply data and intelligence for a municipal police department, which would be much narrower in scope.

Also absent from this chapter is coverage of the many groups that may not be formally recognized as law enforcement; however, they are closely related. Among those are claims/field investigators employed by insurance companies to evaluate potential cases of fraud and other types of misbehavior, and forensic accountants, who investigate cases involving money laundering, fraud, embezzlement, and related financial crimes. Law enforcement agencies often seek the expertise of these individuals to assist with complex financial cases. Chapter 13 addresses other positions related to those found in law enforcement, including private security.

Recruitment, Selection, and Training

Obtaining a position in law enforcement involves the completion of many steps and can be a test of endurance. Law enforcement agencies invest substantial resources in recruiting, selecting, and training employees and struggle with regard to hiring practices when resources are scarce. The recruitment process generally begins with departments establishing the minimum standards required for the position, followed by efforts to locate and attract qualified candidates. The minimum standards typically include physical and age requirements, educational requirements, criminal history restrictions, and medical disqualifiers. Departments establish requirements in these and perhaps other areas for eligibility to be considered for the selection process. About 38% of departments have residency requirements, which mandate that officers live within or in close proximity to the city they will serve (Reaves, 2012).

Actively recruiting candidates is a particularly important component of the hiring process. Departments typically post details of their job openings on their website and/or the city's website, which is where those interested in working for a particular department should begin their search. Police departments may advertise positions in schools, at fairs, on military bases, and at other locations that attract adults and young adults who may be interested in working for their department. The recruitment efforts may be more intense in certain areas and places based on department interests. For instance, a department interested in becoming more diversified in terms of gender may allocate more resources toward advertising in locations often frequented by females (e.g., a women's college or women's workout facility). Recruitment efforts emphasize the many benefits of a career in policing, including the stability of the position, benefits, and opportunities to help others. Chapter 7 includes a job advertisement from the Fort Worth Police Department.

Recruitment efforts hopefully generate a large body of qualified candidates, from which the most promising and qualified will be selected. Much screening and evaluation of the candidates are conducted at this point. Departments want to ensure that they are identifying and hiring highly competent, ethical, and reliable people. Law enforcement officials reported that the following characteristics are related to a successful career in policing (Guffey et al., 2007):

- Dependability
- Physical fitness
- Excellent judgment
- A strong moral character
- Excellent judgment
- An ability to control one's temper under stressful conditions

Those applying for a career in policing should be prepared for the various screening and evaluations required as part of the hiring process. Screening practices involve consideration of a candidate's history and whether or not they meet the requirements for the position. An extensive background check is required, including information on previous jobs and residences. This information should be included in your "me" file, as referenced in Chapter 7. Departments typically consider candidates' driving history, credit history, criminal background, and work history, among other areas. References will be required. The earlier suggestion that one's social media be cleaned and professional is particularly important when applying for positions in policing. Investigation is, of course, a primary function of their job.

Those who make it past the screening stage will proceed to a series of evaluations. The evaluations may include:

- An aptitude test
- A polygraph or voice stress analysis
- A psychological evaluation
- An interview
- A physical agility exam
- A medical exam
- A drug test
- A medical exam

Not every department uses all of these evaluations. The job advertisement often notes which ones are required. Each evaluation provides data for the department to determine candidate suitability for becoming a police officer. Candidates who appear most suitable to the department will be selected and required to undergo training.

Three types of training help ensure that police officers are prepared to meet the requirements of their job. Basic training is provided to the recruits selected as part of the hiring process. This is done at a police academy, which on average consists of 833 hours of classroom education and practical training (Buehler, 2021). Recruits become officers upon graduating from basic training and undergo field training. Field training officers are paired with new officers and are expected to further train the officers while on duty and monitor their progress. The average length of field training was 508 hours in 2018 (Buehler, 2021). In-service training is the final type of training. It may be offered to or required of all officers and is generally designed to keep officers well-trained. For instance, all officers may have to undergo in-service training to learn how to use a new weapon or technology. This type of training is also offered when officers are promoted and need to better understand the responsibilities associated with their new position.

Research is an integral part of any job search, especially law enforcement. Individuals considering a career in the field are strongly encouraged to research the agencies and positions they are considering. Such research could, for instance, involve determining what evaluations are involved, and what is required to successfully complete the evaluations. Consider doing a ride-along with agencies you may be considering. Shadowing someone in the position you're considering is an effective use of time. Be aware that not all departments permit ride-alongs.

Summary

Law enforcement agencies provide many career opportunities for those interested in a career in criminal justice or criminology. The large number of agencies worldwide and wide array of functions performed by law enforcement agencies at all levels make positions in law enforcement attractive to many prospective employees. While many in society associate a career in law enforcement as strictly involving a big-city police officer on patrol, one must not overlook the many positions in all levels of law enforcement, and those in fields closely related to law enforcement.

Of particular importance with regard to a career in law enforcement is experience. Not everyone is interested in a career as a patrol officer; however, the benefits of directly experiencing crime and interacting with individuals who break the law are helpful in many aspects of a career in law enforcement. Accordingly, many higher-level positions in law enforcement require some type of street-level law enforcement.

The wide array of functions performed by law enforcement agents and agencies provides a great opportunity for those interested in the field to utilize their skills and help others. Those interested in law enforcement ought to consider what specific skills they can bring to the job that will enable them to excel. For instance, problem-solving skills and the ability to speak a second language are valuable assets to many law enforcement agencies.

Those interested in a career in law enforcement are encouraged to interview, or simply speak with those in the field. Further, remaining optimistic is very important. The process can be tedious and take much time; however, the benefits may very well be worth the effort.

Discussion Questions

1. At which level of law enforcement would you prefer to work? Why?
2. Which federal law enforcement agency appeals to you the most with regard to a career in law enforcement? Why?
3. What would be the pros and cons of working for a state law enforcement agency?
4. Which level of law enforcement do you believe poses the most danger for those working in the field? Why?
5. What do you believe would be the most effective way for police departments to generate a very large pool of candidates as part of their hiring practices?

Critical Thinking Exercise

Assume you've been tasked with centralizing all law enforcement agencies in the United States. This entails no longer having agencies at different levels. Instead, there would be one, centralized law enforcement group. Describe how you would generally organize this agency and identify the primary positions and their associated responsibilities.

For Further Examination

Basham, S.L. (2020). Campus law enforcement: The relationship between emergency preparedness and community policing. *Policing: An International Journal, 43*(5), 741–753.

Bumgarner, J., Crawford, C., & Burns, R. (2018). *Federal law enforcement: A primer.* Carolina Academic Press.

Diaz, V.M., & Nuño, L.E. (2021). Women and policing: An assessment of factors related to the likelihood of pursuing a career as a police officer. *Police Quarterly, 24*(4), 465–485.

Li, Y., Luo, F., Carey, M.T., & Brown, B. (2021). The desirability of law enforcement careers among college students in a Hispanic community. *Journal of Criminal Justice Education, 32*(2), 234–251.

Wood, M. (2017). Making and breaking careers: Reviewing law enforcement hiring requirements and disqualifiers. *Journal of Criminal Justice Education, 28*(4), 580–597.

References

Ackerman, T.A. (2006). *Federal law enforcement careers* (2nd ed.). Jist Works.

Brooks, C. (2022). *Federal law enforcement officers, 2020 – Statistical tables.* U.S. Department of Justice, Bureau of Justice Statistics. NCJ 304752.

Buehler, E.D. (2021). *State and local law enforcement training academies, 2018 –Statistical tables.* U.S. Department of Justice, Bureau of Justice Statistics. NCJ 255915.

Burcher, M., & Whelan, C. (2018). Intelligence-led policing in practices: Reflections from intelligence analysts. *Police Quarterly, 22*(2), 139–160.

Burns, R.G. (2022). *Criminal justice: The system in perspective.* Oxford.

Clinkinbeard, S.S., Solomon, S.J., & Rief, R.M. (2021). Why did you become a police officer? Entry-related motives and concerns of women and men in policing. *Criminal Justice and Behavior, 48*(6), 715–733.

Collica-Cox, K., & Furst, G. (2019). It's not the CSI effect: Criminal justice students' choice of major and career goals. *International Journal of Offender Therapy and Comparative Criminology, 63*(11), 2069–2099.

Gardner, A.M., & Scott, K.M. (2022). *Census of state and local law enforcement agencies, 2018 – statistical tables.* U.S. Department of Justice, Bureau of Justice Statistics. NCJ 302187.

Guffey, J.E., Larson, J.G., Zimmerman, L., & Shook, B. (2007). The development of a Thurstone scale for identifying desirable police officer traits. *Journal of Police and Criminal Psychology, 22*, 1–9.

Howard, K.A.S., Carlstrom, A.H., Katz, A.D., Chew, A.Y., Ray, G.C., Laine, L., & Caulum, D. (2011). Career aspirations of youth: Untangling race/ethnicity, SES, and gender. *Journal of Vocational Behavior, 79*(1), 98–109.

Hyland, S. (2018). *Full-time employees in law enforcement agencies, 1997–2016.* U.S. Department of Justice, Bureau of Justice Statistics. NCJ 251762.

Johnson, D. (1981). *American law enforcement: A history.* Forum Press.

Mijares, T. C. (2018). *Careers for the criminal justice major.* Charles C. Thomas.

Reaves, B.A. (2012). *Hiring and retention of state and local law enforcement officers, 2009—statistical tables.* U.S. Department of Justice, Bureau of Justice Statistics. NCJ 238251.

Stringer, E.C., & Murphy, J. (2020). Major decisions and career attractiveness among criminal justice students. *Journal of Criminal Justice Education, 31*(4), 523–541.

Yu, H.H. (2018). Gender and public agency hiring: An exploratory analysis of recruitment practices in federal law enforcement. *Public Personnel Management, 47*(3), 247–264.

Chapter 10

Working in the Courts

Courtrooms can be very exciting places in which to work. The drama, opportunities to help others and secure justice, and general unpredictability associated with courtroom proceedings make courts very unique places. Such uniqueness attracts individuals toward the variety of careers in the court system.

Many of us are familiar with courtrooms via media and popular culture images. Most, if not all, of us have seen the courtroom dramas in which the skillful prosecutor outwits the defense attorney or vice versa. We may have seen judges impose unusually harsh sentences upon guilty persons, and juries provide the surprising verdict of either guilty or not guilty. In light of these images, have you ever considered what it would be like to work in a courtroom? Have you considered what being a judge or an attorney would encompass? Have you thought about what is involved with the many other positions in courtrooms?

Many in society restrict their images of courtroom actors to include only judges, defense attorneys, and prosecutors. There are, of course, various other positions in the courts, as discussed in this chapter. This chapter begins with an overview of the organization of the United States' court system, which helps place career opportunities into context. This is followed by coverage of the positions that work toward ensuring smooth and efficient courtroom practices. Those positions include judges, attorneys, court reporters, clerks of court, court administrators, bailiffs, and paralegals. As a primary component of the criminal justice system (along with law enforcement and corrections), courts provide many diverse and rewarding opportunities for those who seek employment in criminal justice.

Organization of Courts

The organization of US courts can be somewhat confusing to describe and understand. At the most basic level, the United States has a dual court system consisting of state and federal courts. Violations of federal laws are processed in federal courts, while violations of state laws are addressed in state courts. Courts can be further categorized according to hierarchical jurisdiction, or whether they are trial or appellate courts. Court structure is also based on subject matter jurisdiction, for instance, as trial courts of limited jurisdiction hear only a limited category of cases (e.g., misdemeanors, traffic offenses, and so on), while trial courts of general jurisdiction hear all other cases (e.g., felonies). Courts are also bound by geographical jurisdiction, as they typically do not have the power to try a person accused of committing a crime in another geographical jurisdiction.

Perhaps the most effective way to describe the organization of US courts is to examine the various types of courts at both the state and federal levels. Discussion of the organization of federal courts is simplified by the fact that there is only one federal court system. Describing the organization of state courts becomes somewhat clouded by the variations that exist among states.

DOI: 10.4324/9781003360162-13

The federal court system, as it relates to criminal cases, consists of US Magistrate Court's, US District Court's, US Courts of Appeals, and the US Supreme Court. Magistrate courts are primarily responsible for the preliminary stages of felony cases and hear cases involving minor crimes committed on federal property. The 94 U.S. District Courts spread throughout the United States and its territories (Guam, Puerto Rico, the Virgin Islands, and the Northern Mariana Islands) are presided over by roughly 670 district court judges. These courts are the trial courts for all major violations of federal law.

The US Courts of Appeals are the primary appellate courts at the federal level. The circuit courts at this level are staffed by roughly 179 judges. The US Supreme Court is the highest court in the United States. It has the discretion to select the cases it chooses to hear and does so by reviewing cases that address the more pressing needs and issues in society. The Supreme Court limits the number of cases it hears to about 75–80 per year and hears cases that originate at both the federal and state levels.

There are many more employment opportunities available in the state courts compared to federal courts, as there are more courts and more cases heard in the states. State-level courts can generally be categorized into the following categories: Trial courts of limited jurisdiction, trial courts of general jurisdiction, intermediate courts of appeal, and courts of last resort (or state supreme courts).

Trial courts of limited jurisdiction, or lower courts, are the busiest of all the courts. They primarily handle preliminary stages of felony cases and address misdemeanor, small claims, and traffic cases. These courts often face multiple obstacles, not the least of which includes inadequate funding, insufficient facilities, and large caseloads.

Trial courts of general jurisdiction, also known as major trial courts, district courts, circuit courts, and superior courts, have legal authority to address the more serious crimes and cases not particularly delegated to the trial courts of limited jurisdiction. The legal authority granted to these courts is determined by law.

Intermediate courts of appeal exist in 42 of the 50 states. The eight states without this intermediate level of appeals are less populated and encounter a smaller number of appeals than their counterparts. Intermediate courts of appeals handle appeals that originate in the trial courts. The state courts of last resort (or state supreme courts) are the highest level courts in the state system. Defendants in the courts are provided the right to one appeal, after which all other appeals are at the discretion of the next highest appellate court. Thus, state supreme courts in states with no intermediate courts of appeal have no discretion to determine which cases they will hear, while those in states with the intermediate level have a discretionary docket. Regardless of the inconsistencies in the court structure, both appellate and trial courts exist in many places, employ many people, and provide very rewarding career opportunities.

Examining the structure and organization of both the state and federal court systems highlights the wide array and large number of employment opportunities available to those with an interest in the field. Each courtroom is filled with various professionals performing a variety of tasks. The level of danger in courts is much lower than it is in law enforcement and corrections, which makes it a more appealing career choice for some people. Further, the specialization and variety of positions found in the courts encourage some to seek careers in this area.

The Courtroom Actors

One of the more interesting aspects of our court system is the interconnectedness of various groups performing different functions. For instance, consider a typical courtroom prepared for a trial. Each individual working in the room has specific, yet differing responsibilities.

Courtrooms are symbolic of society's concern for justice and are the work setting for various individuals who share similar goals.
Source: www.pexels.com/photo/interior-design-of-a-courtroom-5346823/

The end result of this cooperative effort is intended to be justice. The network of ongoing relationships that exist in the courts largely influences the nature of justice and is referred to as the courtroom workgroup (Eisenstein & Jacob, 1977). The cooperation found in the courts is characterized by a series of factors, including mutual independence (e.g., individuals working independently toward justice), shared decision-making among the participants, shared perceptions of crimes and individuals caught up in the system, and sanctioning for those who fail to subscribe to the expectations of the courtroom workgroup. There is much familiarity among the primary actors in the courtroom, which provides for efficiency but could distort justice, for instance, when favors or friendships impact attorney or judicial practices.

Among the primary groups of individuals who work in the courts are prosecutors, judges, bailiffs, court reporters, court administrators, defense attorneys, clerks, translators, and administrators. Careers within each of these areas are certainly possible for those with an interest in crime and justice, and, more specifically, law and the courts.

Judges

Judges perform a variety of functions in presiding over the courts. They are symbolic of justice and hold the most responsibility for ensuring that justice is served in courtrooms.

Judges maintain great power and discretion throughout criminal case processing. They may set bail, determine whether or not probable cause exists to continue processing, rule on pretrial motions, accept or deny plea bargain proposals, preside over bench and jury trials, provide instructions to juries, sometimes set punishment, and conduct many other actions necessary for the day-to-day functioning of the courts. Their duties and power are determined by the jurisdictional levels of the courts over which they preside, meaning that not all judgeships are alike. For example, judges who preside over state courts of limited jurisdiction have heavier caseloads and administrative responsibilities than judges who preside over state supreme courts.

Magistrate judges are used in a similar manner in both state and federal courts. The term "magistrate" refers to different kinds of judges, such as justices of the peace. These court officials typically have limited powers and preside over minor offense and pretrial hearings. They ease the workload for judges, who generally have more legal power than magistrates. States vary in their use of magistrates.

Judgeships are prestigious and command respect, as evidenced in the gown that they wear, their use of a gavel to bring the court to order, the requirement that everyone rise when the judge enters the courtroom, and the elevation of the judge's bench over the rest of the courtroom (Burns, 2022). It is a highly respected position that typically requires much experience in the courtroom.

The work environment of judges largely consists of offices and courtrooms. They typically work 40-hour weeks and spend much time preparing for and hearing cases. A well-rounded education is essential for judgeships, primarily because judges preside over cases addressing every aspect of society. A law degree is required to be a judge in the large majority of jurisdictions.

Federal judges are nominated by the president and must be confirmed by the Senate. It is a lifetime appointment. State court judges are selected via several means. Particularly, some states hold partisan elections while other states use nonpartisan elections to select judges. Judges in some other states are appointed by either gubernatorial or legislative appointment, or the states may use a combination of election and appointment. Judges are generally required to have previously been lawyers, although most states allow nonlawyers to preside as judges in limited instances.

In 2020, there were just under 45,000 judge and hearing officer positions in the United States. The anticipated job growth for judgeships between 2020 and 2030 is expected to be slower-than-average, or 3% (Bureau of Labor Statistics, 2022a). Judgeships typically require extensive experience in the legal arena; thus, anyone considering a career as a judge should expect to first work in the courts as a prosecutor or defense attorney.

Prosecutors

Prosecutors, also referred to as district attorneys or assistant district attorneys, are officials who represent the government in legal proceedings, including criminal cases. They perform important roles with regard to the functioning of the criminal justice system and, more generally, society due to their extensive involvement throughout criminal case processing. For instance, prosecutors influence police practices by communicating with police officers regarding the amount of evidence required to proceed with prosecution. Although many in society associate prosecutors solely with trying cases, prosecutors represent the government throughout all courtroom proceedings, including the initial appearance, bail decisions, charging, the preliminary hearing, grand jury hearings, arraignments, discovery, plea bargaining, sentencing, and appeals.

Prosecutors maintain broad discretion throughout the adjudication process. Among the key decisions made by prosecutors are determining:

- whether or not to file charges,
- what charges to file,
- whether or not to proceed with a case,
- whether or not to engage in plea bargaining,
- what to offer during plea negotiations,
- the approach taken during trial, and
- what sentencing recommendations they should propose.

They are also active in all appellate hearings. Given their extensive role throughout criminal case processing, prosecutors are influential sources of input regarding criminal justice policy.

The US Department of Justice, headed by the US Attorney General, prosecutes cases in federal court. US Attorneys are the main litigators in federal court. The 93 US Attorneys represent different districts throughout the United States and its territories and are assisted by over 5,400 Assistant US Attorneys. A state attorney general exists in each state to serve as the primary legal officer. They provide legal advice and oversight to attorneys in their state and represent the state in legal matters. Prosecution in state court is provided at the state, county, and local levels, with district attorneys and assistant district attorneys handling the cases.

Prosecutors reflect "the knight in shining armor" standing up for justice and representing the general public. They spend much time in the courtroom or their office, either preparing cases or actively prosecuting them. A law degree and successful completion of the state bar exam are required to become a prosecutor.

A Practitioner's View

Sharen Wilson, Criminal District Attorney, Tarrant County

When I began my career as a Tarrant County prosecutor in 1981, I was one of only three female attorneys in the office. Fast forward to 2015 and Tarrant County is the 15th largest county in the nation and I am elected the first female Criminal District Attorney to serve my county. Today, I am one of 90 female attorneys in the office.

Through all the changes in society and law during my over 40 years in this profession – population growth, diversity in the workforce, technological advancements, and evidence analysis to name a few, one thing has remained the same. Seeking justice. Justice for the victim, justice for the accused, and justice for the community. Criminal justice should never depend on gender, race, education, income level, or any of the other attributes that make us unique. Instead, the criminal justice system should only focus on individual conduct and where appropriate, consequences for conduct.

Being a prosecutor, either an assistant or the elected, requires being a lawyer. While law books prepare you as an attorney, real life prepares you for trial and for being able to analyze the conduct of others. Every life experience can give you a glimpse into what people do and think and others' reaction to them. Those experiences help you evaluate conduct but also evaluate potential jurors. Paying attention to how persons not employed in the criminal justice system view and process a crime will prepare you for your first voir dire. You may realize that what is justice in your eyes may not be justice in the eyes of another.

Defense Attorneys

Defense attorneys are viewed by many in society as "representing the guilty." To some extent, this statement is true, as many who enter the criminal justice system are indeed guilty of the crimes for which they are arrested and charged. However, not everyone who enters the system is guilty, and even those who are guilty are entitled to adequate representation and fair treatment throughout the adjudication process. The task of ensuring that the defendant's interests are appropriately recognized by the courts is left to defense attorneys.

A small percentage of defendants represent themselves in court, in what is known as *pro se* legal representation. The very large majority of defendants are represented by a defense attorney. Some defendants hire their own attorney, while others use defense counsel provided by the government. Private counsel is retained by those with the financial means to do so. Most individuals who enter the criminal justice system, however, do not possess the means to secure private counsel and are provided representation by the court, or what is known as indigent representation. The requirement that representation be provided to defendants who cannot afford an attorney is grounded in the Sixth Amendment and was largely impacted by the US Supreme Court's decision in *Gideon v. Wainwright* (1963).

Indigent defense is provided primarily in three ways: public defenders, assigned counsel, and contract systems. Public defenders are salaried attorneys who work in offices solely designed to provide legal representation for indigent defendants. They represent the majority of indigent cases, followed by assigned counsel attorneys and contract attorneys. Assigned counsel systems involve the use of private attorneys who are appointed by judges on a case-by-case basis to represent defendants who cannot afford private counsel. Contract systems involve individuals or groups (e.g., law firms, nonprofit groups) providing indigent representation in a jurisdiction according to a contract they sign with the court. Assigned counsel and contract systems primarily involve individuals who provide indigent representation in addition to providing other legal services, while public defenders solely represent indigent defendants.

The extensive workload of public defenders' offices provides many challenges. A lack of state-provided resources and the general under-appreciation of public defenders by the public, the courts, and defendants are primary obstacles for some public defenders (e.g., Jaffe, 2018). Public defenders' offices are typically located in large cities given the disproportionate number of crimes that occur in these areas, and the higher levels of poverty (indigency). Among the positions found in public defenders' offices are the chief public defender, assistant public defenders, supervisory attorneys, managers, investigators, social workers, paralegals, indigency screeners, and administrative support staff. Each plays important roles in ensuring that defendants' Sixth Amendment rights are protected.

Defense attorneys face other struggles besides large caseloads and limited resources. For instance, their clients (defendants) may not believe their counsel is adequately representing them, and defense attorneys generally lack the power maintained by judges and prosecutors (Neubauer & Fradella, 2019). Further, they are dependent on the actions of prosecutors and judges in the courtroom (Cole et al., 2004), for instance, as judges oversee court hearings, and prosecutors present cases. The job, however, can be very rewarding. Defense attorneys are positioned to help people in a time of need and provide much counselling for their clients. Such counseling may involve guidance on the forthcoming steps in their case, plea bargaining, expected outcomes, and the orientations of the prosecution and judge.

Both defense attorneys and prosecutors are actively involved in research and report writing with the goal of substantiating a particular point or position. Much of their work is done in an office with the assistance of paralegals and legal research tools. Trial court attorneys spend more time than their counterparts in the courtroom.

Many attorneys are generalists in their approach to the law; however, there are many lawyers who specialize in a particular area of the law. For instance, coverage of attorneys in this chapter has focused on criminal attorneys; however, there are many attorneys who specialize in international law, environmental law, civil law, family law, business law, and other areas. All lawyers must pass the bar exam in the state in which they wish to practice law. Candidates must graduate from a law school approved by the American Bar Association or the state authorities to qualify for taking the bar exam. Bar exams are tests administered by bar associations that must be passed in order for attorneys to practice law in the jurisdiction. For instance, the New York Board of Bar Examiners administers the New York State Bar Exam, which is offered twice each year.

Graduation from a law school is a primary step in becoming an attorney. Generally, students seeking to attend law school are required to take the Law School Admission Test, similar to the general need to take the Scholastic Aptitude Test or American College Testing exam for consideration to undergraduate studies. Completion of law school requirements typically takes three years and results in a Juris Doctorate. This is followed by taking the bar exam in the jurisdiction where one wishes to practice law.

There were an estimated 804,200 lawyers in the United States in 2020, and continued growth is anticipated in the field. It is expected that there will be an additional 71,500 lawyers by 2030, a 9% increase. This level of anticipated increase is about average compared to all other occupations (Bureau of Labor Statistics, 2022b).

Court Reporters

Court reporters, or stenographers, document the courtroom proceedings. Their work results in a written transcript of courtroom actions, which is critical for judicial proceedings, for instance, as judges can revisit earlier portions of a trial for clarification. Further, the transcript created in trial courts is used in appellate courts to revisit areas or issues at the center of an appeal. Proceedings in appellate courts primarily involve judicial consideration of the transcript and oral arguments by attorneys. Appellate courts do not conduct retrials of cases.

Court reporting is conducted in several ways. Most commonly, reporters use a stenotype machine to document all statements made in courtroom proceedings. The machine enables reporters to use shorthand to document what occurred. The information entered into the stenotype machine is decoded and often provided on the screen of a television or a computer monitor. Reporters also use electronic reporting, which involves the use of audio equipment to record the proceedings. While taping the proceedings, the reporter documents who is speaking and ensures clarity in the recording. Reporters or transcribers are typically responsible for creating a written transcript of the proceedings. Voice writing is the third method of court reporting. This method involves a court reporter speaking directly into a voice silencer, which is a mask with a microphone. The reporter repeats the testimony into the recorder, although the mask prevents the others in the courtroom from hearing the reporter's voice. A written transcript is then prepared from the recording.

Court reporters typically work in comfortable settings, including courthouses, attorney's offices, or perhaps from home. Speed, accuracy, listening skills, command of the English language, and excellent hearing ability are necessary for court reporters. Hours of sitting in a courtroom can be tiring, and wrist, back, neck, and/or eye strain can be problematic. Further, the pressure of keeping pace with the proceedings can be stressful. Court reporters typically work a 40-hour week. The extent of training required to become a court reporter varies by the type of reporting. For instance, it typically takes less than a year to become a novice voice writer; however, it requires at least two years for one to become proficient at real-time voice writing. Training is provided by various vocational/technical schools and colleges. The National Court Reporters Association (NCRA) provides information, guidance, and support for members and the public in matters pertaining to court reporters.

Certification assists reporters in obtaining jobs and advancing in their careers. The NCRA, the United States Court Reporters Association, and the American Association of Electronic Reporters and Transcribers are among those that provide certification. Some states require voice writers to pass a test in order to earn State licensure. Many states require reporters to be notary publics.

The US Bureau of Labor Statistics (BLS) does not provide anticipated growth data for court reporters alone. Instead, it combines the position with simultaneous captioners, who provide similar services, although not in a courtroom. Captioners may provide transcriptions for television or meetings to assist those who are hard of hearing or deaf. The BLS reported that the job outlook for court reporters and simultaneous captioners is projected to grow at a slower-than-average rate; 3% from 2020 to 2030 (Bureau of Labor Statistics, 2022c). This projection should not discourage one from seeking a career in the field, as courts across the United States and afar will continue to rely on the valuable services of court reporters.

Clerks of Court

Clerks of court are considered the record keepers of the court and are significant contributors to the day-to-day functioning of courtrooms. Sometimes referred to as "register of probate," "clerk," or "prothonotary," clerks of court play a vital role in the administration of courtrooms. They are involved in docketing court cases, collecting fees, administering jury selection, swearing in witnesses, marking evidence, and maintaining custody of evidence and court records. Clerks in some states are permitted limited judicial duties, including issuing warrants. In general jurisdiction courts, they are elected to their position in 27 states and appointed or hired in 18 others. Other states use a combination of approaches (Raftery, 2021). Clerks operate semiautonomously from judges and act as the nonjudicial manager of the courts. They engage in a variety of administrative tasks.

Court clerks may be required to have a law degree or significant administrative experience. The size of a court and the degree of responsibility largely dictate qualifications. Federal courts require court clerks to have extensive training and a master's or law degree. State courts, particularly the smaller ones, may be willing to employ individuals with lower levels of education; however, they prefer a bachelor's degree. Clerks should be familiar with accounting, budgeting, personnel issues, and word processing. Those interested in becoming a clerk of court can hone their administrative skills at local vocational schools and/or by working in other positions within the courts to gain firsthand experience.

Court Administrators

The responsibilities of court administrators are similar, yet different from clerks of court. They both provide services to ensure the smooth functioning of courtroom activities; however, court administrators generally address "big picture" responsibilities (e.g., budgeting), while clerks of court are more directly involved in courtroom proceedings. In smaller jurisdictions, the positions and responsibilities may be merged.

Court administrators perform a variety of tasks that contribute to the efficient operation of courtrooms. They ensure that cases are processed efficiently and timely and perform many tasks earlier performed by judges, clerks of court, and prosecutors. Their responsibilities generally involve scheduling of hearings and cases, maintaining court records, budgeting, planning space utilization, and managing courtroom personnel (Burns, 2022). Some court administrator positions require a bachelor's or master's degree; the minimum requirements vary by jurisdiction and responsibilities. Some courts may require professional certification.

Bailiffs

In June 2022, a court officer (bailiff) was bitten on the hand by a man who was entering court for the first day of his trial. The bailiff was attempting to remove a piece of jewelry from the defendant when he was assaulted. The defendant, who also struck the bailiff in the head and continued to attack him as he sought to escape, was found guilty of killing two police officers and charged for the attack on the bailiff (Dawson, 2022). This incident highlights the potential dangers associated with courts and the important contributions of bailiffs.

Bailiffs, also termed "marshals" or "court officers," provide a law enforcement presence in the courtroom and help maintain safety and order in the courts. Their duties vary by location, but generally include enforcing courtroom rules and regulations, assisting judges, protecting jurors from outside contact including the media, delivering court documents, announcing the judge's entry into the courtroom, preventing defendants from escaping, and providing security for courthouses (Burns, 2022).

Bailiffs are required to have a high school degree, although it is preferred and sometimes required in some locales that bailiffs have a college education. Applicants for a bailiff's position will likely be required to pass a written and oral exam and will be evaluated based upon their ability to use good judgment, courtesy, and tact. Experience working with the public or in a courtroom or court administrator's office is helpful, given that bailiffs regularly interact with attorneys, witnesses, defendants, jurors, and others. Most bailiffs are sworn law enforcement officers, although it is possible to be a bailiff yet not a sworn officer.

Bailiff services are typically provided by the sheriff's departments or some other law enforcement agency in local jurisdictions, although some local bailiffs are nonsworn, unarmed personnel. The US Marshals Service provides security in federal courts, and the US Supreme Court Police provides law enforcement services for Supreme Court Justices and the Supreme Court building. Accordingly, the job requirements for becoming a bailiff generally fall under being a law enforcement officer.

Paralegals

Paralegals, also known as legal assistants, perform administrative and clerical tasks for lawyers. Among other duties, they complete administrative and clerical duties for attorneys, prepare and research cases, research laws, investigate facts related to cases, collect and create legal documents, and interview witnesses and defendants (National Association of Legal Assistants, 2017). Essentially, paralegals are legal assistants who help attorneys prepare for cases, although they do not represent clients in court.

Paralegals have become increasingly vital to the day-to-day functioning of the courts since they first appeared in the mid-1960s. In 2021, there were an estimated 345,600 jobs as paralegals and legal assistants in the United States, with positions largely located in traditional law offices, corporate legal offices, and government and public agencies (Bureau of Labor Statistics, 2022d).

Colleges and paralegal training institutions provide specific training for becoming a paralegal. The roughly 650 paralegal education programs in the United States are offered in a variety of formats and lengths. Among the more common types of programs are those offered at community and some four-year colleges, and certificate programs (which are typically designed for individuals who already have a college/university degree) (National Federation of Paralegal Associations, 2022). Some paralegals are trained on the job.

Those interested in a career as a paralegal should acquire knowledge regarding legal forms, procedures, and terminology. They should be able to write clearly and professionally. Effective verbal skills and the ability to work effectively with others are also important for a career in this area. Paralegals require considerably less schooling than a law degree and sometimes pay very well. They can specialize in different areas of law, including criminal, corporate, or family law. Strong research and organizational skills and attention to detail are necessary to be an effective paralegal.

Others Who Work in the Courts

This chapter does not include a comprehensive account of individuals working in the courts. The positions highlighted above constitute the more commonly known or prominent positions within the courts, although there are others who are closely involved with court proceedings. Among the employment positions associated with the courts not discussed above are:

- Court liaison counselors, who, among other tasks, assist and counsel defendants charged with crimes, evaluate and initiate treatment plans, and make referrals to support agencies.
- Court representatives, who, among other responsibilities, review court papers and ascertain whether those convicted of breaking the law are eligible for alternatives to detention sentences.
- Release-on-own recognizance interviewers, who gather information on defendants who may receive pretrial release and make release recommendations to judges.
- Pretrial services officers, who advise the courts on pretrial detention and release, release condition supervision, monitoring, pretrial diversion, and public safety.

One could also work in the courts by providing counsel to victims. For instance, domestic violence counselors assist and counsel victims of domestic abuse. More generally, victim services personnel provide assistance and counseling to victims of a broader scope of crimes. Chapter 13 more closely examines careers in victim services.

Summary

It is fair to state that the future appears quite positive with regard to many careers in the courts. For instance, annual government expenditures on judicial and legal functions increased from an estimated $41 billion in 1997 to $66 billion in 2017 in the United States. The total number of full-time judicial and legal employees increased by 21% during the same time (Buehler, 2021). Put simply, there are many different careers for those interested in working in the courts.

There is a reason why television and big-screen courtroom dramas are notably popular with the general public. The high levels of unpredictability, significant consequences, interesting content, and uncertainty associated with the courts create and perpetuate public interest in the legal arena. The same factors often attract individuals to seek careers in the courts.

Many students who consider a career in the courts limit their options to being a lawyer or a judge. While these are certainly viable options, there are many other positions for consideration. Accordingly, this chapter highlighted the nature of the work associated with the more traditional career opportunities in the courtroom while identifying and commenting on the less familiar career opportunities in the legal arena. Judges, attorneys, court reporters, clerks of court, court administrators, bailiffs, and others serve significant yet distinct roles in the courts. Their collective efforts are necessary for justice to occur.

Discussion Questions

1. Which position within the courts is most appealing to you? Which is least appealing? Why?
2. What are the responsibilities of judges and attorneys in the courtroom?
3. What contributions do courtroom personnel other than judges and attorneys provide to the court?
4. How are the general functions of lawyers and judges different from law enforcement officers? Discuss how these courtroom personnel and law enforcement are dependent on each other to help secure justice.
5. What would be the most difficult aspect of being a defense attorney? What would be most difficult about being a prosecutor?

Critical Thinking Exercise

Attend a court hearing or watch one online. Notice and record the actions of the various members of the courtroom workgroup. Do they often interact with others in the courtroom? Is discretion a large part of their job? Who does most of the communicating/interacting with others? Are your observations reflective of what you initially believed were the functions and roles of those who work in the courts?

For Further Examination

Baćak V., Lageson S.E., & Powell K. (2020). "Fighting the good fight": Why do public defenders remain on the job? *Criminal Justice Policy Review, 31*(6), 939–961.
Hricik, D. (2021). *Law school basics: A preview of law school and legal reasoning.* Nova Press.
Neubauer, D., & Fradella, H.F. (2019). *America's courts and the criminal justice system* (13th ed.). Cengage.
Ryan, C. (2021). Paying for law school: Law student loan indebtedness and career choices. *University of Illinois Law Review, 1,* 97–138.
Webster, E. (2020). The prosecutor as final safeguard against false convictions: How prosecutors assist with exoneration. *Journal of Criminal Law and Criminology, 110*(2), 245–306.

References

Buehler, E.D. (2021). *Justice expenditures and employment in the United States, 2017.* U.S. Department of Justice, Bureau of Justice Statistics. NCJ 256093.
Bureau of Labor Statistics. (2022a). *Occupational outlook handbook, judges and hearing officers.* U.S. Department of Labor. Available at: www.bls.gov/ooh/legal/judges-and-hearing-officers.htm
Bureau of Labor Statistics. (2022b). *Occupational outlook handbook, lawyers.* U.S. Department of Labor. Available at: www.bls.gov/ooh/legal/lawyers.htm
Bureau of Labor Statistics. (2022c). *Occupational outlook handbook, court reporters and simultaneous captioners.* U.S. Department of Labor. Available at: www.bls.gov/ooh/legal/court-reporters.htm
Bureau of Labor Statistics. (2022d). *Occupational outlook handbook, paralegals and legal assistants,* U.S. Department of Labor. Available at: www.bls.gov/ooh/legal/paralegals-and-legal-assistants.htm
Burns, R.G. (2022). *Criminal justice: The system in perspective.* Oxford University Press.
Cole, G.F., Gertz, M.G., & Bunger, A. (2004). *The criminal justice system: Politics and policies* (9th ed.). Wadsworth.

Dawson, D. (2022, June 16). The man convicted of shooting officers in Delafield has been charged with biting the bailiff. *Milwaukee Journal Sentinel*. Available at: www.jsonline.com/story/communities/lake-country/2022/06/16/man-convicted-shooting-officerscharged-biting-bailiff/7647924001/

Eisenstein, J., & Jacob, H. (1977). *Felony justice: An organizational analysis of criminal courts*. Little, Brown and Company.

Gideon v. Wainwright. (1963). 372 U.S. 335.

Jaffe, S. (2018). "It's not you, it's your caseload": Using *Cronic* to solve indigent defense underfunding. *Michigan Law Review*, *116*(8), 1465–1484.

National Association of Legal Assistants. (2017). *What do paralegals do?* Available at: www.nala.org/about-paralegals/what-do-paralegals-do

National Federation of Paralegal Associations. (2022). How to choose a paralegal education program. Available at: www.paralegals.org/i4a/pages/index.cfm?pageid=3365

Neubauer, D.W., & Fradella, H.F. (2019). *America's courts and the criminal justice system* (13th ed.). Cengage.

Raftery, B. (2021). *FAQ: How many states elect the clerks of their general jurisdiction courts?* National Center for State Courts. Available at: www.ncsc.org/information-and-resources/trending-topics/trending-topics-landing-pg/faq-how-many-states-elect-the-clerks-of-their-general-jurisdiction-courts

Chapter 11

Careers in Corrections

It is unfortunate that we, as a society, need correctional agencies. Nevertheless, people interested in a career in corrections can find a variety of employment involving a wide array of responsibilities. For instance, one could work in a prison or a jail, as a probation or parole officer, in a reentry center, or in a number of other areas discussed in this chapter. Put simply, careers in corrections can be found in the areas of detention, rehabilitation, and administration. A look at the numbers behind the significant recent developments in corrections helps shed light on employment in the area.

As of yearend 2020, an estimated 5.5 million persons were under the supervision of adult correctional systems in the United States. Roughly one in every 47 adults in the United States was under correctional supervision. About 70% of these people were supervised in the community, with the rest confined in jail or prison (Kluckow & Zeng, 2022). These numbers reflect the decrease in the correctional population that emerged in the last 10–15 years, yet it remains that many people in the United States are under some form of correctional supervision. With such a large correctional population comes an assortment of career opportunities.

The imprisonment surge in the United States beginning in the 1980s resulted in an expansion of the correctional workforce. The surge was not restricted to incarceration, as the number of people undergoing community supervision increased substantially as well. There was a demonstrated need to hire for many positions, including both entry level and supervisory. The recent decreases in the correctional population show signs that the expansion has ceased, yet the United States still has a particularly large correctional population, including the highest prison population rate in the world (World Prison Brief, n.d.). This chapter addresses the nature of working in corrections, followed by examination of career opportunities in both institutional and community corrections. Employment positions within corrections may not be as glamorous or safe as many other positions in criminal justice; however, they can be particularly rewarding and the contributions of corrections workers have significant impacts on crime and justice.

The Nature of Working in Corrections

The overall organization of corrections in the United States is difficult to grasp given the wide array of approaches and organizational designs used by the 50 states and the federal government. State correctional systems oversee far more individuals than the federal system, as most crimes are prosecuted at the state level. The organization of corrections also differs by type of services provided and state approaches to corrections.

Discussion of the organization of corrections at the federal level is simplified by the fact that there's only one system of federal corrections. The Federal Bureau of Prisons (BOP) was established in 1930 and has grown from 11 federal prisons to 122 institutions, 6 regional offices,

DOI: 10.4324/9781003360162-14

a headquarters, 2 staff training centers, and 22 residential reentry management offices (Federal Bureau of Prisons, n.d.). The Bureau is responsible for the custody of roughly 157,000 persons in the federal system, including roughly 138,400 individuals in BOP custody, 4,300 in private prisons, and 14,200 in other types of facilities, such as reentry centers (Federal Bureau of Prisons, 2022). The US Probation and Pretrial Services System is responsible for assisting the federal courts with pretrial practices and supervising individuals in the community. The agency also supervises individuals released early from federal prisons.

Describing the organization of state corrections is a bit more complex compared to the federal level primarily because the 50 states use various organizational designs. Simply, institutional corrections primarily consist of prisons and jails. Prisons are correctional facilities that typically hold individuals sentenced to a year or more incarceration. They are administered by the executive branch of each state's government. Jails typically house individuals who have been sentenced to incarceration for less than a year of incarceration or are awaiting trial. Jails are often operated by county-level officials, primarily sheriff's departments.

Probation and parole, also known as community supervision, are the two primary forms of community corrections. The administration of probation varies by state, for instance, as probation can be centralized or decentralized, administered by the judiciary or executive branch, and combined with parole services.

Further clouding the issue of community corrections is the various methods by which community supervision is administered. For instance, probation is administered in various forms, as some individuals may be supervised via electronic monitoring, required to report to a day reporting center, or under intensive supervision probation. The variation adds to some confusion and uncertainty regarding career opportunities in community corrections.

Parole may or may not work in conjunction with probation services and is granted by state parole boards. Parole boards consist of qualified individuals who assess an incarcerated person's suitability for reentry to society, or what is known as discretionary release. Parole boards are generally organized either inside a department of corrections or as an independent agency. There is wide variation among the functions, selection, and responsibilities of parole board members in general. Parole board members are appointed by the state governor in most states that use them.

In some states parole board members serve on a part-time basis; however, most states utilize full-time parole board members. Further, some states require parole board members to have a criminal justice or other social science background, while other states have no statutory qualifications for appointment to parole boards. Membership on a parole board assumedly requires that one can discern whether or not someone seeking parole is prepared for reentry. Not all states use parole boards. Some states use mandatory release instead of discretionary release to determine if and when an individual is to be released early. Mandatory release is based on incarcerated persons earning "good time" credits that reduce the length of their sentence. These inconsistencies regarding parole boards highlight the complexity of the organization of corrections.

Working within corrections, regardless of the area in which one is employed, is attractive for several reasons. For instance, working with individuals convicted of crimes provides excellent opportunities for helping others and protecting society. The high concentration of troubled individuals within correctional systems provides an ideal setting for those seeking a career in which they can assist others and ensure that potentially dangerous individuals cannot harm others. Consider the role of community supervision officers, for example. Primary among their responsibilities are to ensure that individuals abide by the terms of their supervision agreement (which helps provides safety in society), and assisting them in various capacities (for instance, in locating housing, which reflects the helping component). It can be a thankless job, as some may find faults when you help and others may criticize when you enforce the regulations. Nevertheless, community supervision officers provide a much needed service in our communities (Benedictus, 2010).

As stated, corrections agencies provide a variety of positions and areas for employment. For instance, one can work as a prison officer, a counselor, an education specialist, a probation officer, or in an assortment of other areas, many of which are discussed in this chapter. The variety of positions found throughout correctional systems is certainly an attraction to the field. Job security, good benefits, and opportunities to help others and protect society are often associated with many positions within corrections (Thelen, 2009). These and other aspects of the work, such as the opportunities for growth and promotion, are other reasons why some individuals choose a career in corrections.

The correctional workforce relatively recently underwent several changes. Among those changes are the increased use of private prisons, the increased incorporation of technology, enhanced and more strongly enforced external standards regarding correctional facilities, and shifts in the demographics of the correctional workforce. With regard to the latter, increases in the numbers of females and members of racial and ethnic minority groups working in correctional agencies have diversified and improved the field. Each development changed and continues to change employment opportunities within corrections.

Working with persons under correctional supervision can be challenging, and not everyone is suited for a career in corrections. For example, among the challenges associated with employment in institutional corrections are meeting public expectations, the demands of the correctional environment, the cultural influences of the outside world, and addressing the responsibilities expected of each position. Situated within these challenges are dealing with the needs of addressing differing cultural values and expectations (particularly as they relate to supervisees and supervisors) and upholding the goals, missions, and/or expectations of the correctional agency.

When choosing an area of corrections in which to seek employment, individuals ought to keep in mind the primary goals of criminal sentences: retribution, rehabilitation, incapacitation, and deterrence. Particularly, those seeking a career in corrections ought to consider the goals sought by the agencies they are targeting. For instance, one should seek a career in therapeutic services or an agency that focuses on rehabilitation if he or she is especially interested in helping others.

Similarly, one should consider whether or not they wish to work in the public or private sector. Prominent among the opportunities for working in the private sector are opportunities in private prisons. For instance, about 8.2%, or just over 100,000, of persons incarcerated in prison in the United States were housed in private prisons in 2020 (Carson, 2021). Such reliance on private prisons results in many opportunities for those interested in working in corrections to obtain a position in the private sector. Not all states, however, house the incarcerated in private facilities. Some states rely more heavily on private prisons, and some do not use them at all.

The various functions performed by correctional agencies dictates that anyone interested in a career in the field conduct a thorough investigation of the agencies and areas they are considering for employment. Researching a job enables the candidate to know what the position entails, but also impresses the interviewer(s). Studying the credentials, qualifications, and responsibilities of others in the same or similar position one seeks enables individuals to better prepare for particular positions in corrections.

Individuals interested in a career in corrections can begin their search for information regarding the field, including job/position searches, at the websites of various professional corrections associations. Particularly, the American Probation and Parole Association, American Correctional Association, and the American Jail Association are helpful avenues for those interested in the field. Or, one could visit the websites of corrections departments to learn more about their responsibilities and employment opportunities. For instance, the Florida Department of Corrections website has much helpful information and a link to job openings. A close look at positions within institutional corrections provides more insight with regard to working in jails and prisons.

Positions Within Institutional Corrections

Numerous positions exist within institutional corrections. Some of the challenges associated with institutional corrections stem from the frustrations and stress of incarcerated people having severely restricted freedoms, and the overall discouraging work environment which is perpetuated by the disdain incarcerated persons often have for correctional officers and administrators. Conversely, institutional corrections provide a more structured setting in which workers can closely interact with the incarcerated, and a more structured work environment than community corrections, among other benefits.

Employment opportunities within correctional facilities can be categorized into four areas: management, custodial personnel, program personnel, and industry and agricultural personnel. Similar to all major institutions, prisons maintain personnel tasked with ensuring the day-to-day management operations. Management personnel in correctional institutions are responsible for general housekeeping tasks such as purchasing supplies, overseeing financial records, and budgeting. Managers typically have little contact with incarcerated persons and may work in buildings separate from the primary institution. In contrast, custodial personnel, including correctional officers, work directly with the incarcerated (as discussed later). Program personnel are tasked with promoting participation of the incarcerated in educational, treatment, and vocational programs. Industry and agriculture personnel oversee the functioning of any industrial or agricultural programs an institution may provide.

Corrections officer DJ Culkar of the Michigan Department of Corrections commented on the perception of many individuals regarding a career in corrections. Particularly, he suggested that many students do not consider careers in prison due to their belief that working in a prison is distasteful and "done by people of a different class." Culkar added that many people in society mistakenly believe that careers in corrections, particularly jails and prisons, are low paying, offer few rewards, and are filled by individuals who were found to be unsuitable for a career in law enforcement. He noted that "The stereotype of the corrections officer is of a lower-class, authoritarian male who enjoys tormenting and inflicting pain on others." He added, however, that this image, and many related images pertaining to careers in corrections and law enforcement, are notably far removed from reality (2001, 130). Among the many employment opportunities within institutional corrections are positions as a warden, correctional officer, correctional treatment specialist, prerelease correctional counselor, and correctional education specialist.

Wardens

Wardens are responsible for the overall supervision and administration of correctional facilities. They plan, direct, and coordinate programs, and oversee all rehabilitative, security, disciplinary, and educational programs. They supervise institutional staff and, accordingly, must have strong leadership, administrative, and organizational skills.

Wardens should be adept at delegating responsibility, as many contributors are required to effectively administer a correctional institution. Wardens must work closely with their administration for the purposes of establishing and reviewing institutional policies and regulations, reviewing the records and behavior of incarcerated persons, preparing written reports, gathering and analyzing data and statistics, and evaluating all components of the facility.

Historically, wardens were expected to actively engage in a much wider array of activities than is expected today. Particularly, wardens are much more accountable today than in the past, for instance, as they are expected to regularly report to deputy commissioners for institutions in state departments of corrections. Central correctional offices in many states have resolved wardens of their responsibility to prepare budgets, conduct research, engage in legislative relations, and other tasks. Nevertheless, wardens remain the primary contact between the institution and the outside world, and today's wardens and other top correctional administrators are more familiar with administrative and managerial concepts than in years past.

It is expected that wardens will possess thorough knowledge of correctional programs and the day-to-day functioning of their respective correctional facility. Such knowledge encompasses care of the incarcerated, rehabilitative efforts, and issues pertaining to custody. Wardens are expected to have, among other qualities, many years of experience in corrections and at least a bachelor's degree in criminology, criminal justice, or a related field.

Correctional Officers

Correctional officers are responsible for overseeing those being detained in either jail or prison. Jailers across the United States must deal with constantly changing jail populations, as local jails admit roughly nine million people a year (Minton & Zeng, 2021). Correctional officers are charged with maintaining security and accountability of the incarcerated, primarily through preventing disturbances, assaults, and escapes. They monitor and control the behavior of the incarcerated and must report orally and in writing on their behavior. They cannot show favoritism, and are equipped with communications devices in order to summon assistance as needed. Correctional officers have no law enforcement responsibilities outside of the institution in which they work.

Correctional officers perform their duties in several different areas of an institution. For instance, they may work as:

- Block officers, who work directly with the incarcerated in housing units
- Work detail supervisors, who manage the work details of the incarcerated
- Industrial shop and school officers, who ensure that civilians who provide services within the institution (e.g., teachers, counselors, and trainers) are secure
- Yard officers, who monitor incarcerated persons recreating in the prison yard
- Relief officers, who assist with vacancies in the staff

Correctional officer positions may also involve securing administrative buildings, including the visitors' room and prison gates, and standing post at towers aligned along the prison walls (Clear et al., 2016). Correctional officers face many unique challenges and have particularly important responsibilities.

Correctional officers face particular issues with regard to their work environment. An institution's security level should be of particular interest for those interested in a career as a correctional officer in prison. Maximum security prisons house the most dangerous persons, while minimum security prisons house to the least dangerous. Working in a prison or jail can be very stressful and at times dangerous (e.g., Trounson & Pfeifer, 2016). Among other concerns, correctional officers face the risk of physical confrontations on the job. The stress associated with working with individuals who are sometimes antagonistic toward correctional officers poses a particular concern, although stress emerges from other areas of the job, for instance, from a lack of support from other institutional staff (Walters, 2020). Similar to working in other areas of the criminal justice system, correctional officers must be flexible and maintain the ability to not let their work affect their personal life. To do otherwise would be, at the very least, stressful and mentally unhealthy.

Correctional officers may work indoors or outdoors and typically in a noisy and sometimes disruptive environment. The incarcerated are sometimes housed in older facilities, which is another area of consideration for those interested in working as a correctional officer. Both prisons and jails are more dangerous to work in than most other settings; however, prisons are more secure than jails given the officers' familiarity of the individuals they house. The more transient populations found in jails provide additional levels of risk and uncertainty. Correctional officers typically work eight-hour days, five days a week, and on rotating shifts. Officers may be required to work shifts during all hours of the day, weekends, and holidays.

A high school diploma or graduation equivalency degree is required to work in most state prisons as a correctional officer. The BOP requires entry-level correctional officers to have earned at least a bachelor's degree or three years of related experience.

The recruitment and selection of corrections officers somewhat reflect those of police officers, although they are not as intensive and elaborate. Background checks of job candidates are required, as are various assessments used to determine one's suitability for the job. The areas of evaluation generally involve physical agility, reading comprehension, psychological stability, and report writing. Candidates will undergo oral interviews and drug testing (Schmalleger & Smykla, 2009).

Training standards for correctional officers in general are based on guidelines established by the American Correctional Association and the American Jail Association. The required number of academy training for correctional officer trainees varies by states, although they commonly require between 200 and 299 hours. Correctional officer training academies largely resemble police training academies, although they focus more on the challenges associated with institutionalization. Correctional officer training academies typically provide training with regard to (Burton et al., 2018):

- prison programs and services
- supervising the incarcerated
- security counting procedures
- discipline
- cell and body searches
- using force
- controlling contraband
- firearms
- grievances

At minimum, correctional officers should maintain skills in CPR/first aid, stress management, self-defense, the use of prison tools and equipment, and public relations.

An analysis of statutorily prescribed correctional officer hiring qualifications and training requirements across states found that not all states have statutorily defined hiring and training requirements, and there is inconsistency among the ones that do. Based on the findings, it was suggested that training and hiring expectations should be clear, and vagueness in statutes should be removed; hiring and training requirements should be consistent across states; and correctional officers should be trained with regard to mental illness, ethics, and sexual misconduct (Kowalski, 2020).

Inadequate pay, staff shortages, and the difficulty of the work hamper recruitment and retention efforts with regard to correctional officers (Blakinger et al., 2021) and have contributed to high turnover rates and officer dissatisfaction with the job. Prisons and jails sometimes struggle to find and keep employees, and the global pandemic pertaining to COVID-19 and the related shrinking labor market contributed to additional difficulties in finding enough individuals to staff prisons (Kaeding, 2021). Research focused on career stages and job satisfaction among correctional officers found that satisfaction increased with age. It was also noted that levels of job satisfaction were highest during the entry stage of a correctional officer's career (0–2 years), and lowest in the following stage (2–5 years) (Hogan et al., 2017).

Correctional Treatment Specialists

Correctional treatment specialists, also referred to as case managers, provide counseling for individuals in prison and help prepare them for return to society. Correctional treatment specialists assess program needs of the incarcerated, evaluate their progress, and coordinate and integrate training programs. They provide reports to parole commissions and work with probation and parole officers, as well as incarcerated persons and their families regarding an individual's reentry from institutionalization to society.

Correctional treatment specialists work in prisons, jails, or probation or parole agencies. They evaluate the progress of incarcerated persons, for instance, through the use of questionnaires or psychological evaluations and work with multiple groups and individuals to develop reentry plans. Their reports are considered by parole board members and others tasked with making decisions regarding an individual's release. They typically develop treatment plans and create and implement education and training programs targeted toward the betterment of incarcerated people.

Prerelease Correctional Counselors

Prerelease correctional counselors are particularly helpful with regard to reentry practices. These counselors work with residents of state prison prerelease centers and assist the incarcerated prior to their departure from incarceration. For instance, counselors may accompany soon-to-be released individuals to job interviews and assist them in finding employment. They work within the confines of an institution and must be able to work well with incarcerated people.

Corrections Education Specialists

Roughly 65% of individuals housed in state and federal prisons and jails have not finished high school, and about 14% have less than an eighth-grade education ("Economic Perspectives," 2016). Thus, there is a demonstrated need for educators in prison. Corrections education specialists provide a variety of educational services in institutions, as they teach vocational programs, offer academic counseling, and provide in-service training for corrections employees (Whitehead et al., 2013).

Correctional educators must have a bachelor's degree and be certified to teach. Relevant work and/or teaching experience in one's area of specialization is also often required. In addition, familiarity with a variety of teaching techniques designed to assist individuals with attitudinal, behavioral, and learning difficulties is particularly important in the correctional setting.

Generally, many employment opportunities within correctional institutions can be categorized as either line personnel or staff personnel. Line personnel primarily address institutional goals and are in direct contact with incarcerated persons. Positions in this area include the custody force, counselors, medical technicians, and industry and agricultural supervisors. Staff personnel typically work under a deputy warden for management and provide services in support of the line personnel. Staff personnel include accountants, training officers, purchasing personnel, and others who assist with the daily operations of the institution. Aside from positions in institutional corrections, community corrections provides various career opportunities for individuals who wish to work in corrections.

Positions in Community Corrections

Some individuals are attracted to employment in community corrections by the opportunity work outside of institutions with individuals convicted of crimes. They may, for instance, perceive working with persons confined to an institution as somewhat artificial. It may be the case that incarcerated persons will do or say whatever it takes to be released from incarceration, but their words and actions while incarcerated may not be reflective of their actions once they return to the community. Those released from prison face the true test of their ability to stay crime-free outside of a structured institutional setting. The large majority will be supervised in the community following their release, resulting in employment positions providing community supervision. Community supervision officers oversee individuals in the less-controlled setting outside of institutional walls, ensuring that supervisees abide by the terms of their agreement. Among the more prominent positions within community corrections are probation and parole officers, pretrial services officers, and reentry center managers.

A Practitioner's View

Robert Livingston, Community Supervision Officer, Tarrant County Community Supervision & Corrections Department

I am a Community Supervision Officer (CSO) for the Tarrant County Community Supervision & Corrections Department (CSCD). As a CSO, you are responsible for enforcing conditions of supervision imposed by the court, as well as issuing proper referrals, completing assessments, responding to violations, and reporting progress of probationers. In recent years, the field of community supervision has evolved and widely embraced a more rehabilitative approach, focusing on evidence-based practices and progressive responses to violations as they occur. CSOs have access to a variety of tools which aid in the discovery of a client's risk to reoffend, needs, and barriers that preclude success. Through substance abuse assessments, collateral contacts, drug and alcohol monitoring, and counseling services, a CSO can learn what motivates a probationer and identify goals, so that proper referrals and recommendations can be made to enhance prosocial ties and reduce recidivism.

Working as a CSO, days can be typical and routine, and include making face-to-face contact with probationers, completing home visits, writing progress reports, and making referrals to counseling services when necessary. However, a CSO must also be prepared to be flexible and expect the unexpected, from drug relapse, to notification of a new arrest, to unexpected phone calls from a victim. A CSO must be creative with how they intervene when emergencies arise. A CSO's action is imperative as intervention must consider the violation of the conditions and the individual needs of the probationer and any limitations they may have as well. Finally, and most importantly, a CSO must remember probationers are human beings and should be treated with dignity and respect, regardless of the crime for which they are on probation. It is vital to remember their humanity and develop a rapport with clients so a CSO can identify their needs and target criminogenic areas to aid in successful rehabilitation.

Community Supervision Officers

Probation and parole officers, also referred to as community supervision officers, supervise persons in the community. They are more closely involved with their clients and their cases than other criminal justice employees (Schmalleger & Smykla, 2009). Their work largely involves ensuring that their clients abide by the conditions of their agreement to be supervised in the community. Given the similarity of probation and parole (probation is generally supervision provided as an alternative to incarceration; parole is supervision following a period of incarceration), many of the qualities necessary for employment as a probation officer apply to parole officers. Accordingly, much of this discussion regarding careers in probation applies to careers in parole. Probation and parole officers share the many rewards and challenges associated with their job.

Generally, the primary components of community supervision include providing those on probation with guidance and services to facilitate their success (e.g., providing assistance in finding substance abuse counseling, employment, and education), monitoring the activities of individuals on probation, and ensuring that they remain aware of the need to abide by their probation agreement. This also includes effectively responding to those who violate their agreement (Schmalleger & Smykla, 2009). The specific tasks performed by probation and parole officers include (Abadinsky, 2015):

- Ensuring that those being supervised comply with the terms of their agreement
- Investigating client misbehavior
- Offering recommendations regarding probation or parole revocation, or the imposition of stricter conditions
- Writing reports
- Interacting with individuals on their caseload and involved parties (e.g., school and work officials, families)
- Coordinating with fellow probation or parole agencies and other components of the justice system

Needless to say, community supervision officers perform a wide array of duties and have several important responsibilities. Probation officers are primarily charged with ensuring that those convicted of a crime and permitted to remain in the community do not commit additional crimes or violate the terms of their probation agreement. Specifically, probation officers are tasked with managing caseloads, supervising their clients, and making presentence investigation and other reports to the courts.

Probation officers perform a job that entails unique challenges and demands. They interact regularly with individuals who may pose a threat to society or the officers, have access to sensitive information, and carry firearms in some jurisdictions. Community supervision officers are subject to a background investigation, workplace drug testing, and particular medical standards prior to employment. They perform a job that requires skills in many areas, not the least of which are law enforcement and social work. They may be assigned a typical caseload of felons and misdemeanants, or they could be assigned a series of specialized caseloads. For instance, they may supervise individuals convicted of sex offenses, with substance abuse problems, and/or suffering from a mental illness.

Community supervision officers should be effective listeners; have strong speaking, computer, and reading comprehension skills; and be able to make sound judgments. They should also maintain a service orientation and be familiar with the law, especially as it pertains to community supervision. Most state agencies require that they be at least 21 years old.

Community supervision officers meet regularly with clients at the client's home, in the officer's office, and in the client's place of employment or counseling. Officers are expected to perform a wide array of tasks and serve in a variety of capacities, for instance, in roles that reflect those of a law enforcement officer, a caseworker, and a prosecutor. With regard to the latter, they resemble prosecutors at revocation hearings. Officers advise their clients of a plan of action, particularly with regard to educational, vocational, treatment, and housing opportunities. Supervising individuals in the community requires skills pertaining to investigations, surveillance, counseling, and protecting the general public. Officers are charged with correcting their clients' behavior while maintaining constant concern for public safety.

Community supervision officers assist their clients through seeking and employing the assistance of community organizations such as religious groups, community groups, and residents. These groups support community supervision efforts in many ways and provide opportunities for those interested in working in criminal justice or criminology to gain experience and contribute to society.

Both probation and parole officers assist their clients outside of correctional institutions. In doing so, they are able to monitor their clients' behavior in a noncustodial setting, which can be stressful and dangerous. Individuals on parole are assumed to be more dangerous than those on probation, primarily because they've been to prison, which is not necessarily true for individuals on probation. Accordingly, they may require more direct and stricter supervision than individuals on probation.

Research suggests that individuals are attracted to work in community supervision by a sincere desire to help others and the associated job security and adequate salaries. Among other attractions of working in probation or parole are the flexible schedule, lack of direct

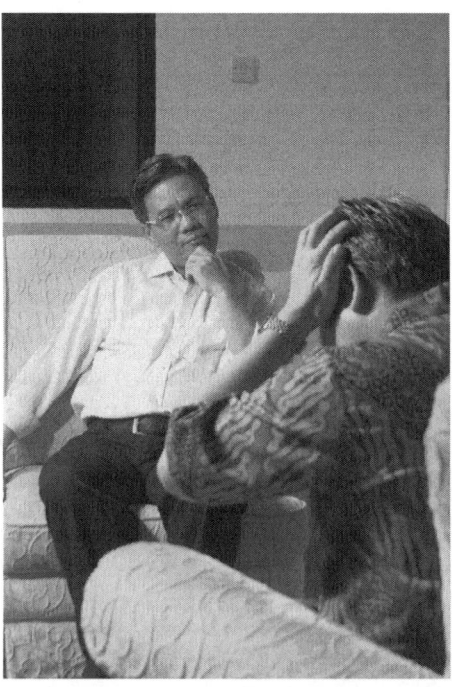

Perceptions of employment in corrections often involve correctional officers. There are, of course, many other positions within the field.
Source: https://pxhere.com/en/photo/1132430

supervision, and ability to guide individuals who are often need of direction and guidance. There are also enhanced opportunities for promotion within probation and parole, and promotions within these fields often come from the ranks (Gibbons & Rosecrance, 2005).

A bachelor's degree in the social sciences is typically required for a career in community supervision, and applicants are typically required to pass oral, written, psychological, and physical exams. Work experience in the criminal justice system is preferred, but not always required, for employment as a probation or parole officer. Volunteering or interning in treatment facilities or other criminal justice facilities undoubtedly increases one's chances of finding employment in the field. Applicants should also be able to effectively write reports and conduct investigations; two of the most important aspects of a community supervision officer's job. The responsibilities of community supervision officers can be stressful due to the regular interaction with individuals who have broken the law, the extensive paperwork required, high caseloads, and deadlines that must be met (Finn & Kuck, 2005). The flexible hours, opportunities to help others, and variety of work involved with community supervision are among the many attractions to the position.

Pretrial Services Officers

Pretrial services officers perform a wide array of duties. Among other responsibilities, they work with defendants prior to trial and help ensure that they do not commit crimes while released prior to their hearings in court. They also conduct investigations for the court by gathering and verifying information about defendants. This information is used to determine the likelihood and conditions under which defendants are released prior to trial.

Reentry Center Managers

Reentry centers, sometimes known as halfway houses, require managers and staff to perform the duties of both correctional officers and prison administrators. Particularly, they maintain custodial responsibility for reentry centers in the community and are accountable for the residents. Managers may perform personal searches, dispense medications and supplies, and oversee the residents' daily domestic responsibilities. They interact with all who enter and leave the building and, accordingly, must be willing to work various shifts and weekends. They must have strong administrative skills and are responsible for writing reports on the overall functioning of the facility and the progress (or lack of progress) regarding the residents.

The above-noted discussion of career opportunities in corrections is by no means comprehensive. The account primarily covers some of the more commonly found positions in various areas of corrections, while providing insight regarding the nature of the work within the field. Among the employment opportunities not mentioned above are positions in the areas of administration, clerical duties, other areas of treatment and counseling, and medical, religion, recreation, and food/maintenance services. Ultimately, there are many positions within corrections.

Summary

Researching an agency or position has the benefit of providing potential applicants detailed information regarding the agency or position under consideration. For instance, caseload numbers and the overall workload are of particular concern for probation or parole officers, as officers in some jurisdictions face larger caseloads than their counterparts. Further, overcrowded prisons make the job of correctional officers even more difficult. Resource allocation is another area of consideration, as is the geographical area in which a position is located, as there are typically differences between urban and rural agencies with regard to travel and caseloads.

There are distinct differences between working in institutional corrections and community corrections. Regardless of these differences, it remains that careers in corrections largely involve interaction with individuals under correctional supervision. While some individuals may be deterred by the thought of spending their career with law violators, others may be attracted to a career in corrections by many factors, not the least of which is the opportunity to help and protect society.

The correctional population has expanded greatly since the early 1980s. Accordingly, there are a variety of positions at various levels within correctional agencies. Many positions within corrections are located in state facilities; however, federal correctional agencies and institutions provide viable, and typically higher-paying options for anyone interested in a career in the field. There are also many local level positions available. As the final component in the criminal justice system, correctional agencies perform many different, vital functions that are required for creating and maintaining a safe and secure society.

Discussion Questions

1 How would you describe the different employment positions within institutional corrections? How does this compare to your description of positions in community corrections?
2 How is working in institutional corrections different, yet similar to working in community corrections?
3 What skills would be particularly helpful for working in institutional corrections? How about community corrections?
4 How would you conduct a job search for a position as a correctional officer?
5 Would you prefer to work in community or institutional corrections? Why?

Critical Thinking Exercise

Interview somebody who works or has worked in corrections. Ask her or him about the dangers, rewards, and challenges associated with their position. Further, ask the interviewee about opportunities for promotion, the hiring process, the training requirements, and whether they are satisfied with their career choice. Is this a position of interest to you? Why or why not?

For Further Examination

Blackwell S. (2021). 'Guys, get your guns out!' – An autobiographical account of a US community corrections training academy. *Probation Journal*, 68(3), 330–346.

Collica-Cox, K., & Schulz, D.M. (2021). Having it all? Strategies of women corrections executives to maintain a work-life balance. *Corrections: Policy, Practice and Research*. DOI:10.1080/23774657.2020.1868360

Einat T., & Suliman, N. (2021). Prison changed me—and I just work there: Personality changes among prison officers. *The Prison Journal*, 101(2), 166–186.

Hillhouse, M., Farabee, D., Smith, K., Nerurkar, J., Sahd, D., Bucklen, K.B., & Hawken, A. (2021). Mindfulness training for correctional staff: A randomized pilot study. *Corrections: Policy, Practice and Research*. DOI:10.1080/23774657.2021.1900756

Sloas L., Lerch, J, Walters S., & Taxman, F.S. (2020). Individual-level predictors of the working relationship between probation officers and probationers. *The Prison Journal*, 100(6), 709–725.

References

Abadinsky, H. (2015). *Probation and parole: Theory and practice* (12th ed.). Pearson.

Benedictus, L. (2010, August 10). A working life: The probation officer. *TheGuardian.com*. Available at: www.theguardian.com/money/2010/aug/21/probation-officer-working-life

Blakinger, K., Lartey, J., Schwartzapfel, B., Sisak, M., & Thompson, C. (2021, November 1). As corrections officers quit in droves, prisons get even more dangerous. *The Marshall Project*. Available at: www.themarshallproject.org/2021/11/01/as-corrections-officers-quit-in-droves-prisons-get-even-more-dangerous

Burton, A.L., Lux, J.L., Cullen, F.T., Miller, W.T., & Burton, V.S., Jr. (2018). Creating a model correctional officer training academy: Implications from a national study. *Federal Probation, 82*(1), 26–36.

Carson, E.A. (2021). *Prisoners in 2020 – statistical tables*. U.S. Department of Justice, Bureau of Justice Statistics. NCJ 302776.

Clear, T.R., Reisig, M.D., & Cole, G.F. (2016). *American corrections* (11th ed.). Cengage.

Culkar, DJ. (2001). The reluctant profession: Being and becoming a corrections officer. Pp. 129–135 in Henry, S. & Hinkle, W.G. (eds.), *Careers in criminal justice* (2nd ed.). Sheffield.

"Economic Perspectives on Incarceration and the Criminal Justice System." (2016). Executive Office of the President of the United States. Available at: https://obamawhitehouse.archives.gov/sites/default/files/page/files/20160423_cea_incarceration_criminal_justice.pdf

Federal Bureau of Prisons. (n.d.). Our locations. Available at: www.bop.gov/locations/

Federal Bureau of Prisons. (2022). Statistics. Available at: www.bop.gov/about/statistics/population_statistics.jsp

Finn, P., & Kuck, S. (2005). *Stress among probation and parole officers and what can be done about it*. U.S. Department of Justice, National Institute of Justice. NCJ 205620.

Gibbons, S.G., & Rosecrance, J.D. (2005). *Probation, parole, and community corrections in the United States*. Allyn and Bacon.

Hogan, N.L., Lambert, E.G., Kim, B., Mendenhall, M., Cheeseman, K., & Griffin, M. (2017). Research note: Career stage and job satisfaction among southern correctional officers. *Criminal Justice Studies, 30*(4), 421–432.

Kaeding, D. (2021, December 21). Jails and prisons have always struggled to find and keep workers. COVID-20 and a nationwide labor shortage made it worse. *Wisconsin Public Radio*. Available at: www.wpr.org/jails-and-prisons-have-always-struggled-find-and-keep-workers-covid-19-and-nationwide-labor-shortage

Kluckow, R., & Zeng, Z. (2022). *Correctional populations in the United States, 2020 – statistical tables*. U.S. Department of Justice, Bureau of Justice Statistics. NCJ 303184.

Kowalski, M.A. (2020). Hiring and training requirements for correctional officers: A statutory analysis. *The Prison Journal, 100*(1), 98–125.

Minton, T.D., & Zeng, Z. (2021). *Jail inmates in 2020 – statistical tables*. U.S. Department of Justice, Bureau of Justice Statistics. NCJ 303308.

Schmalleger, F., & Smykla, J.O. (2009). *Corrections in the 21st century* (4th ed.). McGraw–Hill.

Thelen, R. (2009, July 21). What drives you? Finding the strength to serve every day. *Corrections1.com*. Available at: www.corrections1.com/products/training-products/articles/what-drives-you-finding-the-strength-to-serve-every-day-6OplrjpbzMcGbs7z/

Trounson, J.S., & Pfeifer, J.E. (2016). Promoting correctional officer wellbeing: Guidelines and suggestions for developing psychological training programs. *Advancing Corrections, 1*, 56–64.

Walters, G.D. (2020). Getting to the source: How inmates and other staff contribute to correctional officer stress. *Journal of Crime and Justice, 45*(1), 73–86.

Whitehead, J.T., Dodson, K.D., & Edwards, B.D. (2013). *Corrections: Exploring crime, punishment, and justice in America* (3rd ed.). Anderson.

World Prison Brief. (n.d.). Highest to lowest – prison population rate. Available at: www.prisonstudies.org/highest-to-lowest/prison_population_rate?field_region_taxonomy_tid=All

Chapter 12

Working in the Juvenile Justice System

Many individuals in society are unaware that the *criminal justice system* is primarily reserved for adults accused or convicted of committing a crime. In addition to the criminal justice systems found throughout the United States are juvenile justice systems, which address juveniles accused of or convicted of breaking the law. Accordingly, there are a variety of careers available within the juvenile justice system, many of which are discussed in this chapter.

Working in the juvenile justice system provides many of the same challenges and rewards found working in the criminal justice system. Particularly, the processed individuals in both systems are typically troubled and in need of guidance, support, and help. Employment positions within both systems often entail working within bureaucracies that can sometimes pose particular challenges, for instance, when policy dictates that a particular approach be taken when an alternative approach may seem more appropriate. Working within either the criminal or juvenile justice system also provides ample opportunities to help troubled individuals and help ensure justice.

There are also differences with regard to working in the criminal justice system and the juvenile justice system. For example, juveniles are generally more impressionable than adults and thus the likelihood for rehabilitation is greater with young adults than it is for adults. Along these lines, the philosophical approach to juvenile justice is more focused on rehabilitation or treatment, which has not been an overriding concern in the criminal justice system. Most of the facilities and services provided for justice-involved youth are community based with the hope that troubled youth can better themselves through maintaining positive contacts with schools, families, and other forms of community support. Those who work in the juvenile justice system interact with a wider group of people than do those who work in the criminal justice system. Particularly, cases involving justice-involved youth (or at-risk youth) are more likely than cases in the adult system to involve biological, adoptive, and/or foster parents; teachers or other school officials; friends of the youth; and departments of child and family services. These and other differences warrant particular discussion of the variety of employment opportunities within the juvenile justice system.

Juvenile Involvement in the Justice System

Determining which individuals are considered "juvenile" is important for several reasons, not the least of which relates to the procedures for initiating and engaging in formal court proceedings. In most states, the oldest age for original juvenile court jurisdiction in matters of delinquency is 17. The existence of a distinct system of justice for juveniles reflects the fact that they are indeed different from adults, and should be treated as such when they break the law.

The juvenile justice system provides numerous opportunities for those seeking employment in a field where they can help others and protect society. Akin to adult criminal behavior,

DOI: 10.4324/9781003360162-15

Although the rate of delinquency has dropped in recent years, juveniles continue to break the law at a disproportionate rate. Accordingly, many employment positions exist within the juvenile justice system.
Source: https://pixabay.com/images/search/delinquency/

juvenile offending is not going to cease any time soon, and individuals are needed to work with juveniles in the United States and abroad. Juveniles have historically broken the law at a rate that is disproportionate to their representation in society. Rates of juvenile delinquency dropped significantly in the 1990s, although juveniles commit their fair share of offenses, and accounted for about 7% of all arrests, and 22% of all arrests for robbery in 2019 (Office of Juvenile Justice and Delinquency Prevention, n.d.).

Those who work in juvenile justice perform a variety of tasks centered on preventing delinquency and providing appropriate responses and services to juveniles who break the law. Options within the field include a variety of positions that can be based in schools, facilities, or communities, and they can be focused on delinquency prevention or responses to delinquency. Many efforts have been made to target justice-involved youth and those at risk, given that they are the ones most likely to end up in the criminal justice system. The saying that "you can't teach an old dog new tricks" suggests that you can teach younger dogs new tricks. This infers that juveniles are more impressionable and susceptible to changing their behaviors compared to adults. Working in the field provides many opportunities for rewarding experiences changing the lives of young people who may be headed in the wrong direction. The contributions of those who work in juvenile justice is particularly important given that too many juveniles who enter the juvenile justice system later end up in the criminal justice system.

Working in the Juvenile Justice System

Anyone interested in working in the juvenile justice system should be sincerely concerned for the betterment of youth and, more generally, society. Such concern should be accompanied by patience, flexibility, and the ability to effectively communicate with children and others. Juveniles often differ from adults in their responses to treatment approaches, official sanctions, methods of communication, and various other areas. Accordingly, efforts that may prove successful with adults may not work with juveniles. The move to create and retain a distinct juvenile system was based on the differences between juveniles and adults, and these differences should continue to be recognized by those who work in the field.

The emphasis on rehabilitation, treatment, and counseling found within the juvenile justice system is based on the belief that juveniles are impressionable enough that negative behaviors can be addressed before they escalate into serious crime. This approach has been somewhat abandoned in the adult system, where the focus has largely shifted toward retribution, deterrence, and incapacitation.

The opportunity to assist impressionable, troubled youth is one of the appealing aspects of working in the juvenile justice system. Nevertheless, those entering this field should be aware of the potential for frustration and/or discouragement that may appear when working with youthful individuals. Consider, for example, the juvenile caseworker who has a notable interest in helping others. She encounters a troubled 14-year-old boy whose parents stopped caring for him long ago, and she takes a particular interest in this child as she sees great hope. Unfortunately, the boy has a negative outlook on life, has regularly been involved with the law for several years, and seems immune to counseling, treatment, and therapy. Now, consider that the caseworker regularly encounters many individuals in equally troubling situations.

Or, consider the caseworker who encounters a similar situation, yet instead of the child's parents not caring for the individual, the parents believe they have all the answers to the youth's troubles. School officials, the caseworker's supervisor, police officers, and the youth have offered competing solutions. All of the solutions contrast and conflict in some manner, leaving the caseworker with great confusion.

Part of the frustration involved with working in the juvenile justice system stems from the system being heavily burdened by status offenders. Status offenders are runaways, truants, and other misbehaving youths whose status as juveniles means that they can be brought to the attention of the juvenile justice system for particular noncriminal acts, for instance, running away from home or skipping school. Over 90,000 status offense cases entered the courts in 2019, with truancy cases being most common (Office of Juvenile Justice and Delinquency Prevention, 2021).

Those anticipating employment in the juvenile justice system ought to be prepared to work and interact with a wide array of individuals. As opposed to the adult system of criminal justice in which adults are primarily deemed accountable for their actions and responsible for meeting the terms of their court-imposed sanction, the juvenile justice system involves parents and others who share some responsibility for the child's well-being and justice-based experiences. Family members are more often involved in the proceedings of the juvenile justice system than at the adult level. Family members and family structures contribute much to the prevention of juvenile involvement in the justice system. For instance, juveniles from broken homes are at an enhanced risk of engaging in delinquency (Bosick & Fomby, 2018).

Along these lines, juvenile justice workers must recognize the significance of our increasingly changing society. Particularly, they must be prepared to interact with individuals from a variety of cultural and socioeconomic backgrounds. Our increasingly diverse society dictates that all who work in the justice systems recognize and appropriately respond to cultural differences that may pose particular challenges with regard to formal social control (McNamara & Burns, 2021). The characteristics of the juvenile population in the United States are changing. For instance, it is anticipated that growth in the US juvenile population will increase by about 3% between 2020 and 2035. With regard to race and ethnicity, the number of Asian, non-Hispanic youth will increase by about 17%, and Hispanic youth are expected to grow in number by 6%. The number of white, non-Hispanic youth will decrease by about 4%. By 2030, it is expected that individuals from racial and ethnic minority groups will constitute about 53% of the population under age 18 in the United States (Office of Juvenile Justice and Delinquency Prevention, 2020). With regard to socioeconomic backgrounds, about one in seven juveniles in the United States lived in poverty in 2019, and the poverty rate for juveniles is about 1.5 times higher than it is for adults ages 18–64 (Children's Defense Fund, 2022).

Changes in the juvenile justice system are further evidenced, for example, in the increasing proportion of female juveniles arrested. Arrest rates for both male and female juveniles have largely declined since the mid-1990s, although the decline has been greater for male youths. Male offenders still constitute the majority of arrests of juveniles (and adults). Further, juvenile arrests appear to be related to racial factors, for instance, as 16% of the US population ages 10–17 in 2018 was Black; however, half of all arrests of juveniles for violent offenses involved Black youth (Puzzanchera, 2020). These and related numbers have implications not only for those who work in law enforcement, but for those working in the courts and corrections as well.

Working in the juvenile justice system, akin to working in the criminal justice system, provides many rewarding and troubling opportunities and situations. Juveniles are often viewed as impressionable, and many justice-based decisions may impact future directions for justice-involved youth. Many positions in juvenile justice provide opportunities to help others, but there can be a sense of frustration when youth seem unimpressionable and/or face difficult family or environmental challenges. Concerns regarding safety are another issue to consider, particularly for people who work in juvenile corrections. Researchers found that safety was significantly related to staff turnover in juvenile detention centers (Mikytuck & Cleary, 2016). Personal well-being is an important aspect to consider in any position within the criminal or juvenile justice system.

Employment Opportunities within the Juvenile Justice System

Most careers within juvenile justice have parallels in the adult system, although the terminology used to identify the positions sometimes differ. The distinct terminology used in the juvenile justice system is designed, among other reasons, to distinguish juveniles from adults. With regard to the primary components of the criminal justice system, there is no distinct police or law enforcement group that focuses on juvenile justice. There are, however, specific positions within law enforcement that address issues pertaining to juveniles. Among these positions are school resource officers (SROs) and gang task force officers. SROs are police officers who are assigned by their department to particular schools, and some schools hire their own police officers. They typically specialize in juvenile justice (particularly in relation to the school setting) and in some cases teach safety- and law-related courses in the schools. Gang task force officers are police officers who specialize in anti-gang efforts. They are involved with both prevention and response efforts.

A Practitioner's View

Bernice B. Mack, Deputy Assistant Director – Community Probation Services, Tarrant County Juvenile Services

Juvenile justice responds to adolescent delinquency by recognizing that children are much different than adults. The goal for youth progress is not short-term compliance, but rather long-term behavior change. We understand that to achieve that, confinement of youth is only necessary to the extent of promoting public safety. Institutionalization

> is not a fruitful strategy and juvenile justice efforts focus on positive youth development provided to youth in their natural environments and communities. Being a juvenile justice professional offers individuals the opportunity to right the wrongs of the world and truly invest in the future by making an impact on young lives.
>
> A juvenile justice professional may prepare for such a calling by earning a bachelor's degree and gaining a full year's experience working with adolescents and providing case management assistance. To truly have an impact, juvenile justice professionals must have a heart for service particularly in assisting disadvantaged people. This field provides an opportunity for the world changers and difference makers to promote social capital. Changing lives in juvenile justice helps individuals find a higher purpose by being part of something bigger than themselves.

Employment opportunities in the juvenile justice system can be categorized in many ways. For instance, one could categorize the positions as pertaining to prevention- or enforcement-related; positions dealing with status offenders or youths who commit more serious offenses; or positions involving institutional- or community-based sanctions. The positions could also be categorized according to employment opportunities with court-involved youth or those who have yet to enter the courts but are seemingly on their way toward doing so. Another categorization of employment positions could consist of a three-pronged approach involving early intervention programs, residential programs, and aftercare programs. Various employment positions exist in these and related areas.

Early intervention programs include prevention programs designed to divert troubled youth from the system or encourage them to cease behaving in a manner that contributed to their entrance into the system. Arguably, the most effective early intervention programs incorporate several approaches, including mentoring, employment, job training, college access services, counseling, and afterschool support. An immediate and comprehensive assessment of an individual can help identify which types of support may be most effective in redirecting him or her.

Residential programs include a continuum of care designed to meet each youth's needs and ensure public safety. Such programs include youth development centers, detention centers, and boot camps. These facilities vary in their approaches, focus on the needs of those housed within them, and offer various employment opportunities. Regardless of residential facility type, these programs should prepare youth for reentry, for instance, through counseling, job skills training, education, behavior modification, and positive mentoring. Classification of each youth's needs is particularly important in determining which residential facility is used.

Aftercare programs are essential for a youth's reintegration into society. These programs emphasize employment and training, and follow-up on the skills and lessons learned in residential facilities. Cooperative arrangements between representatives of the juvenile justice system and various community-based institutions agencies or organizations largely contribute to the effectiveness of aftercare programs. Interagency collaboration and cooperation is, however, sometimes lacking, which hampers outcomes for justice-involved youth (e.g., Kubek et al., 2020). Preventing and addressing delinquency requires collaborative efforts from many groups/individuals, and incorporates a wide array of services. Accordingly, there are many career opportunities associated with aftercare services.

The wide array of services and large numbers of individuals affecting juvenile justice dictate that numerous employment opportunities exist in this area. There are a variety of areas in which one can work in the juvenile justice system. The remainder of this chapter highlights several of the many employment positions found within juvenile justice. This is by no means a comprehensive list, although it does address the most prominent positions.

Child Protective Services Worker – Child protective services employees use various strategies to ensure the safety and well-being of children. These workers seek to establish a relationship with the juvenile's family in attempt to minimize the risks to children. They offer direct services to family members and manage cases through coordinating services as needed. They also provide support and care for children when parents are unable or unwilling to do so. Research focused on the stressors associated with child protective services workers noted that mental health, physical health, and work–life imbalance issues were among the negative by-products associated with the job (Griffiths et al., 2018). These positions reflect the interdisciplinary nature of employment opportunities in criminal justice and criminology.

Child Welfare Caseworker – Child welfare caseworkers offer social services to troubled children and young adults with behavioral problems. Caseworkers also work with parents of troubled children, for instance, by recommending appropriate responses to troubling behaviors. Akin to several other employment opportunities provided in this account (e.g., child protection services employees and child welfare consultants), child welfare caseworkers engage in activities that lean toward social work, meaning that those interested in these positions should consider becoming familiar with both criminal/juvenile justice and social work.

Child Welfare Consultants – These individuals help ensure that childcare institutions, placement agencies, foster homes, court facilities, and other components comply with state laws. Consultants also provide guidance and expertise to facility administrators with the intent to improve services and programs.

Juvenile Corrections Caseworker – Juvenile corrections caseworkers are the primary staff treatment personnel in institutional and some community corrections settings. They perform functions similar to caseworkers employed in adult institutions. Among other duties, they assess and evaluate residents to ensure that clients are meeting their treatment requirements.

Juvenile Mental Health Counselor – These individuals assist juveniles with regard to their personal and family problems, functioning in their environments, and dealing with various relationships. They interact directly with troubled youth, including both those who have and have not committed an offense, primarily through helping them identify their concerns, considering effective and alternative solutions, and finding positive solutions. They counsel clients, arrange for services, and monitor progress to ensure that effective services are provided.

Juvenile Court Judge – Juvenile court judges are considered the most important figures in juvenile courts, primarily due to their role as the ultimate decision-maker. Among the many functions performed by juvenile court judges are deciding legal issues in the cases that enter the court, setting standards within the community through their decision-making, ascertaining that juveniles who appear before the court are treated fairly, and understanding how cases that do not reach the juvenile court are being resolved. Juvenile court judges, much like the judges who work in criminal courts, hear pretrial motions, preside over hearings, and are involved in post-conviction processes. In most states they are required to have a law degree, and many have experience as prosecutors or defense attorney (Fuller, 2016).

Juvenile Court Referee – Many juvenile courts employ referees, who are sometimes referred to as the "arm of the court" or a "commissioner." Some states use only juvenile court judges; however, other states use referees and related officials to assist judges in processing youths through juvenile court. Referees ease the burden of juvenile court judges, for instance, through serving as primary hearing officers at the fact-finding stage and sometimes during the detention stages. Judicial dispositions, however, are typically the responsibility of juvenile court judges.

Juvenile Court Prosecutors – Sometimes referred to as petitioners, juvenile court prosecutors are tasked with protecting society while ensuring that troubled youth are protected by their constitutional rights. They perform the same functions as prosecutors in adult courts, for instance, by being involved in all phases of the court proceedings. Among other contributions, juvenile court prosecutors may make recommendations to the judge regarding whether or not a case should be transferred to the adult court, advise judges on adjudication and dispositional alternatives, and determine which cases they will or will not prosecute. Juvenile courts did not use prosecutors until after the due process movement beginning in the 1960s. Until then, juvenile cases were presented directly by police officers, caseworkers, or school officials. Prosecutors today play a particularly important role in the adjudication process, as they make many important decisions (Fuller, 2016).

Juvenile Defense Attorney – Juvenile defense attorneys primarily act as a legal advocate for juveniles who enter court, and serve as a guardian or parent surrogate to the client in court. Specifically, they prepare cases and represent juveniles at all phases of the proceedings. Juveniles may retain private counsel or they may receive representation from the court, similar to what occurs in criminal court. Juvenile defense counsel also wasn't used until the due process revolution beginning in the 1960s (Fuller, 2016), and they too play an integral role in the adjudication process.

Juvenile Diversion Specialist – Juvenile diversion specialists generally work with individuals with no previous involvement in the juvenile justice system, particularly those who may be eligible for some type of diversion program. As an alternative to formal case processing, diversion programs promote specific skills, often involve some type of community service, and encourage conflict resolution and problem-solving. Diversion specialists guide juveniles through these programs, typically with the support of the youth's guardian or family.

Juvenile Justice Detention Officer – Detention officers are responsible for maintaining a safe and secure institutional environment for youth, themselves, and their coworkers. Similar to the role of prison officer, detention officers help prevent youth escapes, abuse of institutionalized youth, sexual harassment, and inappropriate conduct by the staff. Detention officers may also assist their supervisors with ensuring that detained youth's services and programming comply with court orders, department policies, quality assurance standards, and the law.

Juvenile Intake Officer – Intake officers play a key role in determining a juvenile's involvement in the system. Intake is the stage where decisions are made to dismiss the case, address it informally, or handle it formally by processing it through the courts. Intake officers make recommendations to judges regarding the processing of the case. Among the factors considered are the juvenile's personal safety, the risk to the public if the juvenile is released, and the risk of the juvenile not returning to court for processing (Fuller, 2016).

Juvenile Probation Officer – Probation is the most commonly imposed sanction by juvenile courts (Hockenberry & Puzzanchera, 2021). Accordingly, juvenile probation officers serve an important role in the juvenile justice system, and offer another opportunity for individuals to work in juvenile justice. Their role is similar to that performed by adult probation officers. Generally, they supervise juveniles under community supervision, and ensure that the terms of probation are being met. Juveniles on probation are often required to attend classes, counseling sessions, education-based opportunities, and related programs that promote trouble-free living. Compared to adult probation officers, juvenile probation officers are typically more closely engaged with their clients and their cases, including family members and school officials.

School Resource and Other Types of Officers – SROs help school officials curb school violence and ensure that schools remain safe environments conducive to learning. These officers are trained police officers who specialize in juvenile delinquency and related issues. They facilitate safety awareness and provide a positive role model in schools. SROs sometimes teach safety-related courses in addition to deterring delinquency and providing an immediate police response to troubling situations taking place on school grounds. Research suggests that they struggle with role confusion, limited support to complete the most satisfying aspects of the job (e.g., mentorship), and unclear partnerships with schools (Javdani, 2019). Their role has become even more important as several mass shootings at schools across the United States have generated calls for a greater law enforcement presence on campuses.

As noted, this list of employment opportunities in juvenile justice is not comprehensive, and many of the positions within the field are similar to what is found in the criminal justice system. A primary difference between the two is the accentuated focus often placed upon addressing the special needs and concerns of juveniles. There is a focus on addressing the needs and concerns of adults in the system, although it is not as intense. Efforts made to address juvenile delinquency provide many dividends for the criminal justice system, as involvement in our justice systems as a juvenile is related to involvement in the adult (criminal) justice systems (e.g., Copeland et al., 2022). Accordingly, many effective, motivated, and involved employees are needed to fill the variety of positions in the field.

It was earlier argued by some that we should abolish the juvenile justice system on the grounds that there would be reduced financial costs of finding justice, greater continuity of services, and an overall savings in justice-based resources. Eliminating juvenile courts, it was argued, would enhance the protection of the due process rights granted juveniles, and help eliminate the intertwining and sometimes conflicting goals of providing justice and social services for troubled youth (Dawson, 1990; Feld, 1997; Jackson & Knepper, 2003).

There are, however, many strong arguments for preserving the juvenile justice system. For instance, a distinct system for juveniles recognizes the differences between justice-involved youths and adults, and provides enhanced opportunities for rehabilitating troubled youth. The adult system of justice is primarily focused on punishment, deterrence, and incapacitation; approaches that may not be in the best interests of impressionable youths. Certainly, there is room for improvement within the juvenile justice system, as there is in the criminal justice system. The onus is largely on those working in the field, legislators, voters, and others, to recognize and correct the problems.

Summary

Working with juveniles poses particular opportunities and challenges not often found in the adult system. For example, the belief that juveniles are more impressionable and vulnerable to change than adults is primary among the differences. The enhanced focus on rehabilitation and considering the input of various groups (e.g., parents, court officials, social workers, and others) also contribute to the differences between the systems. Further, juvenile justice officials must determine the best approach to addressing juvenile offending, which can be frustrating in several aspects, particularly with regard to the divisiveness in opinions regarding how we should address delinquency.

Working with troubled youth provides an excellent opportunity to change lives in a positive manner. Young adults and children today face numerous problems, not the least of which include drugs, gangs, poverty, suicide, and all forms of abuse. Being able to assist young, impressionable individuals is what attracts many individuals to the field. Recognizing that one can make a substantial difference in the lives of troubled youths prompts workers in the system to fully embrace the value of their work, and strive to continue making a difference.

Anyone interested in working within juvenile justice is strongly encouraged to initially test the waters prior to accepting a job in the area. Such testing could involve volunteer work and/or an internship. The experience will undoubtedly contribute to one's understanding of whether or not working with troubled youth is an appropriate career choice. If nothing else, the work provided will likely contribute toward helping others.

Discussion Questions

1. Should the emphasis within juvenile justice be on rehabilitation or punishment?
2. What two employment positions in juvenile justice are most appealing to you? Why?
3. What would make working with justice-involved youth different from working with adults?
4. How could the positions in the juvenile justice system be categorized? Provide examples of positions for each category.
5. Should we have a distinct juvenile justice system, or should both adults and juveniles be processed in the same system of justice? Why or why not?

Critical Thinking Exercise

List five reasons why someone would want and not want to work in the juvenile justice system. Feel free to search online for information about juvenile justice employee motivations. Have a classmate or friend do the same, and then share and analyze your results. What commonalities and differences emerged? Do the results encourage you to seek a career in juvenile justice? Why or why not?

For Further Examination

Anderson, R., Treger, J., & Lucksted, A. (2020). Youth mental health first-aid: Juvenile justice staff training to assist youth with mental health concerns. *Juvenile Family Court Journal, 71*(1), 19–30.

Fisher, B.W., & Devlin, D.N. (2020). School crime and the patterns of roles of school resource officers: Evidence from a national longitudinal study. *Crime & Delinquency, 66*(11), 1606–1629.

Odessa, L., Anderson, A.A., & Rapp, J.T. (2022). Resident and staff time and activity allocation in a juvenile justice facility. *Residential Treatment for Children & Youth, 39*(2), 135–153.

Rhineberger-Dunn, G., & Mack, K.Y. (2020). Predicting burnout among juvenile detention and juvenile probation officers. *Criminal Justice Policy Review, 31*(3), 335–355.

Sinclair, J., Unruh, D., & Kelly, K. (2021). Relationships matter: The role transition specialists play in youth's reentry from the juvenile justice system. *Career Development and Transition for Exceptional Individuals, 44*(1), 4–16.

References

Bosick, S.J., & Fomby, P. (2018). Family instability in childhood and criminal offending during the transition into adulthood. *American Behavioral Scientist, 62*(11), 1483–1504.

Children's Defense Fund. (2022). *The state of America's children 2021*. Available at: www.childrensdefense.org/state-of-americas-children/soac-2021-child-poverty/

Copeland, W.E., Tong, T., Gifford, E.J., Easter, M.M., Shanahan, L., Swartz, M.S., & Swanson, J.W. (2022). Adult criminal outcomes of juvenile justice involvement. *Psychological Medicine*, https://doi.org/10.1017/S0033291722000393

Dawson, R.A. (1990). The future of juvenile justice: Is it time to abolish the system? *Journal of Criminal Law & Criminology, 81*(1), 136–155.

Feld, B. (1997). Abolish the juvenile court: Youthfulness, criminal responsibility, and sentencing policy. *Journal of Criminal Law & Criminology, 88*(1), 68–136.

Fuller, J.R. (2016). *Juvenile delinquency* (3rd ed.). Oxford University Press.

Griffiths, A., Royse, D., & Walker, R. (2018). Stress among child protective service workers: Self-reported health consequences. *Children and Youth Services Review, 90*, 46–53.

Hockenberry, S., & Puzzanchera, C. (2021). *Juvenile court statistics 2019*. National Center for Juvenile Justice.

Jackson, M.S., & Knepper, P. (2003). *Delinquency and justice*. Allyn & Bacon.

Javdani, S. (2019). Policing education: An empirical review of the challenges and impact of the work of school police officers. *American Journal of Community Psychology, 63*, 253–269.

Kubek, J.B., Tindall-Biggins, C., Reed, K., Carr, L.E., & Fenning, P.A. (2020). A systematic literature review of school reentry practices among youth impacted by juvenile justice. *Children and Youth Services Review, 110*, https://doi.org/10.1016/j.childyouth.2020.104773

McNamara, R., & Burns, R. (2021). *Multiculturalism, crime, and criminal justice* (2nd ed.). Oxford University Press.

Mikytuck, A.M., & Cleary, H.M.D. (2016). Factors associated with turnover decision making among juvenile justice employees: Comparing correctional and non-correctional staff. *Journal of Juvenile Justice, 5*(2), 50–67.

Office of Juvenile Justice and Delinquency Prevention. (n.d.). Juvenile arrests. *Statistical Briefing Book*. Available at: www.ojjdp.gov/ojstatbb/crime/qa05102.asp?qaDate=2019

Office of Juvenile Justice and Delinquency Prevention. (2021). Petitioned status offense cases. *Statistical Briefing Book*. Available at: www.ojjdp.gov/ojstatbb/court/qa06601.asp

Office of Juvenile Justice and Delinquency Prevention. (2020). Juvenile population characteristics. *Statistical Briefing Book*. Available at: www.ojjdp.gov/ojstatbb/population/qa01101.asp?qaDate=2020

Puzzanchera, C. (2020). *Juvenile arrests, 2018*. U.S. Department of Justice, Office of Juvenile Justice and Delinquency Prevention. Available at: https://ojjdp.ojp.gov/sites/g/files/xyckuh176/files/media/document/254499.pdf

Chapter 13
Other Employment Opportunities in Criminal Justice and Criminology

One of the many benefits of studying or having an interest in criminal justice and/or criminology is the variety of employment opportunities available in the fields. An important means by which one can enjoy, and not despise, going to work each day is to enjoy what they do for a living. A career in criminal justice or criminology provides such an opportunity for many individuals. One merely needs to view the television and movie listings any day of the week to recognize that crime and justice are popular topics among many people.

Several employment positions within criminal justice and criminology come to mind when one considers careers in the fields. Particularly, it is often believed that a criminal justice or criminology degree is primarily a ticket to careers as a police officer, corrections officer, or probation officer, or perhaps a researcher. Some also view the degree as a stepping stone to a career practicing law (upon completion of law school). While these careers are undoubtedly options for those who study the fields, there are a wide array of positions that often go unrecognized and thus not considered. The following highlights several of the more "nontraditional" areas of employment related to crime and justice, and demonstrates that there are seemingly endless employment opportunities for those interested in the fields.

Among the positions that often go unrecognized by those interested in a career in criminal justice or criminology are those providing victim services, in the private security field, and conducting crime analyses, including the preparation and sharing of crime mapping reports. Further, one could work in the forensic sciences and many other positions related to the fields. These vast array of employment positions demonstrates the diversity of employment opportunities in criminal justice and criminology.

Victim Services

Working in the criminal justice system, in any capacity, can be both rewarding and discouraging. Consistently interacting with law-breakers and the unfortunate victims of their behaviors can negatively impact one's disposition and outlook on life. This concern is perhaps most recognizable in policing and careers involving victim services. Nevertheless, a career providing services to individuals who have been victimized entails excellent opportunities to help those most in need of assistance.

Historically, victims were overlooked by much of society, including the criminal justice system. The focus on criminal behavior was primarily targeted on those who committed the crime. The victims' rights movements of the 1970s and 1980s altered this approach, and resulted in increased societal and governmental attention focused on the victims of crime. Several key pieces of legislation and the introduction and promotion of victim assistance programs and services have resulted in great benefits to many victims of crime and more employment opportunities. Prominent among the enhancement of victim services are efforts to involve

DOI: 10.4324/9781003360162-16

victims in the criminal justice process. For instance, victims are sometimes permitted to offer a victim impact statement at trial, are more often informed of the progress of the case involving the individual who victimized them, and may be eligible for financial compensation for their losses and harms. These changes have been accompanied by greater opportunities for victims to receive treatment, or assistance by various agencies both within and outside of the criminal justice system. Accordingly, these changes have created additional opportunities for employment for those interested in crime, justice, and the overall well-being of others.

Victims come from all socioeconomic backgrounds, levels of education, races, cultures, ages, and geographical areas. Put simply, nobody is immune to victimization. Victims of crime are often visualized by many in society as having been assaulted or the targets of thieves. However, victimization comes in many forms and occurs in various locations. For instance, one may be the target of racial profiling, sexual harassment, or terrorist activities, among other types of victimization. Such violations may occur at one's home, in the workplace, on school grounds, on a public street, or in a crowded mall. Although the risk of being victimized may increase or decrease according to one's behavior, anyone is vulnerable to harm and violations committed by others.

Providing services to victims may entail investigation, research, profiling, assistance, and counseling. For instance, the work may involve assisting police officers investigating claims of domestic abuse or sexual assault, identifying behaviors that might predict when individuals are in danger of being abused, assessing and sharing protective measures with schools and individuals, or counseling and assisting individuals who have been victimized. Victim services personnel may also assist individuals who are requested to testify in court, for instance, through ensuring that the individual has transportation to the court, is aware of when to be in court, has access to preferred clothing, and is comfortable being on the witness stand.

Anyone seeking to work with crime victims should be prepared to work with all types of individuals facing difficult and challenging situations. Victim services personnel should be sympathetic, caring, and helpful. Further, they should be flexible and recognize the differences among the clients they encounter. Each victim is different and requires specific services and resources to meet their particular needs. Fortunately, there has been increased awareness of those needs and more effective responses and services for crime victims.

The services provided at domestic violence shelters very aptly reflect employment involving victim services. These shelters provide a safe place for victims of domestic abuse to escape initial or continued victimization. They offer counseling and support for victims, and, needless to say, provide very important services. They also provide volunteer, internship, and employment opportunities for those interested in a career in this field.

Various social service agencies provide assistance for victims and others in need of assistance. Social workers help people address and cope with their personal, social, and community problems, which can include substance abuse, chronic disease, employment stress, and family dysfunction. Among those they help are individuals within the criminal justice system, those at risk of entering the criminal justice system, and those impacted by the system (e.g., families of the incarcerated who are in need of assistance). The contributions of social workers assisting crime victims highlight the multidisciplinary nature of criminal justice and criminology.

Requirements for employment in victim services vary by position, nevertheless students interested in working with victims ought to take courses in social work, sociology, and psychology, along with their criminal justice or criminology studies. They should consider minoring or double-majoring in these areas. Some universities and colleges enable students to specialize in victimology or the study of victims. These opportunities undoubtedly provide significant preparation for a career in the field. Anyone anticipating a career assisting crime victims is encouraged to seek volunteer and internship opportunities.

A sample of the more prominent positions available for individuals interested in working in victim services is provided below. The titles and responsibilities may differ slightly among agencies and jurisdictions given the differences among the types of services and terminology used. The outlook for positions in victim services is related to fluctuations in crime rates, public and governmental concern for crime victims, and the level of resources directed toward the area.

> **Victim Advocates** – Victim advocates generally work with victims of all crimes, including those that have been prosecuted and those who have not. Generally, they are responsible for performing crisis intervention work, assisting at the scene of a crime, and following up with victims of crime, for instance, by providing support, referrals, and information about the case. They may specialize in particular areas (e.g., misdemeanors, felonies, juveniles, sexual assault, domestic violence). Crisis counseling is a key component of the position, which generally requires licensing in social work.
> **Victim Services Coordinators** – Coordinators develop and operate programs targeted to assist crime victims. Such programs may include rape crisis services, victim impact panels, victim ministry, and various types of support groups. These programs may be offered in a central location, or provided in surrounding areas.
> **Victim Services Assistants** – These individuals often work with victim advocates to provide victim services such as notification of hearings and review police reports for victims of violent crime when an arrest has not yet been made.
> **Victim Services Office Managers** – Office managers oversee the day-to-day functions of the victims services office, and also assist with hearing notifications, telephone contacts with victims, and other support services as needed.
> **Child and Family Therapists** – Child and family therapists provide assessment and therapeutic services to child victims of crime and non-offending family members. These individuals must be able to assist both young and older children who have been victims of various types of trauma, including sexual abuse, domestic violence, and witnessing a homicide.
> **Human Trafficking Project Manager** – Human trafficking project managers assist with cases involving the illegal movement of people within countries and across national borders. Among their responsibilities are developing, coordinating, and managing human trafficking programs, coordinating services for victims of human trafficking, recruiting and supervising community-based case managers, project evaluation, managing hotlines for reports of human trafficking, and preparing and disseminating reports on the nature and status of human trafficking.

These and related positions are reflective of the need for interdisciplinary studies in best preparing for a career in criminal justice or criminology.

Private Security

To many individuals, a thought of career in private security conjures images of a security officer acknowledging customers who enter or exit a department store. While this image is to some extent accurate in that security officers provide an important service to businesses and customers, it remains that the private security field is vast, is expanding, and has become increasingly professionalized. The more common objectives of private security positions include:

- enforcing the policies and procedures concerning general security, asset and access control, and employee safety

- providing a workplace environment that helps attract and retain personnel, and protecting them from undue pressures
- preventing the compromise and unauthorized disclosure of an entity's technology or assets
- protecting and preserving the entity's assets
- responding to on-site incidents that threaten employees and/or the organization
- reporting conditions that are considered a breach of security or pose a potential security hazard (Hess & Wrobleski, 1996).

These are certainly important tasks that require a notable level of trust and accountability on behalf of security personnel.

The term *private security* is often associated with security officers, or guards as they were once called. In addition to security officers, private security encompasses private detectives and investigators, alarm companies, armed couriers, consultants, and personal bodyguards. Societal concern for crime prevention and recognition of the limited abilities of the police to respond to all crimes have contributed to the extensive expansion of the field both in terms of personnel and the functions they perform. The private security industry has benefitted from the increased need for cybersecurity, as crime has continued to move online in part, and individuals and companies feel vulnerable relying on police protection (Button, 2020). Information security analysts, for instance, provide security measures to secure their organization's computer systems and networks, and have a relatively high median salary (see Appendix E for salary information). Employment growth for information security analysts is expected to increase by 33% from 2020 to 2030 (Bureau of Labor Statistics, 2022a).

Private security officers are perhaps the most visible aspect of the private security industry. These individuals, who are usually uniformed and sometimes armed, provide protective services for commercial and residential establishments. They may control access to private property; maintain order; protect against crime, fire, and other emergencies; and provide a sense of security for customers, employees, and employers. Private security officer positions are considered entry-level positions.

Security officers may work in a variety of locations, including apartment complexes, casinos, department stores, and similar places where resident, customer, and employee protection is required. They may stay at a fixed location, perhaps while monitoring closed circuit security cameras, or engage in patrol functions. Some security officer positions include limited police powers, and licensure requirements vary by states. The licensing requirement is an example of the reform and advancement that has occurred in the field. Flexible hours and limited training requirements are among the reasons why some individuals become security officers, especially those who take the position for a second or part-time job. The salaries for security officer positions are generally low compared to other criminal justice and criminology careers, although they vary depending on geographical considerations, the extent of danger involved, and requirements of the position.

Related, loss prevention specialists provide more elaborate and extensive security services to retail outlets than do security officers. Security officers typically provide a visible presence in establishments, while loss prevention specialists work more behind the scenes preventing theft, inventory shrinkage, fraud, and related losses. They may monitor surveillance cameras, manage video archives, train employees regarding loss prevention, investigate losses, and generally assist with best practices in ensuring the prevention of loss to the company.

Private detectives and investigators are also encompassed under the umbrella term *private security*. These individuals assist businesses, attorneys, and individuals through locating and analyzing information. Accordingly, they engage in the discovery, assessment, and presentation of legal, financial, or personal information. Surveillance is a key component of the work provided by private detectives and investigators, as is conducting research and information gathering. Private investigators are involved in a wide array of cases, including insurance and other types of fraud, marital disputes, harassment cases, and background investigations. The widespread use of technology has assisted private detectives and investigators who regularly access information online to provide services.

Private investigators and detectives often specialize in particular areas. For instance, they may specialize in computer forensics, which involves recovering, analyzing, and presenting information collected from computers as part of an investigation. Some provide assistance in the legal arena, for instance, through assisting with the preparation of criminal defense cases, locating witnesses, serving legal documents, interviewing involved parties, and gathering and reviewing evidence. They may also conduct internal or external corporate investigations, for instance, through investigating claims of employee theft or drug abuse for a corporation. Further, they may conduct financial investigations, which may involve the creation of financial profiles of individuals or companies that are prospective parties to large financial transactions. Private detectives may also work in hotels and convention centers, where they are tasked with protecting guests and employees of the establishment, for instance, through keeping undesirables off the premises and generally providing protection against theft and violence. The US Department of Labor noted that 33,700 private detectives and investigators worked throughout the United States in 2021. This number is expected to increase by about 13% between 2020 and 2030. This growth is faster than the average for all occupations (Bureau of Labor Statistics, 2022b).

Armed courier services assist individuals and businesses in the transportation of money, goods, documents, and/or people as they are transported from one place to another. These services typically use armored vehicles but may use trains or airlines as well. The couriers are armed, uniformed individuals who perform a vital service in many regards. Their work can be dangerous in the sense that they are often openly in possession of valuable goods.

Alarm companies constitute another component of the private security industry. Public concern for personal protection from victimization is evidenced in the extensive and growing use of private alarm companies. For example, the global home security systems market is expected to increase from $56.9 billion in 2022 to $84.4 billion by 2027 (Business Wire, 2021). The market for security alarms and related products is anticipated to increase in the years ahead, for instance, as the Bureau of Labor Statistics (2022c) reported that the anticipated growth for security and fire alarm installers is expected to grow at a faster than average rate. Combined, these reports suggest that many employment opportunities exist and will arise in the area.

Security consultants provide vital services and information for individuals or companies seeking to enhance their personal protection. Generally, consultants offer their professional assessments regarding the types of threats or risks that may affect the person or property to be protected, the likelihood or probability that those threats or risks may be acted upon, and plans to reduce the likelihood of threats, danger, and risks. A career as a consultant requires years of experience in the field and expertise in specific areas of threat assessment. Consultants may be called upon to analyze both internal and external threats. They may assess a company's physical properties as well its procedural components. An example of the services provided by security consultants is evidenced in their work responding to school shootings and other forms of violence at campuses across the United States. Schools employ the services of security consultants to help prevent harms to students, teachers, and others on campuses.

Bodyguards, also known as personal protection specialists, provide security for various groups and individuals, including celebrities, executives, officials, politicians, world leaders, diplomats, and other high-profile or at-risk individuals. Increased globalization of business and the tenacity with which the paparazzi follow celebrities are two of the many reasons why people hire personal protection specialists. Corporate executives charged with visiting foreign countries may be inclined to hire a protection specialist to protect against harm. Personal protection specialists must protect their client while remaining in the shadows and not interfering with them.

Anyone interested in becoming a personal protection specialist is encouraged to peruse the special training courses designed to prepare one for a career in the field. Due diligence should go into researching the various training courses, as some programs may promise much yet offer little. In other words, those seeking to prepare for a career in this area should identify and attend a credible training program. The training should incorporate topics such as first aid, weapons handling, offensive and defensive driving, and assessing and responding to threats. Former military personnel and law enforcement officers who have been trained in security and protection are particularly suitable for a career in personal protection.

The licensing requirements to become a personal protection specialist vary by state, and are designed to ensure that specialists are prepared for the difficult tasks they face. For example, Virginia recognizes a personal security specialist as "... any individual who engages in the duties of providing close protection from bodily harm to any person." The minimum requirements to be a personal protection in the state are being at least 18 years old, successfully completing all initial training requirements, and being a US citizen or legal resident of the United States. The training component of the requirements includes 60 hours of training in personal protection and 14 hours in entry-level firearms training. Additional hours in handgun training may be required (Virginia Department of Criminal Justice Services, 2022).

There are certainly other positions in private security, and opportunities for employment in the field keep increasing. The private security industry is large and growing at a significant pace, which provides appreciable employment opportunities. For example, over 40 countries, including the United States, have more people working in private security than they do in public policing (Provost, 2017). Those interested in working in private security ought to consider whether they are suited for a career working for an employer, or perhaps should start their own private security entity. The market for security services appears to be vibrant and it may be wiser for some individuals to create their own business and be their own boss. Such a decision should be considered only after one has some level of experience in the field, or partnered with individuals who have experience.

Crime Analysis and Mapping

Crime analysis and mapping have become integral components of many law enforcement agencies. Crime analysts are tasked with collecting, compiling, and disseminating information that can be used to address crime fighting, crime prevention, and other important activities. Crime analyses are notably important for policing and academics. The information generated through analyses of crime can be used for research studies, to assist with crime prevention and crime-fighting practices, and to generally improve policing and other aspects of the criminal justice system.

The skills required to become a crime analyst include knowledge of crime analysis basics, the capability to evaluate the integrity of information, an understanding of criminal behavior, comprehension of inferential and descriptive statistics, and familiarity with spatial analysis. In general, crime analysts should be familiar with police practices, maintain advanced research skills, have strong communication skills, and possess technological capabilities. Experience as a police officer is helpful to become a crime analyst, but not necessary. The current trend among police departments is to use civilian crime analysts, primarily because officers tend to shift positions relatively frequently and departments do not wish to continuously invest resources in training analysts.

Crime analysts must be accountable and interact with various groups. For instance, analysts rely on police officers to provide accurate and interpretable reports that are used for analysis. This information may then be shared with police administrators, public officials, and the general public. The manner in which the information is shared by analysts must often be provided in different forms. The information police administrators view may be different from what reaches the public. The reports must be provided in a manner that is interpretable by a wide array of individuals and various groups. Of particular importance, analysts must demonstrate integrity and not simply provide reports based on what they believe others expect to see.

Larger police departments are more likely than smaller ones to have a crime analyst, or a crime analysis unit. Among the employment opportunities in crime analysis units are crime analysis assistants/technicians, entry-level crime analysts, experienced crime analysts, and specialty crime analysts. The latter may specialize in a particular type of crime, for instance, sex crimes, school crimes, or the mapping of crime.

Crime mapping has become an increasingly popular aspect of crime analysis. Historically, crime mapping consisted of police personnel using simplified maps and pins to track crime in their respective jurisdictions. The information generated by pin mapping helped identify "hot spots" of criminal activity. The earlier practice of pin-mapping has largely been replaced by technology-driven geospatial crime-fighting efforts and computers that now provide sophisticated analyses of crime and other behaviors relevant to criminal justice. Geographic information systems (GIS) applications, which drives crime mapping, can convert layers of information into visual form to assist analysts in detecting relationships between times, places, events, and trends.

Police analysts began increasingly using computerized crime mapping beginning in the mid-1980s primarily in response to the accessibility and enhanced abilities of computer systems, the introduction and continuous development of GIS software, and directed crime prevention efforts that heavily consider geographical factors (Paulsen & Robinson, 2004). The increased role and significance of crime mapping information systems in departments worldwide is aptly noted by Roman Kmet (2021, 53), who noted that they are "… a commonly used tool by public authorities, primarily for the police, security forces and services, local and regional government, as well as for inhabitants of a certain territory."

Geospatial crime mapping is used in all components of the criminal justice system. For example, attorneys may use computer-generated maps to present some types of evidence, while community supervision officers use maps to locate the homes of supervisees for the purposes of service area allocation. Geospatial mapping, however, is most commonly used in policing, particularly with regard to patrol, investigation, community relations, and administration.

The continuous incorporation of computerized mapping has assisted criminal justice agencies in many ways. Being able to visually assess where and what types of crimes predominantly occur, in visual form, has assisted many police departments. Courtroom decisions have been assisted through visual depictions of information that can be easily interpreted. Many areas of the criminal justice system have increasingly integrated crime mapping into their crime and justice-based practices, and it is expected that they will continue to do so. Individuals with crime mapping skills will likely encounter an increasing number of employment opportunities in the years ahead.

Crime analysts who incorporate mapping into their work should be prepared to work in an office in front of a computer. Their work is basically information-processing, and critical to continuous progress in the criminal justice system. The use of GIS demonstrates the adaptability of the criminal justice system with regard to technology, and generates many new positions throughout the field. All students with an interest in this area are encouraged to take relevant courses and become notably familiar with GIS programs. Courses may be offered at local colleges and universities, or it may be necessary for students to attend conferences and workshops that provide hands-on instruction. Students may consider double-majoring in criminal justice and computer science, or majoring in one and minoring in the other.

Anyone interested in crime mapping is encouraged to download the free software "CrimeStat" offered by the US National Institute of Justice (at https://nij.ojp.gov/library/nij-funded-software-tools-apps-and-databases#maps) and become familiar with mapping. The site also provides other free software programs that assist with investigations and research in crime and justice. Those seeking a career in mapping or any other technology-based aspect of law enforcement are strongly encouraged to develop skills and interact with the software tools. Further, several books, including *Using Computer Science in High-Tech Criminal Justice Careers* (Hand, 2018) and *Exploring Careers in Cybersecurity and Digital Forensics* (Tsado & Osgood, 2022), provide robust accounts of the role of high technology in criminal justice and criminology careers.

Forensic Science

Career selection is based upon many factors, including media depictions of crime and justice. The effects on viewers of the popular television show CSI has been discussed in terms of whether or not it influences courtroom practices (e.g., Cole & Porter, 2018) and career choices (Collica-Cox & Furst, 2019). Regardless of whether or not the show and related

Careers in forensic science became increasingly popular in response to media depictions of the field. Employment in the area typically requires specialization in specific disciplines.
Source: https://pixabay.com/illustrations/nypd-police-crime-scene-detection-849659/

media accounts impact behaviors and choices, it remains that a career in forensic science offers opportunities to fight crime and secure justice.

The term "forensic science" simply refers to the use of science to detect and solve crimes. It encompasses various areas that require specialization in different areas of the hard sciences, as can be speculated from the titles of the areas within forensic science. Those areas include (Dempsey, 2003):

- Ballistics, which involves the study of bullets, firearms, and other projectiles
- Tool mark comparison, which involves examination of the possibility of particular tools (e.g., hammers or screwdrivers) being used in a crime
- Serology, sometimes referred to as biology screening, it involves analyses of bodily fluids such as blood and semen
- Toxicology, which involves testing biological samples for the presence of drugs and other toxic substances
- Questioned document analysis, which consists of analyses of written and printed documents, including handwriting samples, computer printouts, and ink
- Photo analysis, which involves analyzing photographs, including x-rays and digital imagery
- Forensic pathology, which is the scientific evaluation of dead bodies and involves investigation of sudden and/or unexplained deaths
- Physical anthropology, which involves analyses of skeletal remains of bodies
- Forensic entomology, which involves analyses of insects found on decomposing dead bodies
- Forensic odontology, which involves the study of dental remains of dead bodies
- DNA profiling, which involves examination of DNA samples
- Biometric identification, which involves analyses of physical characteristics that distinguish individuals, for instance, hand geometry and iris scanning.

As noted, these positions require specialization in areas outside of criminal justice and criminology studies. Individuals interested in careers in forensic science should strongly consider specializing in whatever area is most related to their career choice. For instance, those interested in DNA profiling are strongly encouraged to major in chemistry and criminal justice or criminology.

Careers in forensic science are safer than many other positions in criminal justice or criminology. They are also more traditional in the sense that one would be more likely to work in a lab for a prescribed number of hours each day. Testifying in court may be part of the job requirements, and report writing that documents one's findings is often required. The following positions highlight the opportunities available within the forensic science:

- Ballistic specialists, also known as firearms examiners, analyze weapons and bullets used in crimes. Their work is conducted in a lab, and they have specialized skills that enable them to closely analyze, identify, and classify all things related to firearms.
- Toolmark specialists examine tools or objects used in the commission of a crime. They search for specific markings that would connect the tool to the crime scene and/or the accused. They may look for scratches, marks, indentations, or any other distinguishable features in contributing to criminal investigations.
- Serology specialists analyze body fluids (e.g., urine, blood, semen), often to determine if the evidence collected from a crime scene matches the accused.
- Questioned document analysts evaluate handwriting samples, ink, paper, personal documents, and related documents to assist with the investigation of forgery and related

crimes. Their expertise helps identify possible links between documents collected as evidence and the accused.
- Fingerprint specialists collect, classify, and analyze fingerprints. They seek to link evidence collected from a crime scene with persons who may be responsible.

There are, of course, many other positions within the forensic sciences. It is anticipated that this field will continue to grow as the hard sciences are increasingly used in the criminal justice system.

Other Crime and Justice-Based Employment Opportunities

There are, of course, other justice-based employment opportunities not covered in this and preceding chapters. For instance, criminal justice continues to become international in nature, although international opportunities are not often mentioned in discussions of employment in the field. Many of the same opportunities referenced in this book are available in other countries, and several international groups offer exciting employment opportunities to address crime and justice from a more global perspective. For instance, INTERPOL consists of nearly 200 member-countries and facilitates international law enforcement cooperation, and Europol performs many of the same functions in Europe. Further, the United Nations at times addresses issues pertaining to crime and justice, and provides another avenue of employment for those interested in working on a global scale. One could also work for the many nongovernmental organizations (NGOs) that address international crime and social justice issues, yet are operated independent of governments. For instance, employment opportunities exist with Human Rights Watch or Amnesty International, both of which protects human rights internationally. NGOs assist in different areas (e.g., justice, public health), and provide excellent opportunities to gain experience and assist others. A systematic review of the research literature suggested NGOs have positive effects on health and governance (Brass et al., 2018).

Many nonprofit groups offer helpful opportunities for employment for students of criminal justice or criminology. Various positions noted throughout those book (e.g., victim advocate, reentry personnel) are housed within nonprofit agencies. The term "nonprofit" does not mean that employees are not paid. Crime and justice-based agencies often rely on the services of nonprofit groups and agencies.

The justice systems throughout the United States require some level of administration, which in turn generates additional employment opportunities for those with an interest in criminal justice or criminology and public administration. Career opportunities in this area generally require knowledge in both fields, and include positions such as a criminal justice administrator, and criminal justice research and planning analyst. These positions are found in all justice systems, and involve more traditional work environments and traditional work hours compared to many other positions in criminal justice.

The proliferation of the study of criminal justice and criminology across the United States dictates that additional teachers will be needed at high schools, colleges, and universities to offer criminal justice and criminology instruction. Such programs are growing at a notable rate in higher education (Stringer & Murphy, 2020), and becoming increasingly popular at the high school level. A master's degree and preferably a Ph.D. is required of most who wish to teach criminal justice or criminology at colleges and/or universities. A master's degree and some experience may suffice for employment at most two-year colleges and some universities, however, a terminal degree is required by many four-year universities. Those interested in a career in academia need to assemble a curriculum vitae instead of a resume. A vita is similar to a resume as it highlights one's professional experience and history; however, it focuses more on research, teaching, and service to the community and field. Many helpful resources exist to prepare for a career in academia, including some focused on criminal justice and criminology (e.g., Radatz & Slakoff, 2021). Appendix F highlights the categories of information that are included in a vita.

> **A Practitioner's View**
>
> Michael J. Lynch, Professor and Graduate Director, Department of Criminology, University of South Florida
>
> There are different kinds of professors. My career has focused more on research and mentoring graduate students at the highest-level research University. For example, the University I work at is classified as a Carnegie Very High Research Activity (R1) Doctoral University, which is the top of the University classification scale. One-hundred and thirty US Universities are classified as R1 institutions. While I spend a good deal of time mentoring graduate students, I often teach undergraduate courses. I have directed 26 doctoral dissertations and 25 MA theses, which is quite a few, and doing so is one way I assist students but also shape the field.
>
> In terms of shaping the field, I am an unusual criminologist since I created an area of research that has expanded and is now recognized as a legitimate part of criminology (i.e., green criminology, which didn't exist before I defined it). Other portions of my research examine radical criminology (e.g., class and crime, and class biases in criminal justice processes and the application of law), corporate crime and its control, environmental injustice, environmental sociology, and racial biases in criminal justice processes. To do research appropriately requires correct training (i.e., getting a Ph.D.) and then practicing your trade consistently over the course of your career. For criminologists working in Ph.D. programs, being average means having about two publications a year, while being among the top criminologists in the world requires publishing several articles or books a year, and having others in your field cite those works.

The requirement for additional degrees may discourage some students from seeking a career in academia. Research in the area found that women; students who are encouraged to attend graduate school; students less averse to writing, reading, and statistics; and students who perceive more diversity intolerance were more likely to be interested in graduate education in criminal justice or criminology (Cooper et al., 2019). Anyone with an interest in attending graduate school should conduct their own research, speak with faculty, and visit graduate programs to learn more.

Encouragement for Career Advancement

Complicating matters in this attempt to document the opportunities for employment in criminal justice and criminology is the fact that positions are created on an ongoing basis. In other words, more opportunities for employment in the fields will emerge as time goes on. Consider the number and variety of jobs in criminal justice and criminology in the 1950s. Now, consider all that are available today. There are substantial differences in terms of the quantity and quality of positions, due in large part to the social and technological changes we've experienced.

Today's criminal justice and criminology students are strongly encouraged to consider ways that they can contribute to and enhance our understanding of crime and justice-based practices. For example, today's young adults are more skilled with technology than their predecessors. This enhanced familiarity with technology could be applied to criminal justice practices and services. In other words, students entering the criminal justice and criminology workforce should continuously consider ways to enhance the system. Further, they should continuously consider means by which they can perhaps start their own business that provides a unique or advanced justice-based service, or patent a particular crime prevention or crime-fighting product. For instance, police departments are continuously seeking new less-lethal weapons in efforts to subdue uncooperative suspects without taking their lives. The onus is on the forthcoming generations to improve current practices. Strongly consider, and continue to consider ways that you can contribute to the improvement. Creativity, entrepreneurship, and initiative will help tomorrow's justice-based employees be successful and create a better society.

The term "think outside the box" has become somewhat cliché in society. Students, workers, politicians, and the like are often encouraged to "think outside the box." But what, specifically, does that mean? The term refers to the encouragement of thoughts that are not mainstream, or status quo. It promotes creativity in the form of critical thinking (another term that has become cliché) and consideration of alternatives. Such encouragement of creativity and consideration of alternatives are notably suitable for those considering a career in criminal justice or criminology. Particularly, the areas of crime and justice are ripe for entrepreneurship. Consider these critical factors: a public that is willing to spend resources for protection; behavior (i.e., criminal behavior) that is not going to drastically change in the near future; and a criminal justice system that continuously needs reform. These market factors are encouraging for anyone who wishes to make a change and create a fulfilling and lucrative career providing services as they relate to crime and justice.

Consider, for example, the low-tech, yet highly popular (and profitable) crime prevention device known as The Club. There's not much to The Club other than reinforced steel and locks used to secure automobile steering wheels. Its creator, James E. Winner, Jr., was savvy enough to mass produce The Club and his efforts paid off. Winner, Jr. started marketing The Club after his Cadillac was stolen, even though it had a factory-installed alarm. Winner, Jr. was an Army veteran, and recalled how he used a secured chain to prevent the theft of his vehicle while serving a tour of duty in Korea. He later created and sold The Club, a profitable and helpful contribution to crime prevention practices (TheClub.com, 2020). It is important for tomorrow's criminologists and criminal justice professionals to continuously consider what they can contribute to the fields. Simply, they should remain optimistic, and consider how things "can be done," as opposed to why things "can't be done." This basic change in mindset will likely pay substantial dividends.

The interdisciplinary nature of criminal justice and criminology results in crime and justice-based employment positions found in many subject areas. Positions in the fields often require familiarity with the principles of, and information generated by other disciplines, including sociology, business, biology, psychology, chemistry, computer science, economics, social work, and political science. Accordingly, employment opportunities related to crime and justice are found in science and medical labs, in computer labs, in offices, on the streets, in courtrooms, in homeless shelters, and in many other areas. Those interested in a career in criminal justice or criminology shouldn't have tunnel vision and assume that they are simply restricted to being a police officer, judge, attorney, or corrections officer. These can be wonderful careers and there are many of them; however, tomorrow's workers should seek to create new positions and products that will facilitate improvement of the day-to-day operations of the criminal justice system, and create a more orderly and just society.

Summary

Criminal justice and criminology have become increasingly popular areas of study in colleges and universities across the United States. The increase may be attributable to the influences of popular culture, or the discipline may simple be coming of age and students and employers are truly recognizing the benefits of a criminal justice or criminology education. Or, perhaps, there are other reasons for the increased academic interest in the fields. Regardless, much of the increase has come when, arguably, many criminal justice and criminology students are largely unaware of the vast array of positions within the field.

Some of the more nontraditional employment and internship opportunities with regard to crime and justice involve providing services to victims, working in the private security field, and analyzing crime. International and administrative positions are also available, as are a host of other opportunities. Each of these areas may be overlooked by criminal justice and criminology students, which is unfortunate given that preparation for a career in these areas generally occurs throughout one's academic career, and arguably their life; not simply when they receive a diploma.

The futures of criminal justice and criminology are unknown, although one thing can be sure. Change will occur and new products and services will be marketed to improve justice-based, crime prevention, and crime-fighting efforts. Tomorrow's employees should not be content to sit back and wait for others to make the change.

Discussion Questions

1. What are the benefits and challenges of working with victims of crime? Are you interested in a career in the area? Why or why not?
2. What services are provided by the private security industry? Do you believe society values the industry's contributions as much as it should? Why or why not?
3. Do you believe crime analysis and crime mapping will increasingly impact police departments and other groups in the future? Why or why not?
4. Do you believe the media and popular culture misrepresent the duties and responsibilities of forensic scientists? Why or why not?
5. What skills do you believe will be particularly important for criminal justice professionals and criminologists in the next ten years?

Critical Thinking Exercise

Do an online search using the term "crime news" to identify recent accounts of crime. Read the articles and record the names of the jobs mentioned in the first seven articles. For instance, do they mention police officers, judges, prison officers, or prosecutors? See which positions are most commonly referenced. Which positions that were likely involved are not mentioned? Also, note the actions of the criminal justice officials involved in the account. For instance, was a police officer making an arrest? Was a judge imposing a sentence? Were there any unexpected findings?

For Further Examination

Button, M. (2020). The "new" private security industry, the private policing of cyberspace and the regulatory questions. *Journal of Contemporary Criminal Justice, 36*(1), 39–55.

Ellis, C., & Knight, K.E. (2021). Advancing a model of secondary trauma: Consequences for victim service providers. *Journal of Interpersonal Violence, 36*(7–8), 3557–3583.

Hamlin, C. (2021). What's scientific about forensic science? Three versions of American forensics, 1903–1965, and one modest proposal. *Academic Forensic Pathology, 11*(1), 24–40.

Piza, E.L., Szkola, J., & Blount-Hill, K-L. (2021). How can embedded criminologists, police pracademics, and crime analysts help increase police-led program evaluations? A survey of authors cited in the evidence-based policing matrix. *Policing: A Journal of Policy and Practice, 15*(2), 1217–1231.

Walters, G.D., Runell, L., & Kremser, J. (2022). Career aspirations, influences, and motives in undergraduate criminal justice majors: A comparison of two student cohorts assessed seven years apart. *Journal of Criminal Justice Education, 33*(4), 605–619. DOI:10.1080/10511253.2022.2025875

References

Brass, J.N., Longhofer, W., Robinson, R.S., & Schnable, A. (2018). NGOS and international development: A review of thirty-five years of scholarship. *World Development, 112*, 136–149.

Bureau of Labor Statistics. (2022a). Information security analysts. U.S. Department of Labor. Available at: www.bls.gov/ooh/computer-and-information-technology/information-security-analysts.htm

Bureau of Labor Statistics. (2022b). Private detectives and investigators. U.S. Department of Labor. Available at: www.bls.gov/ooh/protective-service/private-detectives-and-investigators.htm

Bureau of Labor Statistics. (2022c). Data for occupations not covered in detail. U.S. Department of Labor. Available at: www.bls.gov/ooh/about/data-for-occupations-not-covered-in-detail.htm

Business Wire. (2021, June 7). Global home security systems market (2022 to 2027). Available at: www.businesswire.com/news/home/20220607005949/en/Global-Home-Security-Systems-Market-2022-to-2027---Implementation-of-AI-and-Deep-Learning-in-Home-Security-Systems-Presents-Opportunities---ResearchAndMarkets.com

Button, M. (2020). The "new" private security industry, the private policing of cyberspace and the regulatory questions. *Journal of Contemporary Criminal Justice, 36*(1), 39–55.

Cole, S.A., & Porter, G. (2018). The CSI effect. In Cole, S.A. & Porter, G. (eds.), *The Routledge international handbook of forensic intelligence and criminology* (pp. 112–124). Routledge.

Collica-Cox, K., & Furst, G. (2019). It's not the CSI effect: Criminal justice students' choice of major and career goals. *International Journal of Offender Therapy and Comparative Criminology, 63*(11), 2069–2099.

Cooper, M.N., Updegrove, A.H., & Bouffard, J.A. (2019). Predictors of criminal justice undergraduates' intentions to pursue graduate education in criminology or criminal justice. *Journal of Criminal Justice Education, 30*(1), 46–70.

Dempsey, J. S. (2003). *Introduction to investigations* (2nd ed.). Wadsworth.

Hand, C. (2018). *Using computer science in high-tech criminal justice careers.* Rosen Publishing.

Hess, K.M., & Wrobleski, H.M. (1996). *Introduction to private security* (4th ed.). West.

Kmet, R. (2021). Analysis of current practical solutions of crime mapping information systems. *Defense and Security Studies, 2*, 53–62.

Paulsen, D.J., & Robinson, M.B. (2004). *Spatial aspects of crime: Theory and practice.* Allyn and Bacon.

Provost, C. (2017). The industry of inequality: Why the world is obsessed with private security. *TheGuardian.com.* Available at: www.theguardian.com/inequality/2017/may/12/industry-of-inequality-why-world-is-obsessed-with-private-security

Radatz, D.L., & Slakoff, D.C. (2021). A practical guide to the criminology and criminal justice job market for doctoral candidates: Pre-market preparation through offers and negotiations. *Journal of Criminal Justice Education.* DOI: /10.1080/10511253.2021.1966061

Stringer, E.C., & Murphy, J. (2020). Major decisions and career attractiveness among criminal justice students. *Journal of Criminal Justice Education, 31*(4), 523–541.

TheClub.com. (2020). The CLUB legacy. Available at: https://winner-intl.com/the-club-legacy/

Tsado, L.K., & Osgood, R. (2022). *Exploring careers in cybersecurity and digital forensics.* Rowman & Littlefield.

Virginia Department of Criminal Justice Services. (2022). Personal protection specialist. Available at: www.dcjs.virginia.gov/licensure-and-regulatory-affairs/personal-protection-specialist

Chapter 14

Epilogue

Having read the previous chapters you should feel prepared for a career criminal justice or criminology. However, you're probably not quite there. Reading about working in criminal justice or criminology and actually doing so are two different things. For instance, I can read a war novel, yet could never truly understand what it's like to fight in a war without having done so. Nevertheless, I could say that after reading the novel I better understand what it's like to be a soldier, and that alone is helpful. Similarly, you can state that you better understand what to expect upon beginning your career after reading about careers in criminal justice and criminology.

The term epilogue refers to "a concluding part added to a literary work." Accordingly, this concluding section adds to the previous chapters by offering advice regarding promotions and overall career development. Much of the information earlier shared in this work guided readers in anticipation of working in criminal justice or criminology. This epilogue provides assistance regarding employment *after* getting a job, and what one can generally expect and prepare for throughout their career. Largely through the use of scenarios, the information regarding promotions offers direction for career progression, while the section on career development addresses the expectations associated with progressing through a career.

Promotions

Promotions can be viewed as a reward for a job well done, recognition of one's abilities, and opportunities to further demonstrate competency or perhaps mastery in one's field. Most employees exert significant efforts working toward a promotion. Workers sometimes may lose sight of organizational goals as personal goals, including job promotion and salary increases take precedence. Promotions and salary are certainly important, as are enhanced job responsibilities, greater supervisory power, and perhaps greater opportunities to make a difference, which typically accompany a promotion. The benefits of a promotion are certainly real; however, there may be unanticipated intangibles associated with a promotion. Consider the following scenarios as they pertain to promotions.

Francisco worked as a probation officer for six years. In that time, he demonstrated continuous improvement and his annual evaluations were above the average of his coworkers. Francisco was told he was targeted for promotion to a supervisory position within his agency. The news encouraged Francisco to perform his job even more professionally. Francisco applied for the supervisor position and thought for sure that he would get the promotion. He was disheartened to hear that the position was given to one of his coworkers. He felt even worse when he found out that the coworker who was promoted had less experience than Francisco, and the recipient's annual evaluations were average at best. Even worse, the coworker would be Francisco's immediate supervisor.

Francisco initially continued working in the manner he had prior to being denied the promotion. However, he soon became less enthusiastic about his work and felt he was in a dead-end position. He was distant from his new supervisor and resented the fact that the less qualified candidate received the job. His performance slipped a bit over the next few years, and Francisco chose not to apply for the two supervisor position openings that arose during that time. Francisco truly believed he would end his career in his current position.

This scenario highlights an unforeseen challenge associated with opportunities for promotion and demonstrates how not being promoted can impact workers. What could Francisco have done to improve his chances for promotion? How could he have better handled not getting promoted? What were his options following being passed for promotion? There are many acceptable responses to these questions. To begin, Francisco could have improved his chances for promotion in many ways. He instead took an unprofessional approach to not being promoted. Sure, he was disappointed; who wouldn't be? Tuning out, becoming disinterested in one's work, and giving up on promotion simply because one feels cheated, however, does little good for anyone. Francisco could have assessed his situation and sought the most effective and opportunistic options. Perhaps most important, he could have scheduled a meeting with whoever was in charge of hiring to perhaps gain an understanding of where he was lacking and why he was overlooked for the position. Such meetings are not always comfortable, for instance, because Francisco doesn't necessarily want to hear about his shortcomings and supervisors typically don't want to directly tell someone about their shortcomings. Nevertheless, this type of meeting would help Francisco redirect his efforts and increase his likelihood of being promoted the next time an opportunity arose. Perhaps Francisco was next in line for a supervisory position, yet was passed over because of the manner in which he responded to being overlooked for the initial promotion. Francisco could have also approached the situation by embracing the change and continuously improving in his position. Or, he could have sought employment with a different agency.

The repercussions of being promoted are sometimes as difficult as the effects of not being promoted. In other words, one should be careful of what they wish for. Consider another scenario involving Francisco. Let's suppose he received the initial promotion and was now the office supervisor. Francisco was now "in charge" of his friends/colleagues and had to ensure that they were accountable and responsible. He knew much about his friends/colleagues having worked with them for years. He knew their strengths and weaknesses. Personally, he liked the fact that he was recognized for his accomplishments by being promoted, yet he was uncertain of his leadership skills. How would he handle supervising his close friends? Would they still treat him the same? As it turns out, Francisco's friends slowly distanced from him. Francisco was less and less frequently invited to social outings and things just weren't the same. He was also given much more work and many new responsibilities, so being dismissed from the social network wasn't as painful simply because he seemingly was always working and stressed to meet deadlines.

In this scenario, the much sought-after promotion eventually changed Francisco's life for the worse. Yes, he was recognized for his diligence; however, he lost his primary group of friends and found himself working more than he anticipated. This scenario is not provided to discourage anyone from seeking a promotion. One should always seek opportunities to advance professionally. The scenario was provided, however, to encourage individuals to anticipate some of the often overlooked effects and changes associated with a new position. A promotion typically results in many changes, and things will not remain the same upon receiving one. Determining what type of promotion best suits your needs requires a thorough evaluation of all that the promotion entails. Simply being promoted is not, in and of itself, necessarily a good thing. The same research skills used to investigate new jobs should be used to learn about new positions.

Promotions benefit the employee in many ways, which is essentially workers seek them. Many steps can be taken by employees who wish to improve their chances of being promoted. Career advice expert Angela Copeland (n.d.) offered ten strategies for getting promoted. These strategies include:

1. **Developing mentoring relationships with someone higher in the company** – Mentors can help spread positive information among the administration and can be an effective source for information and career guidance.
2. **Quantifying results** – Make a strong case for promotion by showing detailed information about your past success. Quantify your results to demonstrate how you have assisted the overall well-being of your agency or company. Emphasize your accomplishments through the use of evidence.
3. **Practicing self-promotion** – Make people aware of your accomplishments in subtle, but effective manners. Modesty is indeed virtuous, but there comes a point at which a bit of self-promotion assists with getting promoted. Be sure to avoid overpromoting yourself, as this may come across to others as bragging.
4. **Establishing bonds with superiors** – It makes sense to befriend and earn the respect of those who have some level of control over your career progression. Superiors can be the ones who decide whether or not you get promoted, for instance, by offering positive or negative feedback regarding your work performance. Demonstrate to your superiors that you are competent, are interested in progressing through the ranks, and maintain a sincere interest in the well-being of the company, agency, or business. Bonding with superiors may entail learning more about their personal interests and chatting with them about the topics in various informal settings.
5. **Acquiring knowledge and skills** – One of the most effective aspects of career development is the acquisition of skills or knowledge that makes you critical to the well-being of the agency. Obtaining skill sets and knowledge germane to the industry make employees more marketable in many ways. Keeping abreast of developments with regard to industry news, events, and changes within one's area of specialty largely contribute to effectively performing one's job. This, in turn, should impress supervisors and contribute to getting promoted. Be an expert in your area of concentration.
6. **Building a network** – It is commonly suggested by career professionals that landing the perfect job and getting promoted is not necessarily based on what you know, but who you know. Networking with others both within and outside of one's place of employment is particularly helpful in getting a promotion. Building a strong reputation in your field has many positive impacts.
7. **Asking for more responsibilities** – Volunteering to take on new projects or helping fellow employees makes you appear as a team player and expands your knowledge base and skill sets. One should only request additional responsibilities, however, when the added work won't interfere with their current workload. It is not always a good idea to be a "jack of all trades, yet master of nothing," and a slippage in one's work performance may be detrimental to promotion opportunities. It may appear, for instance, that you cannot handle an extensive workload.
8. **Acting professionally at all times** – Professionalization is required in one's appearance, demeanor, work performance, timeliness, interaction with others, and various other aspects of employment if one expects a promotion. Problem-solving is an often overlooked aspect of professionalism. Supervisors generally prefer employees who can effectively handle problematic situations without the assistance of others. Focus on solving problems and not creating them.

9. **Being a team player** – It may be the case that personal goals or interests may be temporarily sacrificed for the benefit of the agency, business, or department. Teamwork is essential for the completion of many tasks, and being an effective team player will likely pay long-term dividends, including a promotion.
10. **Creating your own opportunities** – "Critical thinking" has been a buzzword at universities and colleges across the United States. Accordingly, students are often taught to critically assess various situations. Use critical thinking skills to determine and respond to neglected areas in your field or place of employment. For instance, consider whether technological developments could enhance service efforts. Is there a product currently on the market that could improve agency performance and save company resources? If so, bring it to the attention of your supervisors.

Dr. Copeland's strategies are indeed effective in working toward promotion and overall career development. The onus is on employees to proactively engage these strategies, with particular concern for their current employment situations; changes and developments in their workplace, field, and society in general; and their own personal makeup. It may be easier for workers to employ some of these steps, yet not others. For instance, one may not be able to easily quantify their accomplishments. Regardless, anyone interested in a promotion should adopt as many of these strategies as possible throughout their career.

Setting goals and aiming for promotions are often vital components of one's overall career development. Those in or entering the workforce should have some idea of where they wish to be in five, ten, or even twenty years. Understanding the steps necessary to attain those goals involves recognition of the accomplishments, including promotions, needed for success. Mapping one's anticipated career development is challenging and filled with uncertainty; however, it is necessary.

Networking, remaining flexible, being timely and diligent, making yourself especially valuable, and seeking excellence are among the steps required for promotions and overall career development.
Source:https://pixabay.com/photos/entrepreneur-begin-start-up-career-3245868/

Career Development

The likelihood of success in one's career development is contingent upon a series of good decisions. For instance, consider mapping the course your life has taken thus far. If you're like most others in society, you were faced with critical points in life in which you were forced to make key decisions. Hopefully, you always made and continue to make the most appropriate decisions; however, we're all not so fortunate. Everyone has made an inappropriate decision at some point. The key to effective career development is to not make poor career-related decisions and to minimize any negative impacts associated with the decisions you make. Doing this is sometimes easier said than done and requires luck, intuitiveness, and effort. How one responds to difficult and challenging situations reflects their true character. One of the best ways to minimize poor decisions in the workforce is to become educated in the area of career development.

Numerous books, programs, podcasts, websites, and articles offer advice for getting hired, getting promoted, retiring early, and various other aspects of employment. One could easily be overwhelmed by sheer amount of available material; nevertheless, the resources can certainly enhance one's career development. The quality of these works must be taken into consideration by individuals anticipating successful career development. For instance, rarely is one going to find an employment-based resource or outlet that directly relates to their position and the circumstances they currently, or will potentially, face. There is no "one size fits all" resource when it comes to employment self-help materials. Accordingly, it is important for those interested in learning about career development competently consider how their situation best relates to what they read or hear.

One can read multiple books on career development and apply what they've read to their situation in the workforce. Nevertheless, one must remember to set goals, remain focused on those goals (or change them as needed), and be content with who they are and what they're doing. Much like businesses and corporations set goals and make substantial efforts to attain them, those entering and in the workforce should also set clear goals, identify objectives required to meet those goals, conduct periodic assessments of their progress, and establish a timetable to meet those goals. To be sure, one must remain flexible when trying to reach goals, as unanticipated personal, professional, and societal changes could certainly impact goal attainment.

The need to remain flexible with regard to setting and reaching professional goals is important. Flexibility in setting and reaching goals is vital for effective career development. For instance, consider a situation in which a young professional set goals and is on track toward reaching those goals, yet unexpectedly has to move home and take care of their parent who is in need of medical assistance. Their goals may be put on hold, or in need of change. Strict rigidity in goal attainment is admirable, but at some point being practical and responding to life challenges may need to take precedent.

Too often, a college degree is sought simply as a means to obtaining a preferred job. Lost in the student's development is a true desire for learning. In an ideal world, tests wouldn't be dreaded by students. Students would welcome exams as opportunities to demonstrate the vast amount of information they have attained. Enjoying the experience of learning and being an "information gatherer" undoubtedly contribute to career development. Aside from simply better understanding one's job, gatherers of information can speak to and interact with a variety of individuals on numerous topics. They will generally garner far more respect than those who know little other than the minimum expectations of their employment position.

Career development is largely facilitated by continuously growing and learning; remaining thirsty for knowledge. Keeping abreast of current events, understanding the latest technological developments, remaining in touch with the job market in one's field, and keeping abreast of industry trends in one's professional area of employment are among the most important areas in which one should remain knowledgeable. In sum, one should never stop wanting to learn.

The economy will likely have an impact on your professional career given that it can impact much of entire workforce. The impacts may be positive or negative. Either way, it is beyond your control. Preparing for economic changes requires both knowledge and flexibility, which contribute to effective career development. Particularly, understanding how financial market shifts directly impact one's current position and future employment opportunities is important for informed decision-making. Flexibility is required as changes of this nature bring about levels of uncertainty. For instance, cutbacks, layoffs, and/or decreased budgets could easily generate the need for employees to alter goals, find new jobs, or generally prepare themselves for a life that differs from what they anticipated. Having a plan for times of trouble or uncertainty is a key component of professional development.

Economic changes are not the only wildcards that influence career development. Chapter 3 focused on critical areas of change that will likely impact careers in criminal justice and criminology. For instance, changes in criminal behavior, technological changes, increased globalization, political developments, and other factors were identified as potentially impacting careers in the field. The global pandemic surrounding COVID-19 beginning in 2020 was largely unexpected and had substantial impacts on careers in the field. Working from home, social distancing, illnesses, cutbacks, quarantining, and many other factors affected many jobs, people, and agencies (e.g., Baldwin et al., 2020). Effective career development is dependent upon consideration of these and related factors as one prepares for changes and developments.

Universities and colleges regularly prepare students with a knowledge base in a variety of areas. Sometimes overlooked in the information is the ability to enter, survive, and prosper in the workforce. Unfortunately, students are often left on their own to prepare for a career in the field, and how to progress once they have one. Perhaps this limitation stems from the barriers that sometimes exist between academics and practitioners. For example, academics may not be overly concerned with the practical side of criminal justice, and practitioners are not always overly concerned with the theoretical underpinnings of crime and justice. Or, perhaps it exists because criminal justice and criminology programs are not always clear with regard to what they expect of their graduates. In other words, are criminal justice and criminology programs preparing theorists, practitioners, or both? Regardless, it is the responsibility of the individual who enters an academic program to make the decisions that are best for them. Such decision-making is enhanced through knowledge and an understanding of one's expectations and goals. Hopefully, this work assists your admirable efforts toward creating a better understanding of crime and justice, and a more effective criminal justice system that better protects society and truly ensures justice for all.

The future is not predetermined. Accordingly, one cannot predict what tomorrow will bring. Nevertheless, forecasters use various techniques, including quantitative and qualitative analyses, to identify anticipated changes in society. Those entering or already working within criminal justice or criminology are strongly encouraged to keep abreast of the changes and be flexible enough to adapt to any unforeseen challenges. Doing so will provide benefits in one's professional, social, and family life.

Perhaps most importantly, try to enjoy your career preparation, job search, job, and all else career-related. Some level of stress will certainly be involved at various points, but always take a step back and try to place things into proper perspective. If a job makes you miserable, consider finding one that doesn't. A positive outlook and perseverance will help in many ways with your career development. Life is too short to be unhappy with your career. Make efforts to find enjoyment in your career, or reboot and seek a career elsewhere. There are plenty of jobs and careers to choose from, and with a positive attitude and effort, you should be able to find a career that meets your needs.

Summary

Entering or progressing through the criminal justice or criminology workforce can be intimidating, rewarding, and challenging. How to best navigate your way through career development requires knowledge, and much of it. Too often, students gather knowledge simply for the sake of passing exams and earning high grades. Knowing how and what to learn are vital for any type of employment. For instance, it is important for those working in criminal justice or criminology to use their research skills to investigate employment positions, agencies, markets, promotions, and various other components related to the workforce. Learning facts are helpful if one plays the game show *Jeopardy*, but the ability and yearning to learn, and understanding how, what, and why to learn provide greater rewards throughout one's career and lifetime.

Well-roundedness, intuitiveness, motivation, professionalism, integrity, and high ethical standards are what employers seek in candidates. Studying what is needed for a job, how to obtain a job, what a job entails, and how to succeed in a position within criminal justice or criminology requires more than knowledge about crime and justice. The information attained in sociology courses could help students anticipate current, emerging, and future social problems. Political science programs offer government-focused courses in which students learn how politicians shape the direction of justice-based practices. Preparation for a career in the fields should entail serious consideration and understanding of the various areas both directly and indirectly related to criminal justice and criminology. It should also involve understanding of the most effective measures of locating and landing a preferred job, and how to progress beyond that position, if indeed that is what you seek. Such career development is part of a continuous process requiring efforts on your behalf, that in turn benefit you. Cutting corners, being lazy, and disinterest will have the largest impacts on you. Here's hoping you don't take that approach.

References

Baldwin, J.M., Eassey, J.M., & Brooke, E.J. (2020). Court operations during the COVID-19 pandemic. *American Journal of Criminal Justice, 45*, 743–758.

Copeland, A. (n.d.). How to get promoted: Strategies for moving up the corporate ladder. *LiveCareer.com*. Available at: www.livecareer.com/resources/careers/planning/getting-promoted-strategies

Appendix A

Sample Cover Letter, Resumes, and Follow-up Letter

SAMPLE COVER LETTER

July 8, 2022

Sergeant James Bollinger
Adberg Police Department
4397 Maytown Street
Adberg, CO 76502

Dear Sergeant Bollinger:

I am responding to your online advertisement for the position of Dispatcher. My familiarity with the Adberg Police Department prompted me to apply for this position. Several officers in the department with whom I have spoken suggested I would be an asset to the agency and community.

With a Bachelors of Science in Criminal Justice and dispatcher experience through my internship with the Baytown Police Department, I believe I am well-prepared to effectively fulfill the requirements of your position. I received an exceptional evaluation from my internship site supervisor, who suggested that I should strongly consider a career in this field. A resume highlighting my background, education, work experience, and general qualifications is enclosed.

I thank you for your consideration of my application and credentials, and look forward to hearing from you. Please contact me should additional information be required.

Sincerely,

Kevin Bielen
2397 Winscott Lane
Barbrook, TX 88752

Encl. Resume

SAMPLE RESUME – CHRONOLOGICAL RESUME

Bradley Whitlock
198 South Ocean Street | Carroll, FL 85428 | (555) 555-5555 | bwhitlock@mail.com

Education
Master of Science in Criminal Justice   May 2019

- President of Criminal Justice Graduate Student group
- 3.93 GPA

Bachelor of Science in Criminology and Criminal Justice   May 2016
Eastern Pennsylvania University, Talbot, Pennsylvania

- Dean's list on five occasions
- Outstanding Criminal Justice Undergraduate Award recipient, Spring 2017
- Alpha Phi Sigma National Criminal Justice Honor Society member, 2014–Present
- Internship, Jackson County District Attorney's Office, Fall 2015

Experience
    Cardwell's Hardware, Talbot, Pennsylvania
    Director of Assets Protection   March 2019–Present

- Manage staff of five loss prevention personnel
- Assist in the day-to-day protection of store assets and protection of customers and employees
- Work directly with store managers and local criminal justice agencies
- Promoted twice, and attended three work-related training seminars focused on various aspects of loss prevention and security
- Helped reduce loss by 19% in 2020, and 25% in 2021

    Dayton's Department Store, Grandview, Arkansas
    Security Officer   May 2017–March 2019

- Provided protective, uniformed services for large retail store
- Monitored closed-circuit cameras and customer behaviors
- Contributed to 18% reduction in loss to the store
- Worked closely with local law enforcement agencies in various capacities, including attendance at two-day training seminar offered by police department

Honors

Cardwell's Hardware Employee of the Month, April 2020, November 2021
Dayton's Department Store Most Valuable Asset Award, *recipient*, 2018
Outstanding Criminal Justice Undergraduate Award, *recipient*, Spring 2015
Alpha Phi Sigma National Criminal Justice Honor Society, *member*, 2014–Present

Involvement

ASIS International, *member*, March 2018–Present
Midwestern Association of Criminal Justice, *member*, February 2017–Present
Society of Young Professionals, *member*, March 2020–Present

SAMPLE RESUME – FUNCTIONAL RESUME

Bradley Whitlock
198 South Ocean Street | Carroll, FL 85428 | (555) 555-5555 | bwhitlock@mail.com

Experience

Cardwell's Hardware, Talbot, Pennsylvania
Director of Assets Protection   March 2019–Present

- Manage staff of five loss prevention personnel
- Assist in the day-to-day protection of store assets and protection of customers and employees
- Work directly with store managers and local criminal justice agencies
- Promoted twice, and attended three work-related training seminars focused on various aspects of loss prevention and security
- Helped reduce loss by 19% in 2020, and 25% in 2021

Dayton's Department Store, Grandview, Arkansas
Security Officer   May 2017–March 2019

- Provided protective, uniformed services for large retail store
- Monitored closed-circuit cameras and customer behaviors
- Assisted as needed in preventing and responding to emergency situations
- Worked closely with local law enforcement agencies in various capacities, including attendance at two-day training seminar offered by local police department

Jackson County District Attorney's Office, Jackson Pennsylvania
Student Intern   June 2015–December 2015

- Researched cases and generally assisted attorneys in case preparation
- Observed courtroom proceedings and discussed practices with attorneys
- Shadowed attorneys as they handled cases

Education

Master of Science in Criminal Justice May 2019
Bachelor of Science in Criminology and Criminal Justice May 2016
Eastern Pennsylvania University, Talbot, Pennsylvania

Honors

Cardwell's Hardware Employee of the Month, April 2020, November 2021
Dayton's Department Store Most Valuable Asset Award recipient, 2018
Outstanding Criminal Justice Undergraduate Award recipient, Spring 2017
Alpha Phi Sigma National Criminal Justice Honor Society member, 2014–Present

Involvement

ASIS International member, March 2018–Present
Midwestern Association of Criminal Justice member, February 2017–Present
Society of Young Professionals member, March 2020–Present

SAMPLE FOLLOW-UP LETTER

August 24, 2022

Jack Weatherbee, Director of Operations
New Hampshire Department of Probation and Parole
90823 Altamonte Drive
Worcester, NH 76312

Dear Mr. Weatherbee:

Thank you for your consideration of my application for the probation officer position with your agency. I hand-delivered my application packet to your office on July 24 and am sorry to have missed you.

I remain particularly interested in the position and look forward to hearing from you. Please contact me if you need any further information as you proceed through the hiring process.

Sincerely,

Braylen Edwards
3904 Third Street
Wainscott, NH 88793
872-984-0623
bedwards@mail.com

This will also be available to download on the book page on Routledge.com.

Appendix B

State Labor Offices

The following is a listing of state agencies that are helpful with regard to employment in the criminal justice system.

Alabama
Alabama Department of Labor
www.labor.alabama.gov

Alaska
Alaska Department of Labor and Workforce Development
www.labor.state.ak.us

Arizona
Industrial Commission of Arizona
www.azica.gov

Arkansas
Arkansas Department of Labor & Licensing
www.labor.arkansas.gov

California
California Department of Industrial Relations
www.dir.ca.gov/contactus.html

Colorado
Colorado Department of Labor and Employment
www.coloradolaborlaw.gov

Connecticut
Connecticut Department of Labor
www.ct.gov/dol

Delaware
Delaware Division of Industrial Affairs
www.delawareworks.com

District of Columbia
Washington D.C. Department of Employment Services
www.does.dc.gov

Florida
Florida Department of Economic Opportunity
www.floridajobs.org

Georgia
Georgia Department of Labor
www.dol.state.ga.us

Hawaii
Department of Labor & Industrial Relations
www.labor.hawaii.gov

Idaho
Idaho Department of Labor
www.labor.idaho.gov

Illinois
Illinois Department of Labor
www2.illinois.gov/idol

Indiana
Indiana Department of Labor
www.in.gov/dol

Iowa
Iowa Workforce Development
www.iowaworkforcedevelopment.gov/

Kansas
Kansas Department of Labor
www.dol.ks.gov

Kentucky
Kentucky Labor Cabinet
www.labor.ky.gov

Louisiana
Louisiana Workforce Commission
www2.laworks.net

Maine
Maine Department of Labor
www.maine.gov/labor

Maryland
Maryland Department of Labor, Licensing and Regulation
www.dllr.state.md.us

Massachusetts
Massachusetts Executive Office of Labor & Workforce Development
www.mass.gov/eolwd

Michigan
Michigan Department of Labor and Economic Opportunity
www.michgan.gov/lara

Minnesota
Minnesota Department of Labor and Industry
www.dli.mn.gov

Mississippi
Mississippi Department of Employment Security
www.mdes.ms.gov

Missouri
Missouri Department of Labor and Industrial Relations Commission
www.labor.mo.gov

Montana
Montana Department of Labor and Industry
www.dli.mt.gov

Nebraska
Nebraska Department of Labor
www.dol.nebraska.gov

Nevada
Nevada Department of Business and Industry
Labor.nv.gov

New Hampshire
New Hampshire Department of Labor
www.nh.gov/labor/

New Jersey
New Jersey Department of Workforce Development
www.nj.gov/labor/

New Mexico
New Mexico Department of Workforce Solutions
www.dws.state.nm.us

New York
New York State Department of Labor
www.labor.ny.gov

North Carolina
North Carolina Department of Labor
www.labor.nc.gov

North Dakota
North Dakota Department of Labor
www.nd.gov/labor

Ohio
Ohio Department of Commerce
com.ohio.gov

Oklahoma
Oklahoma Department of Labor
www.labor.ok.gov

Oregon
Oregon Bureau of Labor and Industries
www.oregon.gov/boli

Pennsylvania
Pennsylvania Department of Labor and Industry
www.dli.state.pa.us

Rhode Island
Rhode Island Department of Labor and Training
www.dlt.ri.gov

South Carolina
South Carolina Department of Labor, Licensing & Regulations
www.llr.state.sc.us

South Dakota
South Dakota Department of Labor and Regulation
www.dlr.sd.gov

Tennessee
Department of Labor & Workforce Development
www.tn.gov/workforce

Texas
Texas Workforce Commission
www.twc.state.tx.us

Utah
Utah Labor Commission
www.laborcommisssion.utah.gov

Vermont
Vermont Department of Labor
www.labor.vermont.gov

Virginia
Virginia Department of Labor and Industry
www.doli.Virginia.gov

Washington
Washington Department of Labor and Industries
www.lni.wa.gov

West Virginia
West Virginia Division of Labor
labor.wv.gov

Wisconsin
Wisconsin Department of Workforce Development
dwd.wisconsin.gov

Wyoming
Wyoming Department of Workforce Services
www.wyomingworkforce.org

Source: U.S. Department of Labor. (2021). State labor offices. Available at: www.dol.gov/agencies/whd/state/contacts

This will also be available to download on the book page on Routledge.com.

Appendix C

Federal Criminal Justice and Criminology Employment Resources

Many individuals interested in criminal justice and criminology wish to work at the federal level, particularly federal law enforcement. Unfortunately, there is much uncertainty among the general public, including criminal justice students, regarding federal-level criminal justice in the U.S. The following information highlights a variety of resources available for better understanding, and applying for positions in criminal justice at the federal level. Some of the information pertains directly to employment; other resources provide supporting and background information that helps readers better understand the nature of working in criminal justice at the federal level. The material assists with preparing for, and obtaining careers in all aspects of federal criminal justice.

Articles/Reports

Brooks, C. (2022). *Federal law enforcement officers, 2020 – statistical tables.* U.S. Department of Justice, Bureau of Justice Statistics. NCJ 304752.

Collica-Cox, K., & Furst, G. (2019). It's not the CSI effect: Criminal justice students' choice of major and career goals. *International Journal of Offender Therapy and Comparative Criminology, 63*(11), 2069–2099.

Kowarski, I. (2020, September 24). How to become an FBI agent and why. *USNews.com.* Available at: www.usnews.com/education/best-colleges/articles/how-to-become-an-fbi-agent-and-why

Obert, J. (2017). A fragmented force: The evolution of federal law enforcement in the United States, 1870–1900. *Journal of Policy History, 29*(4), 640–675.

Roufa, T. (2019). Federal government criminal justice and law enforcement careers. *Thebalancecareers.com.* Available at: www.thebalancecareers.com/federal-law-enforcement-jobs-974533

Walker, J.T., Burns, R.G., Bumgarner, J., & Bratina, M.P. (2008). Federal law enforcement careers: Laying the groundwork. *Journal of Criminal Justice Education, 19*(1), 110–135.

Yu, H.H. (2015). An examination of women in federal law enforcement: An exploratory analysis of the challenges they face in the work environment. *Feminist Criminology, 10*(3), 259–278.

Yu, H.H. (2020). Glass ceiling in federal law enforcement: An exploratory analysis of the factors contributing to women's career advancement. *Review of Public Personnel Administration, 40*(2), 183–201.

Books

Alsup, W. (2019). *Won over: Reflections of a federal judge on his journey from Jim Crow Mississippi.* NewSouth Books.

Bumgarner, J., Crawford, C., & Burns, R. (2018). *Federal law enforcement: A primer.* Carolina Academic Press.

Comey, J. (2021). *Saving justice: Truth, transparency, and trust.* Flatiron Books.

Federal Law Enforcement Training Center. (2016). *F.L.E.T.C. legal division practice exams.* Department of Homeland Security. Penny Hill.

Lord, T. (2020). *… And justice for all: Life as a federal prosecutor upholding the rule of law.* Dorrance Publishing.

Slyker, J.E. (2020). *Outside looking in: My 29 year career as a federal employee at the Federal Bureau of Prisons.* Bowker.

Zupan, A. (2015). *FBI special agents are real people: True stories from everyday life of FBI special agents.* CreateSpace.

Links

Federal Bureau of Prisons, Careers – www.bop.gov/jobs/
Federal Public Defense Jobs – www.fd.org/employment
Federal Law Enforcement Training Centers – www.fletc.gov
Offices of the United States Attorneys, Career Center – www.justice.gov/usao/career-center
USAJOBS.gov – www.usajobs.gov
U.S. Department of Homeland Security Jobs – www.dhs.gov/homeland-security-careers
U.S. Department of Homeland Security Jobs, Students and Recent Graduates – www.dhs.gov/homeland-security-careers/student-and-recent-grads
U.S. Department of Justice Careers – www.justice.gov/careers/search-jobs
U.S. Department of Justice Careers, Interns, Recent Graduates, and Fellow – www.justice.gov/careers/interns-recent-graduates-and-fellows
U.S. Probation & Pretrial Services, Careers – www.uscourts.gov/careers/who-works-judiciary/us-probation-pretrial-services-careers
This will also be available to download on the book page on Routledge.com.

Appendix D

Careers in Criminal Justice and Criminology

The following is an extensive account of employment opportunities in all aspects of criminal justice. Each listing is accompanied by a brief job description. Be aware that some positions are titled differently across jurisdictions, and some positions are collapsed or separated. The following is a general overview of positions throughout the criminal justice system. Additional information on many of these positions is provided in the preceding chapters.

LAW ENFORCEMENT

Air Safety Investigator – Investigate aircraft accidents and prepare factual reports of findings. Pilot-in-command (flight time) hours, and knowledge of aircraft design and aviation practices required.

Arson Specialist – Investigate and determine origins and causes of fire through the collection of evidence. They are employed by police, fire departments, and insurance companies.

Ballistics Specialist – Examine weapons used in the commission of crimes. They use standardized principles, practices, and procedures to examine, analyze, classify, and identify firearms to determine usage in particular crimes.

Canine Officer – Sworn officers who use and care for police canines. They keep updated with regard to training, and are prepared to respond to a variety of calls for service.

Chief of Police – Oversees the day-to-day operations of their police department. They are responsible for a wide array of duties, most of which involve various forms of administration.

Crime Prevention Specialist – Performs public service functions providing crime prevention programs and building citizen and law enforcement awareness. They perform public relations, administrative and operational duties, and other tasks specific to the position.

Crime Scene Investigator – Collects evidence at crime scenes, and preserves evidence for processing. They may have to testify in court proceedings.

Deputy Sheriff – Uniformed law enforcement position similar to police officers and state troopers, but often with court and corrections responsibilities. They work in departments with county-wide jurisdiction.

Dispatcher – Receives and dispatches emergency and routine calls to patrol units. They also perform record checks, maintain computerized and written reports, and operate sophisticated computer equipment.

Document Specialist – Evaluate handwriting samples, ink, paper, personal documents, and related items to assist with the investigation of forgery and related crimes. Their expertise helps identify possible links between documents collected as evidence and the accused.

Environmental Conservation Officer – Ensure the conservation and preservation of natural resources, including protected lands and parks. Outdoor work is required, and officers often work independently. Working long and irregular hours is common.

Federal Agent – Law enforcement professional who enforces federal laws. The nature of their work is determined by the jurisdiction of the agency for which they work.

Fingerprint Specialist – Collect, classify, analyze, and identify fingerprint impressions. They may have to testify in court proceedings.

Intelligence Analyst – Provide statistical data for law enforcement agencies. They also prepare and analyze reports that assist with investigations and general law enforcement practices.

Investigator – Provide investigative support to agencies with specific responsibilities to enforce both civil and criminal laws.

Police Officer – Uphold laws, promote public safety, provide services, and maintain order within their jurisdictions.

Police Officer Training Coordinator – Performs administrative tasks to schedule and coordinate various types of training classes for sworn and civilian employees. They are responsible for analyzing, researching, and developing training courses independently or jointly with other law enforcement organizations.

Police Training Officer – Develop, implement, and provide training programs in law enforcement academies. They ensure consistency with development needs for law enforcement, and teach, update, and revise courses regarding currency and relevance to policing.

Polygraph Specialist – Examines individuals to discern truthful and false responses. They may have to testify in court proceedings. Familiarity with polygraph machinery is required.

State Highway Patrol Officer/State Trooper – State-level law enforcement agents that maintain public safety and enforce laws on highways, interstates, freeways, and other areas within their jurisdiction.

Serology Specialist – Perform laboratory analyses of body fluids such as blood, urine, and semen. They conduct extensive chemical tests to determine levels of drugs or alcohol, and may have to testify in court proceedings.

Sheriff – Oversee the enforcement of laws, maintenance of order, and provision of services in their specified county of jurisdiction. Akin to police chiefs, sheriffs oversee the day-to-day functioning of their law enforcement agency.

State Police Officer – Public safety responsibilities and patrol activities on state and interstate highways. They are responsible for the enforcement of motor vehicle and criminal laws. They have statewide criminal investigation authority.

Toolmark Specialist – Examine tools or objects used in the commission of a crime. They search for specific markings that would connect the tool to the crime scene and/or the accused. They may look for scratches, marks, indentations, or any other distinguishable features in contributing to criminal investigations, and may have to testify in court proceedings.

COURTS

Attorney (criminal cases) – Practice in criminal law in the role of prosecuting or defense counsel. They interpret and apply the law through identifying and presenting facts of a case. They must have a law degree and be able to work well with various groups and different types of individuals.

Bailiff – Uniformed law enforcement officer entrusted to provide courtroom security and escort prisoners and jury members into and out of the courtroom. They are the law enforcement presence in the courtroom. U.S. Marshals serve as bailiffs in the federal courts; sheriff's deputies largely provide bailiff services in other courts.

Court Administrator – Perform administrative and management functions within the court system. They ensure that cases are processed efficiently and timely. Their responsibilities generally involve scheduling hearings and cases, maintaining court records, budgeting, planning space utilization, and managing courtroom personnel.

Court Clerk – Provides clerical assistance for a variety of administrative responsibilities. They are involved in docketing court cases, collecting fees, administering jury selection, swearing in witnesses, marking evidence, and maintaining custody of evidence and court records. Clerks in some states are permitted limited judicial duties, including issuing warrants.

Court Compliance Representative – Oversee compliance and the collection of court judgments, including fines and court costs. They offer alternatives to citizens with extenuating circumstances who may default in paying their court-ordered fines.

Court Interpreter/Translator – Provides interpretation and translation services to the courts to assist with case proceedings. They interpret various languages and assist with closed-captioning and real-time translation for hearing-impaired participants.

Court Liaison Counselor – Provides assistance and counsel for defendants charged with crimes. They evaluate and initiate treatment plans and provide referrals to support agencies. They also monitor information on court continuances, subpoena cancellations, plea changes, and other factors that impact the status of scheduled court appearances.

Court Reporter –Work both within and outside of courtrooms for both legal and private organizations, documenting proceedings as official transcripts. They transcribe spoken or recorded speech into written form.

Judge – Apply the law and ensure that hearings and trials are conducted with fairness to all involved parties. They oversee the legal process in courts of law, safeguard rights, determine legal positions, instruct juries, and determine sentences, conditions of pretrial release, and damages. They serve the role of juries in bench trials.

Mediator – A neutral third party who seeks to resolve disputes without reliance on more formal court processes. They offer suggestions for resolutions, but agreement with the suggestions rests with the parties. They are used primarily in civil cases, although criminal cases sometimes are sent to a mediator.

Paralegal – Assist lawyers in doing much of the background work for cases. They are responsible for researching laws and prior cases, investigating facts and evidence, writing legal documents and briefs, coordinating communications, and keeping records of all documents. They perform clerical and administrative duties for lawyers, and conduct research in preparation for cases.

Pretrial Services Officers – Investigate the backgrounds of persons who come before the court for arraignment and sentencing. They prepare the reports that the court relies on to make release and sentencing decisions, and supervise individuals the court releases to the community on pretrial supervision or other types of supervised release.

Public Information Officer – Provides resources that educate the public about courts, law, and the procedures required for different types of cases. They communicate with the media to ensure that accurate information reaches the public.

Release on Own Recognizance Interviewer – Interviews and obtains background information on defendants eligible to be released on recognizance prior to their trial. They offer release recommendations to judges based on the interviews.

CORRECTIONS

Caseworker/HIV Specialist – Provides assistance to incarcerated HIV-infected persons coping with their emotional and health-related concerns. Care and concern for others, particularly those infected with HIV, and familiarity with the virus are required.

Classification and Treatment Director – Plans correctional programs, assigns incarcerated persons to particular programs, and reviews their case reports. In some facilities, the responsibilities of classification and treatment director are distinct.

Clinical Psychologist – Conduct psychological evaluations of the incarcerated, and provide plans of action based on their assessments. Specialization in clinical psychology is required.

Correctional Education Supervisor – Plans and administers academic, vocational, and social education programs in correctional facilities. They prepare courses of study and training materials designed to aid in the rehabilitation process.

Correctional Officer – Monitor arrestees awaiting trial and people who are incarcerated. General duties include monitoring activities of incarcerated people, enforcing rules, maintaining order, and inspecting correctional facilities and persons for illegal materials. They generally provide care, custody, and control of the incarcerated.

Correctional Treatment Specialist – Provides guidance, support, and rehabilitative services to incarcerated persons. They identify and respond to their special needs, particularly as they relate to psychological issues, behavioral challenges, social skills, education, and job training.

Corrections Counselor – Provides guidance and support for individuals during their incarceration. They evaluate their cases, assess their needs for rehabilitation, identify programs to aid with their rehabilitation, and prepare case reports for evaluation. They also facilitate individual and group counseling sessions.

Corrections Education Specialist – Coordinates adult education services, including literacy and writing classes, and degree preparation and guidance. They plan and update lessons, ensure work is completed by students, and perform many of the same functions as educators outside of correctional facilities.

Detention Deputy – Enforce security rules, and supervise and control detainees in jails. They perform many of the same functions as correctional officers, although they primarily work with individuals detained in jails.

Parole Officer/Community Supervision Officer – Assume the legal custody of persons after they are released from incarceration, and ensure that they abide by the conditions of their parole. They also investigate parole violations.

Prerelease Program, Corrections Counselor – Counsel clients and help them transition from custody to society. They help ensure that individuals successfully transition by assisting with locating housing, employment, and community resources.

Prerelease Program, Employment Counselor – Provides vocational guidance for those soon to be released from incarceration. They ensure that individuals released from prison have job skills that will increase their likelihood of success upon return to society.

Probation Officer/Community Supervision Officer – Monitor persons sentenced to probation. They meet with those under community supervision regularly to monitor their activities and behavior, and evaluate their progress. They make reports to the courts about their behavior, and may arrange substance abuse treatment or vocational training for their clients.

Recreation Therapist – Lead, instruct, and encourage the incarcerated in individual and therapeutic group activities. They provide treatment through recreation, assist with therapy, and monitor and evaluate client progress.

Reentry Center Managers – Maintain custodial responsibility for reentry centers/halfway houses and are accountable for the residents. They may perform personal searches, dispense medications and supplies, and oversee the residents' daily domestic responsibilities.

Substance Abuse Specialist – Provides individual and group counseling for incarcerated substance abusers. They conduct intake evaluation interviews, provide substance abuse education, and prepare and maintain case reports for their clients, including their personal history, treatment plan, and progress. Specialization in substance abuse counseling is required for this position.

Vocational Counselor – Provides guidance with regard to vocational opportunities and programs within various correctional institutions. They help incarcerated people understand their capabilities and develop goals for employment upon their release from prison.

Warden – Oversees the administration of prisons. They plan, direct, and coordinate institutional programs, and are responsible for the administrative and organizational control of prisons.

VICTIM SERVICES

Child and Family Therapists – Provide assessment and therapeutic services to child victims of crime and to non-offending family members. They must be able to assist both young and older children who have been victims of various types of trauma, including sexual abuse, domestic violence, and witnessing a homicide.

Human Trafficking Project Manager – Assist with cases involving human trafficking. They are responsible for developing, coordinating, and managing human trafficking programs; coordinating services for victims of human trafficking; recruiting and supervising community-based case managers; project evaluation; managing hotlines for reports of human trafficking; and preparing and disseminating reports on the nature and status of human trafficking.

Victim Advocates – Provide various types of assistance to victims. They provide crisis intervention work, assist at the scene of the crime, offer information regarding support services and court hearings, attend hearings with victims, and provide emotional support and counseling.

Victim-Offender Mediator – Facilitate various restorative justice approaches by offering victims, those who committed the crime, and community members the chance to meet in person to discuss the impacts of the crime on the victim and the community. They oversee these processes with the goal of repairing the harm done, and are trained third party neutrals who facilitate the communication process between all parties.

Victim Services Assistants – Work with victim advocates to provide victim services. Their tasks include providing notification of hearings, and reviewing police reports for victims of violent crime in which an arrest has not yet been made.

Victim Services Coordinators – Develop and operate programs targeted to assist crime victims. Such programs may include rape crisis services, victim impact panels, victim ministry, and various types of support groups.

Victim Services Office Managers – Oversee the daily functions of victims services offices, and assist with hearing notifications, telephone contact with victims, and other support services as warranted.

JUVENILE JUSTICE

Child Protective Service Worker – Ensure the safety and well-being of children. They attempt to establish a relationship with the juvenile's family to minimize the risks to children, offer direct services to family members, and manage cases through coordinating services.

Child Welfare Caseworker – Offer social services to troubled children and young adult with behavioral problems. They also work with parents of troubled children, for instance, by recommending appropriate responses to troubling behaviors.

Child Welfare Consultants – Help ensure that child care institutions, placement agencies, foster homes, court facilities, and other components comply with state laws. They also provide guidance and expertise to facility administrators to improve services and programs.

Juvenile Corrections Caseworker – Perform functions similar to caseworkers employed in adult institutions. They assess and evaluate residents to ensure that clients are meeting their treatment requirements, and are the primary staff treatment personnel in institutional and some community corrections settings.

Juvenile Court Judge – Serve as the ultimate decision-maker in juvenile courts. They decide legal issues in the courts, set standards within the community through their decision-making, and ascertain that juveniles who appear before the court are treated fairly.

Juvenile Court Prosecutors – Also known as petitioners, they help protect society by representing the government in juvenile court matters, while ensuring that troubled youth are protected by their constitutional rights. They are involved in all phases of the juvenile court proceedings.

Juvenile Court Referee – Also known as the "arm of the court," a "commissioner," and/or a "master," referees are used in some states to assist judges in processing youths through juvenile court. They ease the burden of juvenile court judges.

Juvenile Defense Attorney – Act as a legal advocate for juveniles who enter court. They advise clients and their parents about their legal options, offer strategies and advice, and prepare clients for being in the courtroom.

Juvenile Diversion Specialist – Determine a juvenile's suitability for diversion, and often work with first-time justice-involved youth who are eligible for some type of diversion program.

Juvenile Justice Detention Officer – Maintain safe and secure institutional environments. Similar to the roles of correctional officers, they secure and protect the rights and safety of institutionalized youth.

Juvenile Mental Health Counselor – Assist juveniles with regard to their personal and family problems, functioning in their environments, and dealing with various relationships. They counsel clients, arrange for mental health and other services, and generally ensure that effective services are provided.

Juvenile Probation Officer – Similar to the role played by adult probation/community supervision officers, they oversee individuals sentenced to probation. They meet with clients regularly to monitor and guide their activities and behavior, evaluate their progress, and prepare reports for the courts regarding their behavior. They may work closely with the families or caregivers to monitor and help their client, and may accompany them to court hearings, therapy sessions, and/or volunteer work.

School Resource Officers – Help school officials curb school violence and ensure that schools remain safe environments conducive to learning. They are trained police officers who specialize in juvenile delinquency and school safety issues. They facilitate safety awareness and are positive role models in schools.

PRIVATE SECURITY

Alarm Installation Technician – Install alarms in residential and commercial facilities. Familiarity with alarm systems and technology is generally required for this position.

Couriers – Assist individuals and businesses in the transportation of money, goods, documents, and/or people. They are armed and uniformed, and typically use armored vehicles, but may also use trains or airlines.

Cybersecurity Analyst – Protect sensitive digital data and critical assets from threats. They manage data, identify threats and vulnerabilities, and create initiatives to protect information.

Data Analyst – Collect, manage, and analyze data to assess agency performance and identify problems or concerns, and assess agency performance. They provide data-based results to offer guidance for the agency.

Loss Prevention Specialist – Provide extensive security services to retail outlets and related facilities. They often conduct surveillance, offer recommendations to enhance security and reduce loss, train new personnel, conduct safety evaluations, interview suspects, and provide other tasks related to loss prevention.

Personal Protection Specialist/Bodyguard – Provide security for various groups and individuals. The licensing requirements vary by state.

Private Detective/Investigator – Investigators who are usually employed by public and private organizations and government agencies to protect their businesses and employees, although may also be hired by people searching for missing persons. They engage in the discovery, assessment, and presentation of legal, financial, or personal information. Surveillance is a key component of the work provided by private detectives and investigators, as is research and information gathering.

Private Security Officer – Officers hired by private businesses, transportation facilities, and public operating organizations to enforce safety-related policies and procedures. They help maintain a safe and productive workplace environment, and assist with safety-related concerns.

Security Consultants – Provide services and information to best protect individuals or companies. Generally, they offer professional assessments regarding the types of threats or risks that may affect the person or property, the likelihood that those threats or risks may be acted upon, and plans to reduce the likelihood of threats or risks.

OTHER AREAS

Coroner/Medical Examiner – Study non-living organism to determine the cause of death. In cases of violent crime not involving death, medical examiners may assist in sexual assault examinations, blood and DNA analyses, and thorough evaluations to identify injuries.

Crime Analysts – Collect, compile, and disseminate information that can be used to address crime fighting, crime prevention, and other justice-related activities. The information generated through crime analyses is used to assist with crime prevention and crime fighting practices, and generally improve policing and other aspects of the criminal justice system.

Crime Mapping/GIS Specialist – Provide analyses of criminal behavior and other aspects of criminal justice using Geographic Information Systems (GIS) applications, specifically computerized crime mapping. They convert layers of information into visual form to assist analysts in detecting relationships between times, places, events, and trends.

Criminalists – Identify, analyze, and interpret physical evidence. They use scientific training, analytical skills, and practical experience to collect and analyze evidence to identify information that will be useful in an investigation and/or at trial. They typically have extensive training in areas of biology, chemistry, anthropology, or other lab sciences.

Criminal Justice Administrator – Directs, oversees, and monitors the activities of various offices and programs related to government initiatives. The position requires executive-level managerial skills and the ability to develop and incorporate an effective management style with multiple agencies. They are responsible for introducing innovative strategies and best practices in order to improve justice-based practices.

Criminal Justice Research and Planning Analyst – Conduct research and incorporate the results and other information into their planning efforts. Expertise in research and statistical methods, and familiarity with planning processes are required.

Criminal Psychologists – Develop psychological profiles that can help law enforcement officials identify and understand the behavior and actions of suspects and those found guilty of committing a crime. They may also help identify areas where a suspect lives or works, and/or how their victims are chosen. They typically have an advanced degree in psychology and other social sciences.

Criminologist – Social scientists who study crime, criminal justice, and justice-based activities. They seek to reduce crime and delinquency through science-based analyses of data and the application of theory. They offer recommendations regarding crime prevention and responses to crime.

Cryptographers – Write or crack encryption code in efforts to secure information, or to gain access to secured information. They convert plain data into encrypted form in efforts to provide security.

Cyber Forensics Analyst – Use investigative techniques to identify or store evidence on computers. They analyze digital data and information to identify means to protect against network intrusions.

Forensic Accountants – Investigate complex financial crimes, including embezzlement, money laundering, and fraud. They may work for or be hired by law enforcement agencies at all levels.

Forensic Psychiatrist – Offer expert professional opinions in legal cases or civil matters. They are often involved in decisions about whether a defendant is competent to stand trial. These licensed psychiatrists or psychologists typically work in private practice, correctional facilities, and/or hospitals.

Forensic Scientists – Discover, document, and protect evidence that can be used to answer questions arising from crime or litigation. They photograph, draw, measure, reconstruct activities, and perform other related tasks needed to accurately record crime scenes. Generally, they document evidence at crime scenes, usually specialize in one area, and work in public or private crime labs, hospitals, or coroners' offices.

Insurance Fraud Investigator – Investigate cases involving insurance fraud. They examine cases involving deceitful claims by investigating possible frauds, building cases, and recommending further action to legal authorities and compliance officers.

Social Worker – Help people address and cope with their personal, social, and community problems, which can include substance abuse, chronic disease, employment stress, and family dysfunction.

This will also be available to download on the book page on Routledge.com.

Appendix E

Salaries for Select Criminal Justice and Criminology Positions

The following provides an overview of salaries for various positions in different areas of criminal justice. Be aware that these are estimates taken from various outlets and they cover different years. Actual salaries vary by jurisdiction, years of experience, education, and location. Salaries, of course, may be supplemented by bonuses, overtime pay, and other means. The information is provided as a guide to help readers gauge the mean and sometimes median salaries associated with various positions. Readers are encouraged to further investigate each of these positions for greater salary-related details.

Law Enforcement

Deputy Chief – Mean salary $91,030 in 2022 (Payscale.com, www.payscale.com/research/US/Job=Deputy_Chief%2C_Police_Department/Salary)

Detectives and Criminal Investigators – Mean salary $90,370 in 2021 (U.S. Department of Labor, www.bls.gov/oes/current/oes333021.htm)

Police Captain – Mean salary $82,772 in 2022 (Payscale.com, www.payscale.com/research/US/Job=Police_Captain/Salary)

Police Chief – Mean salary $113,900 in 2022 (Salary.com, www.salary.com/research/salary/alternate/chief-of-police-salary)

Police Corporal – Mean salary $62,130 in 2022 (Talent.com, www.talent.com/salary?job=police+corporal)

Police Dispatcher – Mean salary $47,428 in 2022 (Indeed.com, www.indeed.com/career/police-dispatcher/salaries)

Police Lieutenant – Mean salary $69,306 in 2022 (Comparably.com, www.comparably.com/salaries/salaries-for-police-lieutenant)

Police Officers – Mean salary $60,600 in 2022 (Comparbly.com, www.salary.com/research/salary/alternate/police-officer-salary)

Police Sergeant – Mean salary $76,721 in 2022 (Comparably.com, www.comparably.com/salaries/salaries-for-police-sergeant)

Courts

Bailiffs – Mean salary $52,340 in 2021 (U.S. Department of Labor, www.bls.gov/oes/current/oes333011.htm)

Court Administrators – Mean salary $55,740 in 2022 (Comparably.com, www.comparably.com/salaries/salaries-for-court-administrator)

Court Clerk – Mean salary $37,251 in 2022 (Indeed.com, www.indeed.com/career/court-clerk/salaries)

Court Reporters and Simultaneous Captioners – Mean salary $65,240 in 2021 (U.S. Department of Labor, www.bls.gov/oes/current/oes273092.htm)

Judges and Hearing Officers – Median salary $128,710 in 2021 (U.S. Department of Labor, www.bls.gov/ooh/legal/judges-and-hearing-officers.htm)

Lawyers – Median salary $127,990 in 2021 (U.S. Department of Labor, www.bls.gov/ooh/legal/lawyers.htm)

Paralegals/Legal Assistants – Median salary $56,230 in 2021 (U.S. Department of Labor, www.bls.gov/ooh/legal/paralegals-and-legal-assistants.htm)

Corrections

Correctional Officers/Jailers – Mean salary $53,420 in 2021 (U.S. Department of Labor, www.bls.gov/oes/current/oes333012.htm)

First-Line Correctional Officer Supervisors/Managers – Mean salary $69,750 in 2021 (U.S. Department of Labor, www.bls.gov/oes/current/oes331011.htm)

Probation Officers and Correctional Treatment Specialists – Median salary $60,250 in 2021 (U.S. Department of Labor, www.bls.gov/ooh/community-and-social-service/probation-officers-and-correctional-treatment-specialists.htm)

Warden – Mean salary $90,977 in 2022 (Payscale.com, www.payscale.com/research/US/Job=Prison_Warden/Salary)

Juvenile Justice

Child Welfare Consultant – Mean salary $81,797 in 2022 (GovSalaries.com, https://govsalaries.com/salaries/child-welfare-consultant-a-salary)

Juvenile Court Counselor – Mean salary $60,559 in 2022 (salary.com, www.salary.com/research/salary/recruiting/juvenile-court-counselor-salary)

Juvenile Court Judge – Mean salary $115,857 in 2022 (Comparably.com, www.comparably.com/salaries/salaries-for-juvenile-court-judge)

Juvenile Detention Officer – Mean salary $54,000 in 2022 (Zippia.com, www.zippia.com/juvenile-detention-officer-jobs/salary/)

Juvenile Probation Officer – Mean salary $47,707 in 2022 (Salary.com, www.salary.com/research/salary/recruiting/juvenile-probation-officer-salary)

Security

Information Systems and Cyber Security Specialists – Mean salary $110,784 in 2022 (Salary.com, www.salary.com/research/salary/posting/information-systems-and-cyber-security-salary)

Loss Prevention Officer – Mean salary $51,632 in 2022 (Indeed.com, www.indeed.com/career/loss-prevention-officer/salaries)

Private Investigator – Mean salary $48,911 in 2022 (Indeed.com, www.indeed.com/career/private-investigator/salaries)

Security Officer – Mean salary $54,555 in 2022 (Indeed.com, www.indeed.com/career/security-officer/salaries)

Other Positions

Crime Lab Analyst – Mean salary $60,538 in 2022 (Salary.com, www.salary.com/research/salary/posting/crime-lab-analyst-salary)

Crime Victims Advocate – Mean salary $37,999 in 2022 (www.salary.com/research/salary/posting/victims-advocate-salary)

Criminal Justice Planner – Mean salary $72,789 in 2022 (GovSalaries.com, https://govsalaries.com/salaries/criminal-justice-planner-salary)

Cyber Forensics Analyst – Mean salary $78,123 in 2022 (Salary.com, www.salary.com/research/salary/posting/cyber-forensics-analyst-salary)

This will also be available to download on the book page on Routledge.com.

Appendix F

Curriculum Vitae Shell

The following highlights the categories included in a curriculum vita. The organization of the content depends on the nature of the position for which one is applying. For instance, teaching accomplishments may be emphasized over research when seeking a position at a teaching-focused institution.

- Name/Contact Information
- Education
- Professional Competencies (e.g., areas of expertise/concentration)
- Teaching Interests/Experience
- Research Interests
- Professional Experience (e.g., consulting experience, administrative positions, academic appointments)
- Academic Service (e.g., service to the university, college, and department)
- Professional Development (e.g., service to the profession and community, advisory committees/boards)
- Conference Participation (e.g., research presentations, workshop attendance)
- Publications
- Research Grants
- Awards (e.g., scholarships, fellowships, honors, professional recognition)
- Professional Memberships
- Professional/Certification (e.g., certifications, licensure)
- International Experience (e.g., study/travel abroad, international works, languages spoken)

This will also be available to download on the book page on Routledge.com.

Index

Ackerman, T. 112
Adler, F. 5
American Association of Electronic Reporters and Transcribers 132
American College Testing (ACT) 131
American Correctional Association 139–40, 142
American Dream 17
American Jail Association 139–40, 142
American Probation and Parole Association 139–42
American Revolution 15
applying for jobs 34, 75, 87–9, 91–2, 115, 122
Asset Forfeiture Program 114
Assistant Federal Public Defender 100–1; *see also* defense attorney
Attorneys 9, 27, 30, 33, 44, 58–64, 66–7, 125, 128–31, 134–5, 156, 166, 191, 199; defense attorneys 8, 30, 49, 63, 67, 125, 127–8, 130–1, 155–6, 191, 195; indigent defense 41, 43, 59, 64, 100–1, 130, 133; law school 49, 66, 77–8, 101, 131, 160; prosecutors/district attorneys 8, 30, 36, 46–7, 59, 63, 65, 125, 127–30, 132, 146, 155–6, 195

bailiffs 30, 125, 127, 133, 135, 191, 198
Bell, A. G. 84
Berkeley Police School 22
Bold, M. 50
Branson, R. 70
bureaucracies 6, 40, 44–5, 51, 102, 150

campus events 79–80, 82, 85–7
canine officers 29, 111, 118, 120, 190
career centers 79, 85, 87, 95
career fairs 79, 87
case managers 58, 60–1, 64, 143, 162, 194
C^4 model 51
Chenoweth, L. 50
childcare workers 32, 155
child protective services 58, 63
Civil War 15–16, 24
Civil War Era 16
clerks of court 8, 30, 59, 61, 65, 125, 127, 132, 135, 192, 199
The Club 171
Colonial Era of Criminal Justice 13–15

communications and electronics personnel 113
community corrections 8, 30–1, 58, 137–8, 140, 144–8, 155, 195; *see also* parole; probation; community supervision officers
community policing 20, 33
community service coordinators 61
community supervision officers 30–1, 43, 45–6, 66, 138–9, 144–7, 168, 193, 195; *see also* parole; probation; attractions to the job 138, 146–7; nature of the work 43, 45–6, 66, 145–7; requirements for position 145–7; responsibilities 138–9, 144–6, 168, 193, 195
compliance inspectors and specialists 113
Conley, J. 13
constables 14, 16, 117; *see also* local law enforcement
convict criminology 48
cooperative education programs 99–100, 107
Copeland, A. 176–7
corporal punishment 14
correctional reform 15, 17, 100
correctional treatment specialists 33, 140, 143, 193
corrections 5, 8–9, 26, 30–2, 41–5, 63, 137–48, 192–4, 199; attractions 31, 44, 138–9; challenges 31, 42–3, 103, 139, 142; changes 15, 17, 20, 45, 139, 148; nature of work 30–2, 137–48; organization 137–8
corrections/correctional officers 9, 31, 63–4, 66, 138–43, 193, 199; attractions 60–1, 63–4, 66, 138–9; challenges 9, 31, 43, 58–9, 140–3, 147; positions 27, 141; requirements 142; responsibilities 36, 140–2, 193; training 66, 142
corrections education specialists 143, 193
county law enforcement 28–9; *see also* sheriffs
coursework 70–2, 74–7, 81, 86, 99, 101–2, 105
court administrator 61, 125, 127, 132–3, 135, 192, 198
court liaison counselors 134, 192
court mediator 30, 60, 62, 65, 192
court reporter 8, 30, 59, 61, 65, 125, 127, 131–2, 135, 192, 199
court representatives 134
courts 8, 29–30, 46–8, 100–1, 125–35, 166–8, 191–2, 198–9; appellate courts 29, 30, 100, 125–6, 129, 131; history 14–18, 20; intermediate courts of

appeal 29–30, 126; juvenile 150, 152, 154–7, 195, 199; organization 29–30, 125–6; trial courts 29–30, 100, 125–6, 130–1; trial courts of general jurisdiction 29, 125–6, 132; trial courts of limited jurisdiction 29, 125–6, 128; U.S. Circuit Courts of Appeals 29–30, 100, 126; U.S. District Courts 29, 100, 126; U.S. Supreme Court 29–30, 46, 100, 126, 130, 133
cover letters 6, 8, 88–9, 92, 181
COVID-19 104–5, 143, 179
crack cocaine 20
creativity 51, 58, 62, 90, 144, 171
crime analysis/mapping 8, 102, 160, 165–7, 196
crime prevention specialists 42, 60, 65, 67, 77, 120, 190
crime scene investigator 120, 167–9, 190
CrimeStat 167
criminal investigators/detectives 27, 35, 47, 59–60, 112, 191, 196, 198
criminal justice/criminal justice system 4–6, 8, 12–27, 33–7, 41–2, 50, 76–8, 100, 111, 119, 138–9, 157, 163, 169–71; as an academic discipline 5, 21–4, 179; career trends 4, 33–7; compared to criminology 4–5; defined 4–5; growth 4–5, 26; history 6, 12–27; primary components 8, 14; reasons for seeking a career in 8, 41–2, 111, 119, 138–9, 160, 163; reform 15, 17–19, 100, 171; teaching, 12, 50, 76–8, 157, 169–70
criminal law 14–15, 22, 101, 161
criminologists 17, 19, 21, 32–4, 36, 51, 60–3, 65–7, 71, 77, 91, 170–1, 197
criminology 4–5, 21–3, 170, 179; compared to criminal justice 4–5; defined 4–5
Crisis Era 18
cryptography/cryptographers 35, 197
Culkar, D. 140
curriculum vita 91, 169–70, 201
cybercrime 27, 29, 32, 34, 38, 114–15
cyber forensics 35, 197, 200
cybersecurity 35, 163, 195
Cybersecurity and Infrastructure Security Agency 114
cybervetting 92

danger 29, 64–5, 67–8, 106, 118, 126, 133, 138, 141–2, 146, 163–4
deputy sheriff 14, 16, 28–9, 33, 116, 120, 190–1; *see also* local law enforcement
DeRosa, A. 86
detectives/criminal investigators 27, 35, 47, 59–60, 112, 191, 196, 198
differential association theory 85
discretion 30, 40, 44, 62, 70, 126, 128–9
dispatcher 65, 67, 113, 120, 190, 198
diversity 36, 71, 74, 129, 160, 180

economy 5, 12–20, 34, 38, 46, 59, 68, 114, 171, 179
educators 12, 32, 47, 50, 63, 76–8, 143, 150, 157, 164, 169–70, 193

England 13–16
Era of Security 21
ethics 6, 40, 49–51, 74, 90, 104, 106, 121, 142, 180; ethical codes 50; ethical dilemmas 50, 106
experiential learning 7, 72, 98–100, 105, 107

fear of crime 19, 26, 33–6
federal law enforcement 21, 27–8, 58–9, 89, 112–15, 121, 188–9; careers 27–8, 112–15; relocation 28, 113; travel 28, 58–9, 73
Federal Witness Security Program 114
Florida Department of Corrections 140
Floyd, G. 111
foreign language 3, 36–7, 41, 74, 76–7, 81, 89, 102, 104, 123, 192
forensic science 8, 27, 35, 76, 121, 160, 164, 167–9, 190–1, 196–7, 200; ballistics 28, 168, 190; biometric identification 168; DNA profiling 168; fingerprint specialists 113, 169, 191; forensic entomology 168; forensic odontology 168; forensic pathology 168; photo analysis 168; physical anthropology 168; questioned document analysis 168–9; serology 168, 191; toolmark specialist 168, 191; toxicology 22, 168
Fort Worth Police Department 92–3, 121
Friedman, T. 37

Gates, B. 70
general and compliance investigators 113
Geographic Information Systems (GIS) 166–7, 196
Gideon v. Wainwright 130
Gilded Age 17
Glassdoor.com 87
globalism 5, 21, 26–7, 34, 37, 77, 115
Graduate Record Examination (GRE) 77
graduate school/graduate studies 23, 66, 77–80, 169–70
Great Depression 18

Handshake 87
higher education 17, 22–3, 61, 67, 71–2, 75, 77, 80, 84, 99, 101–2, 169
Hilgenberg, J. Jr. 13, 20
Homeland Security Act 27

immigration 17, 21, 27, 36, 115
Indeed.com 87–8
Industrial Revolution 24
institutional corrections 8, 31, 138–44, 148; *see also* prisons; jails; custodial personnel 140 (*see also* corrections officers; jailers); industry and agricultural personnel 140, 143; management 140; program personnel 140
insurance examiner/investigator 32, 65, 121, 197
intelligence analysts 27, 112, 120–1, 191
international crime 37, 169
internships 3, 6–8, 24, 48–50, 72, 80, 96, 98–107; benefits 48, 72, 80, 99–104; concerns 49–50,

104–5; ethics 49–50, 106; expectations 98, 104–7; historical development 98–9
interpersonal skills 60–1, 92
INTERPOL 37, 169
interviewing 6–7, 59–60, 65, 73–4, 82, 86, 88, 90–2, 94–6, 100, 106, 122–3, 139, 142–3, 164; cultural differences 94; preparation 91, 94; questions 94–5; teleconferencing 94; things not to do 91, 94; things to do 92, 94–5
Italian Mafia 18

Jacksonian Era 15–16
jailers 31, 58, 62, 66, 141, 199
jails 15, 18, 28, 31, 100–1, 138, 140–2; *see also* institutional corrections; history 15, 18
job searches 84–90, 94, 106, 103, 122, 179
Jones, M. 12, 24, 36
judges 8–9, 14, 26, 30, 40–1, 44, 46–8, 58–64, 66, 74, 125–8, 130–5, 155–6, 171, 192, 195, 199
juvenile justice/juvenile justice system 4, 6–8, 14, 17–19, 32, 58, 150–8, 194–5, 199
juvenile probation officers 32, 156–7, 195, 199

Kerner Commission 19

laboratory technicians 28, 61, 65
Law Enforcement Assistance Administration (LEAA) 23, 99
Law Enforcement Education Program (LEEP) 23
law school 49, 66, 77–8, 101, 131, 160
Law School Admission Test (LSAT) 77, 131
leadership 3, 6, 17, 46, 72, 74, 77, 80, 85, 90, 101, 140, 175
legal aid counselors 66
letters of recommendation 50, 77–8, 81, 85, 106
LinkedIn 86–7, 89
Lipsky, M. 45
local law enforcement 9, 15–23, 27–9, 33, 36, 57, 115, 117–21, 166, 190–1, 195, 198; differences 29, 115, 118; nature of the work 9, 29, 36, 57, 111, 117–21, 166, 191, 195; patrol 29, 111, 118; pros and cons 119

majors/minors 4, 7, 23, 41, 72, 74–6, 105, 161, 167–8
mandatory release 138
media 5, 35, 46, 125, 133, 167–8, 192
mentorship 78, 80, 98, 154, 157, 170, 176
Michigan Department of Corrections 140
morality 46, 49–51, 122

National Court Reporters Association 132
Nationalization Era 19–20
Native Americans 15
networking 6, 35, 60, 72, 78–82, 84–7, 96, 101–2, 105–6, 176–7
New York Board of Bar Examiners 131
night watchmen 14, 16
nongovernmental organizations 23, 37, 169; Amnesty International 169; Human Rights Watch 169

offices of inspector general 115
Oliver, W. 13, 20, 23
Omnibus Crime Control and Safe Streets Act 23
organizational culture 98, 105
organizational design 44, 115, 137–8
organizational skills 61, 80, 91, 134, 140

paralegals 8, 27, 30, 59–62, 65–7, 125, 130, 133–4, 192, 199
parole 26, 31, 59–63, 66, 137–8, 143–7, 193; *see also* community supervision officers; parole boards 138, 143
Peace Officer Standards and Training 23
physical activity/fitness 7, 64–5, 96, 121–2, 141–2, 147
planning and policy development 13, 20, 46, 59, 61–2, 65, 67, 129, 169, 196
police 9, 15–23, 27–9, 33, 36, 46, 57, 61, 66, 86, 93, 115, 117–23, 142, 144, 166, 190–1, 195, 198; *see also* local law enforcement; county law enforcement; state law enforcement; chiefs 46, 61, 120, 190–1, 196; corruption 16, 18; history 15–23; recruitment 93, 121–2, 142; ride along 86, 122–3; selection 121–2; training 23, 28, 66, 115, 121–2; training officers 120, 122, 144, 191
politics 5–6, 9, 12–13, 15–19, 34–5, 40, 45–7, 51, 65, 102, 113, 164, 171, 179, 180
pre-release correctional counselors 140, 143, 193
pretrial services officers 134, 138, 144, 147, 192
private prisons 67, 138–9
private sector 44, 59, 67, 85, 117, 139
private security 4, 8, 26–7, 32, 34–5, 37, 57–9, 62–3, 65–7, 160, 162–5, 172, 195–6, 198–9; alarm companies/specialists 65, 67, 163–4, 195; armed courier services 163–4, 195; bodyguards/personal protection specialists 163–5, 196; functions 32, 37, 57–8, 162–5; loss prevention specialists 163, 195–6, 199; private detectives and investigators 32, 62, 65–7, 163–4, 196, 199; security consultants 35, 65, 164, 196; security officers 8, 32, 67, 162–3, 198, 199
probation 31–3, 50–1, 59–63, 66, 138–9, 143–7, 156–7, 193, 195, 199; *see also* community supervision officers
professional meetings 78–9, 81
Progressive Era 17–18
Prohibition 18
promotions 44, 59, 66, 68, 86, 139, 147, 174–8, 180

Reagan Era 20–1
reconstruction 16
reentry center managers 137–8, 144, 147, 193
release-on-own recognizance interviewers 134, 192
researchers 21, 26, 33, 42, 60–2, 65–6, 79, 160
resumes 74, 76–7, 81–2, 84, 88–92, 96, 169, 181–3; affiliations 90; chronological and functional 90, 182–3; contact information 89–90; education/certifications 89; employment history 89; employment objective 89; format 89–91, 182–3;

honors/awards 90; master resume 91; references 89–90; scanning/tracking 91; skills 89; submitting 89–91
Roth, M. 24
Ryniker, M. 99

salaries 43–4, 58, 88, 95, 134, 146, 163, 174, 198–200
Santayana, G. 6
service learning programs 98–100
Sgroi, C. 99
sheriffs 14, 16, 28–9, 33, 61, 65, 116–17, 120, 133, 138, 190–1; *see also* county law enforcement; local law enforcement
shift work 66
SimplyHired.com 87
simultaneous captioners 132, 199
social media 86–7, 92, 104, 122
social unrest/rioting 5, 15–19, 21, 36, 111
social workers 63, 76, 86, 130, 145, 155, 157, 161–2, 171, 197
sociocultural changes 34, 36–7
sociology 4–5, 21–2, 76, 161, 170–1, 180
special jurisdiction police 29, 111, 117, 120–1
state law enforcement 7, 28, 111, 115–17, 191; functions 28, 111, 115–17, 191; organization 115–17
street-level bureaucrats 45
student associations 79–80
substance abuse counselors 63, 193
Sutherland, E. 85

technology 5, 7, 21, 26–7, 34–5, 57–9, 77, 79, 86–7, 91–2, 94, 115, 122, 129, 139, 163–7, 170–1, 177, 179, 195
terrorism 7, 21, 24, 26–7, 34, 46, 57, 111–12, 114, 116, 161
tolerance 49–50, 61, 170
training academy 28, 41, 66, 119, 122, 142
translators 127, 192

United Nations 37, 169
United States Court Reporters Association 132
USAJOBS.gov 87, 115, 189
U.S. Attorney General 15, 114, 129
U.S. Bureau of Alcohol, Tobacco, Firearms and Explosives 114; *see also* federal law enforcement
U.S. Bureau of Diplomatic Security 114; *see also* federal law enforcement
U.S. Bureau of Engraving and Printing 115; *see also* federal law enforcement
U.S. Bureau of Justice Statistics 5, 29, 112, 117
U.S. Bureau of Labor Statistics 33, 71, 132, 164
U.S. Bureau of Land Management 58; *see also* federal law enforcement
U.S. Capitol Police 114; *see also* federal law enforcement
U.S. Customs and Border Protection 113–14; *see also* federal law enforcement
U.S. Department of Education 4
U.S. Department of Homeland Security 21, 27, 34, 113–14, 189; *see also* federal law enforcement
U.S. Department of Justice 17, 21, 27, 33, 113–14, 129, 189; *see also* federal law enforcement
U.S. Drug Enforcement Administration 114; *see also* federal law enforcement
U.S. Environmental Protection Agency 115; *see also* federal law enforcement
U.S. Federal Bureau of Investigation (FBI) 7, 17, 27, 40–1, 112, 114; *see also* federal law enforcement
U.S. Federal Bureau of Prisons 113, 137–8, 189
U.S. Federal Law Enforcement Training Center 114–15, 189
U.S. Fish and Wildlife Service 58; *see also* federal law enforcement
U.S. Food and Drug Administration 115; *see also* federal law enforcement
U.S. Immigration and Customs Enforcement 113–14; *see also* federal law enforcement
U.S. Internal Revenue Service 114; *see also* federal law enforcement
U.S. Marshals Service 114, 133, 191; *see also* federal law enforcement
U.S. Mint 114; *see also* federal law enforcement
U.S. National Advisory Commission on Criminal Justice Standards and Goals 23
U.S. National Institute of Justice 167
U.S. National Park Service 58, 114
U.S. Office of Personnel Management 87, 115
U.S. Pentagon Force Protection Agency 114; *see also* federal law enforcement
U.S. Postal Inspection Service 114; *see also* federal law enforcement
U.S. President's Commission on Law Enforcement and Administration of Justice 23
U.S. Probation and Pretrial Services System 138; *see also* federal law enforcement
U.S. Secret Service 73, 114; *see also* federal law enforcement
U.S. Supreme Court Police 133; *see also* federal law enforcement
U.S. Task Force on the Police 23
U.S. Transportation Security Administration 114; *see also* federal law enforcement

victim services 4, 8, 60, 62–3, 65, 134, 160–2, 169, 172, 194, 200; child and family therapists 150, 162, 194; human trafficking project manager 162, 194; nature of the work 160–2; requirements 63, 161; victim advocates 60, 63, 162, 169, 194, 200; victim services assistants 60, 62, 65, 134, 162, 194; victim services coordinators 162, 194; victim services office managers 162, 194
violence 9, 16, 20, 43, 47–8, 119, 157, 162, 164
Vollmer, A. 22–3
volunteering 35, 48, 63, 72, 74, 78, 80–1, 91, 147, 158, 161, 176

Walker, S. 19
wardens 16, 31, 62, 140–1, 143–4, 194, 199
war on drugs 20, 46
War Years (era) 19
Weber, M. 44–5
white collar crime 27, 111–12, 114, 170
White, R. 81

Winner, J. E. Jr. 171
World War I 18
World War II 18–19, 23
writing skills 44, 61, 74, 78, 88–9, 105–6, 119, 130, 133–4, 141–2, 147, 168

ZipRecruiter.com 87
Zuckerberg, M. 70–1